The Republican South

THE REPUBLICAN SOUTH

DEMOCRATIZATION AND PARTISAN CHANGE

David Lublin

PRINCETON UNIVERSITY PRESS

PRINCETON AND OXFORD

Copyright © 2004 by Princeton University Press
Published by Princeton University Press,
41 William Street, Princeton, New Jersey 08540
In the United Kingdom: Princeton University Press,
3 Market Place, Woodstock, Oxfordshire OX20 1SY

All Rights Reserved

ISBN: 0-691-05041-4

British Library Cataloging-in-Publication Data is available

This book has been composed in Janson
Printed on acid-free paper. ∞
pup.princeton.edu
Printed in the United States of America
10 9 8 7 6 5 4 3 2 1

To my sister, Jennifer Lublin

Contents

Figures

Tables

Preface

SINCE THE FOUNDING of the United States, the South has always been a unique region of the nation. The bloody conflict between the Union and the Confederacy in the nation's only civil war only served to accentuate regional distinctions. The view of the South as a special or different part of the United States has been reflected in the works of scholars on American politics. While one does occasionally come across books on the politics of other regions, like the Midwest or New England, there are far more on southern politics. Moreover, political science works examining American politics often divide the nation into the South and the non-South because politics has historically been so different in the South. Despite the undoubted differences between regions outside the South, scholars appear to feel the need to examine them far less often.

The South's political distinctiveness has its roots in racial questions. During the writing of the Constitution, southern delegates were careful to protect slavery against interference by the proposed strengthened federal government. Battles over the counting of slaves in the apportionment of the House of Representatives centered on how much weight the South would have in the national legislature. The infamous three-fifths compromise protected the interests of both regions by giving the South enough seats to protect slavery but insufficient seats to force its extension to other areas.

Battles over the spread of slavery to new territories led to regional political polarization prior to the Civil War and ultimately to the war itself. The defeat of the South freed the slaves but devastated the region. The politics of the region potentially appeared to be revitalized, largely due to the participation of the emancipated blacks in politics. However, the rise of mass disfranchisement of most blacks and many whites, ultimately accepted by the North, led to the seemingly permanent overwhelming domination of the Democrats, who were united in their goal of protecting white supremacy.

The Civil Rights Movement finally ended this racial and political order, capping its success legislatively with the Civil Rights Act of 1964 and the Voting Rights Act of 1965. The implementation of these two laws ultimately shattered the old racial economic and political order. Although the region's blacks remain significantly less affluent than the region's whites, many blacks have entered the middle class. Moreover, the region as a whole has become far wealthier with the income gap between the South and the rest of the nation rapidly closing.

The immediate impact on politics was both more and less dramatic than expected. The Voting Rights Act rapidly led to mass enfranchisement of southern African Americans in areas where they had previously been prevented from casting ballots. The share of whites that registered and voted greatly increased as well. On the other hand, the political impact on southern politics appeared quite small in many ways. While increasing numbers of southern politicians adapted to black participation by accepting the basic gains of the Civil Rights Movement, the partisan impact of the great changes of the 1960s was perhaps smaller than expected. Outside of presidential elections, the Democrats retained their dominance of southern politics far after the racial conflicts of the 1960s.

Political change eventually did arrive in the South. Republicans finally won a majority of the region's U.S. House and U.S. Senate seats in 1994. More recently, Republicans have won control of many of the region's state legislative chambers. Despite major gains, Republicans still do not hold a majority of the region's state legislative seats as of this writing in 2003. Republicans have found it even more difficult to dislodge the Democratic grip on local offices.

This slow progress by the Republicans in the wake of the Civil Rights Movement raises a number of fiercely debated questions surrounding southern politics. Racial issues were long central to southern politics, but do they explain Republican gains over the past several decades? If so, why have the Republicans taken so long to capitalize on the solid shift of national Democrats to racial liberalism?

In this work, I argue that scholars have often misunderstood the process of partisan change in the South. Scholars of partisan change have often described this change as the result of the ability to convert existing voters or to mobilize new ones based on new pressing issues that override existing partisan ties and old issues. This process of partisan change might well describe normal partisan change in an established democratic system. However, it does not describe the South very well at all. The Voting Rights Act of 1965 resulted in the enfranchisement of huge numbers of new voters and revitalized the meaning of elections in the South. One must consequently view the changes in the South not merely as one of partisan change but one of democratization.

In order to explain why the Democrats retained dominance of the region's politics for so long after the racial conflicts of the 1960s, one must look beyond their existing control of power and offices, as important as that was, to the interrelated role of elites, institutions, and issues. White Democratic elites adapted to the enlarged electorate by adopting conservative to moderate stands on racial issues. Republican presidential candidates may have been able to gain white southern support based on their racial conservatism, but the conservative to moderate positions of most

Democratic candidates made it extremely difficult for Republican candidates to capitalize on the issue in other elections for decades. On the other hand, the racial liberalism of national Democrats combined with the racial conservatism of the Republicans quickly cemented the political loyalties of most African Americans to the Democrats.

The suppression of racial disagreements between the parties by the Democrats combined with the arrival of mass enfranchisement led to the increasing normalization of southern politics. The collapse of disfranchisement along with the end of the institutional role of the Democratic Party as the protector of white supremacy in the South opened the way for political competition. Rather than centering on racial questions, political divisions in the South between Democrats and Republicans focused on the economic questions that had divided the two parties nationally since the New Deal.

Democrats could not maintain their dominance forever through this formula of moderation on race and populism on economics. Institutional rules governing politics, especially party primaries and racial redistricting, increasingly encouraged white political elites to seek election as Republicans, and they often won. The growing prominence of African Americans within the Democratic Party finally led to the delayed emergence of racial issues as well. As Democrats became increasingly liberal on racial issues, a real divide emerged between the two parties on race. Republicans attracted more white votes on this basis. The importance of racial issues for black voters meant that Democrats retained the political support of the vast majority of African Americans in the region.

The rise of social issues like abortion, gay rights, and gun control in the 1980s increasingly attracted religious and social conservatives to the banner of the GOP. Democrats attempted to stifle major partisan divides on these issues as they had racial issues in the past. As with racial issues, they experienced some success, especially in rural areas. However, the rising liberalism of Democrats on social issues combined with the staunch conservatism of Republicans on these same questions allowed for partisan change centered on social issues to occur as well.

In sum, racial and social issues allowed the Republicans to make new inroads among southern whites in the 1980s and 1990s even as economic questions remained the prime source of division between the two parties. Democrats were able to delay this regional shift to the Republicans but could not stave it off forever. The increased funneling of white conservatives by both issues and institutions into the GOP eventually broke the back of Democratic dominance. Despite retaining the support of the overwhelming share of blacks, Democrats find it increasingly difficult to attract sufficient numbers of whites to win southern elections.

Republicans may read this story like a fairy tale with a happy ending.

After much struggle, the GOP emerged triumphant. However, unlike fairy tales, politics never really arrives at "The End." On the other hand, like many stories, this one contains a warning. The African-American and Latino share of the southern electorate continues to rise at a rapid pace. The decline of white supremacy and the rise of southern economic prosperity have reversed the trend of African-Americans migration from the South. Moreover, blacks have a higher birthrate than whites. Latinos have immigrated to the United States in large numbers, including the South. Their political participation remains limited, but the support of most non-Cuban Latinos for the Democrats poses a real threat to continued Republican regional ascendance. Unless the Republicans can capture a greater share of the minority vote, Democrats will need a smaller and smaller share of the region's relatively shrinking white vote to win southern elections.

Acknowledgments

I OWE A GREAT DEBT to the incredible number of people who contributed to this work in so many ways. I ought to first thank the many southerners who were so giving of their time and whose observations helped inform my own. They are so numerous that I could not possibly name all of them. However, I would especially like to mention my good friend, Robert Ellis, who shared his insights on the South with grace and good humor. Our discussions are some of my fondest memories of Columbia, South Carolina.

Many people in offices around the South helped me obtain election data. In Alabama, Janice MacDonald in the Elections Division of the Alabama Secretary of State's office invariably did her best to help me locate Alabama election returns. My colleague, Jay Barth, of Hendrix College helped me both to find election results from Arkansas and then to understand them. The offices of many supervisors of elections around Florida kindly responded to my numerous requests for election returns from their counties. I am also indebted to members of the staff of the reapportionment committees, especially Mark Welsh of the Florida legislature who assisted me in locating Florida election results. In Georgia, Linda Meggers and many other staff members of Georgia Reapportionment Services graciously provided me with Georgia election data without fail on numerous occasions. I am also grateful to the staff of the Elections Division of the Georgia Secretary of State. The Division of Elections of the Office of the Louisiana Secretary of State collects unusually detailed election information for which I remain extremely grateful. The Elections Division of the Mississippi Secretary of State's Office and the Mississippi Department of Archives and History both were very helpful in my search for Mississippi election returns. In North Carolina, the overworked staffs of several different sections of the Secretary of State's office as well as that of the legislative library and the reapportionment committees took time out of their work to help me with mine. The South Carolina Division of Elections keeps impressive election information and graciously welcomed me each of the many times that I stopped by to collect election data and ask questions. I remain especially thankful for Liz Simmons, who continues to answer my requests for information even though I can no longer drop by to say hello in person. Lee Bandy of *The State* repeatedly shared his encyclopedic knowledge of South Carolina politics with me. Jack Austin and Sam Davenport of the Texas Legislative Counsel's Office generously helped me locate and understand the election data from their populous state. In Virginia, I owe much to the Virginia Division of Elections and the Virginia State Archives.

I could not have completed this work without generous financial support provided by an award (#9710058) from the Program in Political Science of the Division of Social and Economic Sciences of the National Science Foundation.

I originally conceived this book during my appointment at the University of South Carolina and am grateful to my former colleagues, many of whom are now elsewhere, who encouraged and helped me, especially Maryjane Osa, William Mishler, William G. Jacoby, Saundra Schneider, Harvey Starr, George Krause, and Blease Graham. My colleagues at American University encouraged me to bring this work to completion. I remain indebted to Karen O'Connor not only for bringing me to AU but for doing her best to provide me with both research and moral support after I arrived. William LeoGrande let me bend his ear and gave me good advice on many occasions in addition to helping with the research support in his capacity as dean. James Thurber repeatedly shared the resources of the Center for Congressional and Presidential Studies without hesitation over the last five years. Nathan Dietz was very giving in his willingness to answer many questions on methodological issues. Similarly, Christine DeGregorio and Joe Soss provided thoughtful comments on early findings from this work that helped me to substantially improve it.

Several people and organizations let me present slices of this work and then commented on it in ways that aided its improvement. Charles Bullock III invited me to present work related to redistricting at a conference at the University of Georgia. I remain grateful for the welcome he and his students provided me in addition to his patience in answering my seemingly endless questions on Georgia politics. I benefited enormously when the Department of Political Science at SUNY Stony Brook lived up to its well- deserved reputation for sharp analysis when they critiqued an early presentation of my argument. It is always a pleasure to find an excuse to return to Charleston and I am grateful that my colleagues at The Citadel allowed me to present early findings at their valuable biannual conferences on southern politics.

Conversation and collaboration with Lisa Handley and Bernie Grofman aided my thoughts on redistricting. I am fortunate to live near Lisa, a valued friend, so we can regularly joust over redistricting and other topics. Even when we disagree, I learn a tremendous amount from her insights. Moshe Haspel, a good friend and scholar, shared his thoughts on southern politics and applied his GIS wizardry to produce maps for me with amazing speed. He also graciously welcomed me to Atlanta on many occasions, including his wedding to a wonderful southerner, Rebecca Baget.

I am thankful to Malcolm Litchfield for bringing this and my previous book to Princeton University Press and for giving me so much helpful, clear advice on the mysterious task of publishing a book. Chuck Myers, the current editor at Princeton, patiently shepherded this book toward completion. His thoughtful suggestions, along with those of Harold Stanley, have improved it greatly.

I owe a special thanks to Steve Voss as my ideas on southern politics benefited repeatedly from my conversations and collaborations with him.

Sue Ikenberry, a dear friend and colleague, provided tremendous support throughout this project. Besides reminding me why politics is fun, she saved me from countless errors of judgment in my attempts to analyze politics.

My grandmother, Rosalyn Weiss, is probably the most northern person I know. However, that did not stop her from taking me out for welcome breaks and encouraging me along the way as I studied southern politics.

I dedicated my previous book to my parents, Janet and Edward Lublin. That thanks does not begin to convey the level of love and support they have continuously provided. I can only express a small portion of my love and thanks for them here.

I was very lucky to meet Eric Hostetler shortly after moving back home to the Maryland suburbs of Washington, D.C. As in all things, Eric's warmth and affection helped sustain me throughout this long project. I am extremely fortunate to have someone so special with whom to share my work and my life. I am also grateful to Eric's parents, Zona and Jim Hostetler, for having been so welcoming and continually expressing so much interest in my work.

I remain very close to my sister, Jennifer Lublin, to whom I have dedicated this book. I am very happy that we now live near each other and can share so much of our lives. Jennifer does not have my love of politics, but I hope that does not prevent her from knowing how much I love and admire her. I know I can always depend on determined love and support from her, especially when the going gets rough. She has always been the extra special spark in my family. I could not have finished this book without her constant enthusiasm and love.

The Republican South

CHAPTER ONE

Introduction

SCANNING SOUTHERN POLITICS for signs that the Republicans would replace the Democrats as the majority party used to be as futile as waiting
for Godot.[1] In *The Emerging Republican Majority*, Kevin Phillips foresaw
that Republicans would quickly gain an edge in presidential elections.[2]
However, the pace of Republican gains below the presidential level was
exceedingly slow in the former Confederate states as Democrats maintained their edge in all offices. The Democratic edge, moreover, was not
a small one. For nearly three decades after the Civil Rights Movement
transformed southern politics, the Democrats held the preponderance of
governorships as well as congressional seats. Democratic dominance appeared even greater at the state legislative and local levels. In some
southern states, located primarily in the Deep South, Republicans held
almost no local or state legislative offices as late as 1980. A wealth of
books and articles appeared trying to explain why the Democrats remained in power and Republican growth was so slow or elusive.[3]

The waiting finally appeared to end in the watershed year of 1994. In a
backlash against the unpopular Clinton administration, Republicans won
a majority of the region's U.S. Senate and U.S. House seats for the first
time. Their share of state legislative seats also leaped upward, and Republicans took control of several state legislative chambers for the first
time. Many analysts expected that Republicans would finally consolidate
their majority during the remains of the 1990s. And yet, the Democrats
did not collapse. The 1994 results did not represent a fluke, and Republi-

[1] Everett Carll Ladd, "Like Waiting for Godot: The Uselessness of 'Realignment' for
Understanding Change in Contemporary American Politics," in *The End of Realignment?
Interpreting American Electoral Eras*, ed. Byron E. Shafer (Madison: University of Wisconsin
Press, 1991), 24–36.

[2] Kevin P. Phillips, *The Emerging Republican Majority* (New Rochelle, NY: Arlington
House, 1969), 187–289.

[3] Charles S. Bullock, III, "Creeping Realignment in the South," in Robert H.
Swansbrough and David M. Brodsky, eds., *The South's New Politics: Realignment and Dealign-
ment* (Columbia: University of South Carolina Press, 1988), 220–37; Edward G. Carmines
and James A. Stimson, *Issue Evolution: Race and the Transformation of American Politics*
(Princeton: Princeton University Press, 1989); James M. Glaser, *Race, Campaign Politics, and
the Realignment in the South* (New Haven: Yale University Press, 1996); Gary C. Jacobson,
The Electoral Origins of Divided Government: Competition in U.S. House Elections, 1946–1988
(Boulder, CO: Westview, 1990).

cans did make further gains. However, by the end of the decade, signs appeared that the Democrats would not go gently into a political coma. Democrats actually gained seats in some state legislative chambers and won back control of North Carolina's lower house. At the same time, Democrats ceased losing seats at the congressional level and even temporarily won back some governorships.

Core Questions

While undoubtedly dismaying Democrats, the scope of these changes places scholars of southern politics today in an advantageous position relative to their predecessors. Enough has changed that one can now talk about the southern partisan shift away from the Democrats and to the Republicans as a largely accomplished fact, rather than a matter for future speculation or even a process in its early stages. This book explores the following questions related to partisan change in the South:

- How should one measure partisan change and what has been the nature of partisan change in the South?
- What issues spurred Republican gains? Scholars have heatedly debated the comparative importance of racial and economic issues in driving Republican growth. More recent work suggests additional attention needs to be paid to social issues.
- Even if economic and social issues explain Republican growth more than previously thought, how does racial context influence southern politics? In a political system in which African Americans overwhelmingly support the Democrats and Republicans derive the vast majority of their support from whites, one suspects that racial context plays a key role even if nonracial issues play important roles in shaping the South's political terrain.
- What is the role of political elites in propelling or slowing partisan change? More pointedly, how do the actions of strategic politicians systematically affect the pace of partisan change? How much have issue differences between Democratic and Republican officeholders sharpened on the issues that propelled partisan change?
- How have institutions shaped partisan change in the South? In the wake of Reconstruction, the South created many new institutions to assure white and Democratic dominance. How have these older institutions, like the primary, that survived the Civil Rights Movement operated in the altered political environment? How have new institutions, like racial redistricting and term limits, aided the Republicans?
- Finally, what are the prospects for the future? Are the Republicans destined to continue their inexorable gains and dominate southern politics as the

Democrats did during the Solid South era? Or will the Democrats stage a comeback?

Describing Partisan Change

In their seminal and provocative work *Issue Evolution*, Edward Carmines and James Stimson argue that "realignment" is no longer a useful concept to describe or explain partisan change.[4] They contend that its meaning has been so debated and its definition tweaked so often to accommodate the latest theory that the term is no longer very useful. In a recent work, David Mayhew forcefully argues that the traditional theory of realignment, in which a critical election surrounding the new issue results in major changes in the composition of party coalitions and in the relative level of partisan support, poorly explains partisan change in American history.[5] While it is tempting to simply utilize "realignment" as shorthand for "major partisan change" here, I avoid using the term to prevent confusion with the theories of other scholars or their particular use of the term.

Even if one does not discuss partisan change in the context of "realignments," one can nevertheless attempt to develop a typology of partisan change in order to more accurately describe and classify different types of partisan shifts. To prevent this typology from eliding into merely classifying various occurrences of partisan change according to which theory they appear to fit, it should depend largely on easily observable data rather than on theories about the causes of partisan change. Of course, different theories may explain the appearance of particular types of partisan change.

A Typology of Partisan Change

The first major means of classifying partisan change is how rapidly it occurs. Realignments that occur in one election might be identified as *rapid* realignments. In *Dynamics of the Party System*, James L. Sundquist outlines his version of "critical election" theory in which the voting be-

---

[4] Carmines and Stimson 1989, 19–26. The chapters in Byron E. Shafer, ed., *The End of Realignment? Interpreting American Electoral Eras* (Madison: University of Wisconsin Press, 1991) further discuss the usefulness of realignment as a concept. The final chapter, Harold F. Bass Jr., "Background to Debate: A Reader's Guide and Bibliography," 141–78, provides an excellent overview and bibliography of work on realignment through 1990.

[5] David R. Mayhew, *Electoral Realignments: A Critique of an American Genre* (New Haven: Yale University Press, 2002). See also Walter Dean Burnham, "Critical Realignment: Dead or Alive?" in *The End of Realignment? Interpreting American Electoral Eras*, ed. Byron E. Shafer (Madison: University of Wisconsin Press, 1991), 101–39; Carmines and Stimson 1989, 156–58.

havior of the electorate quickly shifts due to the arrival of a new issue cleavage in the electorate.[6] The support base of each party changes as does the overall level of support for each party—to the detriment of one and benefit of the other. In some cases, a new party displaces one of the existing parties. Although inspired by past scholarly observations of critical elections, I refer merely to "rapid" rather than "critical" partisan change in order to focus on the pace of partisan change and not on the much more complex question of whether or not a new issue cleavage explains the change.

In contrast, partisan change that occurs over the course of several decades can be labeled *gradual*. (I avoid the term *secular*, often used in the realignment literature, because this implies that partisan change is due to generational replacement.) Although partisan change is often described in the context of quick electoral upheavals, analogous to earthquakes, other scholars believe that partisan change can occur more gradually. Robert Speel, for example, argues that the shift toward the Democrats in presidential elections in New England was a slow process over several decades.[7] As described here, rapid and gradual realignments are extreme types and some realignments may be accomplished relatively quickly over a few elections even if they are not wholly rapid or gradual.

The second major distinction among types of partisan change may be made between *uniform* and *split-level* partisan change. Partisan change has conventionally been conceived as the result of major events that cause shifts in elite and mass partisanship and alter voting behavior at all levels of government. In partisan change that is uniform, the shift in voting behavior and partisan officeholding occurs at all levels of government. However, increasing numbers of scholars have identified cases in which, at least temporarily over several elections, voters cast their ballots for different parties at different levels of government. Speel, for example, notes that New Englanders increasingly voted for Democrats at the fed-

---

[6] James L. Sundquist, *Dynamics of the Party System: Alignment and Realignment of Political Parties in the United States* (Washington, DC: The Brookings Institution, 1983), 11–12, 19–34. Note, however, that Sundquist specifically acknowledges that realignment often occurs over an extended period but argues against viewing critical elections as a type of realignment: "Like magnitude, pace of change is a less than satisfactory criterion for classifying realignments. A single realignment may have both abrupt and slower paced phases, but it is still one phenomenon, one process of change. Critical elections, in sum, are episodes in most realignments; they do not define a type" (11). The great scholar of southern and American politics, V. O. Key, was the originator of the concept of critical versus secular realignments. See V. O. Key Jr., "A Theory of Critical Elections," *Journal of Politics* 17 (February 1955): 3–18; V. O. Key Jr., "Secular Realignment and the Party System," *Journal of Politics* 21 (May 1959): 198–210.

[7] Robert W. Speel, *Changing Patterns of Voting in the Northern United States: Electoral Realignment, 1952–1996* (University Park: Pennsylvania State University Press, 1998).

eral level but often supported Republicans for state and local offices.[8] Split-level partisan change may result in different voting behavior, and perhaps even different partisanship, for various levels of government. The Republicans may dominate in federal elections, while the Democrats usually win state and local elections.

Scholars have heatedly debated whether the very nature of partisan change has fundamentally shifted in America in the latter half of the twentieth century. Phillips and Sundquist separately argue for partisan change in the more conventional sense of a major shift in the preferences of voters and which party wins elections.[9] However, Norman Nie, Sidney Verba, and John Petrocik and Martin Wattenberg argue that the electorate has increasingly become independent and less tied to any political party.[10] Gary Jacobson's work on the rise of the incumbency advantage due to increasingly candidate-centered campaigns tends to support these conclusions.[11] Harold Stanley suggests a way out of this dilemma.[12] The voting behavior of the electorate may be classified not only according to their central tendency but also their variance. Electorates with a large number of truly independent or candidate-centered voters who often split their tickets have a relatively high variance in their support for candidates of a party and are relatively *dealigned*. Alignments in which most voters present strong partisan attachments and tend to vote a straight-party ticket are *strongly aligned*. Note that rather than being forced to dissect the partisanship of the electorate, which may be heavily subject to disputes over question wording on surveys, one can measure the intensity of the partisan commitment by looking at the variation in election returns. Rather than being at odds, the realignment and dealignment literatures are compatible with one another as both the central tendency and variance of the electorate can change over time. The average level of a party's support can remain the same even if there is greater variation between elections and support for individual candidates.

In line with this discussion, changes in voting behavior must persist for several elections in order to be considered a *long-term* partisan change

---

[8] Speel 1998, 14–15, 65, 181–83, 197–98, 200–203; see also Charles D. Hadley, "Dual Partisan Identification in the South," *Journal of Politics* 47 (February 1985): 254–68.

[9] Phillips 1969, 25–42; Sundquist 1993, 1–19.

[10] Norman H. Nie, Sidney Verba, and John R. Petrocik, *The Changing American Voter*, enlarged ed. (Cambridge, MA: Harvard University Press, 1979), 47–73; Martin P. Wattenberg, *The Decline of American Political Parties, 1952–1994* (Cambridge, MA: Harvard University Press, 1996).

[11] Gary C. Jacobson, *The Politics of Congressional Elections*, 5th ed. (New York: Addison Wesley Longman, 2001), 21–40, 105–21.

[12] Harold W. Stanley, "Southern Partisan Changes: Dealignment, Realignment, or Both?" *Journal of Politics* 50 (February 1988): 66–67.

rather than merely a *deviating* election. Temporary circumstances may cause voters to depart from their normal voting behavior. However, if they quickly return to the previous partisan pattern, it seems reasonable to classify the election as deviating.

Classifying Partisan Change in the South

Certain aspects of partisan change in the South are relatively easy to classify according to this typology. First, it is easy to declare that the South has experienced long-term partisan change rather than a few deviating elections. The Democrats have often bounced back after an especially dreadful election performance, such as 1980 or 1994, but they almost always have not regained fully their previous level of support. Nor have the Democrats been able to prevent the Republicans from achieving steady long-term gains. Even the Watergate scandal and the election of southern Democrat Jimmy Carter as president in the mid-1970s gave the Democrats only a temporary boost. The detailed description of Republican gains at the local, state, and federal levels presented in the next chapter shows that Democratic gains during this period were ephemeral and did not derail the steady process of Republican growth.

Although southern partisan change has been punctuated by elections of especially impressive Republican success, it is also not especially difficult to classify partisan change in the South as gradual.[13] Since the mid-1960s, scholars have searched high and low for a specific election that transformed southern politics with nearly the intensity of Indiana Jones's search for the Ark of the Covenant. Claims have been made for many different presidential elections: 1948, 1964, 1968, 1980, and 1994. Much like cubic zirconia lacks the lustre of a real diamond, none of these elections quite fits the bill. In most cases, Democrats still held far too many offices in the wake of the election. Alternatively, the GOP made too many gains prior to 1994 for one to argue convincingly that rapid partisan change centered around this particular contest. Tracing the pace of Republican gains (see chapter 2) strongly suggests that partisan change was gradual. The pace of GOP gains may have varied over time in response to events with periods of relatively slow growth punctuated by impressive gains in one election, but they made relatively steady headway over several decades. Perhaps more important, they were clearly not the product of any one election. Many scholars suspect that even rapid parti-

---

[13] Thomas L. Brunell and Bernard Grofman, "Explaining Divided U.S. Senate Delegations, 1788–1996: A Realignment Approach," *American Political Science Review* 92:2 (June 1998): 397.

san change tends to be accomplished over the course of several elections rather than a single contest.[14]

The debate over whether dealignment has accompanied partisan change in the South is a fierce one. Voters certainly became more likely to split their tickets in the 1970s compared to the 1950s.[15] Scandals and a highly critical media encouraged voters to take a negative view of government and political parties.[16] New scholarly evidence suggests that dealignment was relatively temporary and that partisanship is once again on the rise. Dealignment may have been a temporary side effect of the process of gradual realignment. Older conservative Democrats may split their tickets to express displeasure with national Democratic nominees. Alternatively, young conservative voters inclined to support the Republicans due to their stances on issues may often split their tickets if one or both of their parents are Democrats. Republicans frequently do not offer candidates for local or state offices, making it difficult to express support for the GOP for all office levels. Voters from the Solid South generation have joined the heavenly electorate in ever larger numbers as time has passed, so the share of southern white voters with strong long-term ties to the Democrats has shrunk. Additionally, the Republicans have run more candidates at all levels of government. Both trends likely have a positive effect on the willingness and the ability of new voters entering the electorate to both identify with and vote for Republicans.[17]

Larry Bartels contends that split-ticket voting reached its height in the late 1970s and that partisan voting has steadily grown since then.[18] In the 2000 election, southern Democrats and southern Republicans both overwhelmingly supported their party's nominee for president. Unlike in the past, it is now widely acceptable for whites to identify with Republicans. Indeed, it is more common than not, especially among middle- and upper-class white voters. The remaining whites who identify with the

[14] Carmines and Stimson 1989, 19–26; Mayhew 2002; Bruce A. Campbell, "Change in the Southern Electorate," *American Journal of Political Science* 21:1 (February 1977): 37–64; John R. Petrocik, "Realignment: New Party Coalitions and the Nationalization of the South," *Journal of Politics* 49:2 (May 1987): 347–75.

[15] Larry M. Bartels, "Partisanship and Voting Behavior, 1952–1996," *American Journal of Political Science* 44 (January 2000): 35–50; Nie, Verba, and Petrocik 1979, 47–73; Wattenberg 1996, 17–23.

[16] Thomas E. Patterson, *Out of Order* (New York: Vintage, 1994), 3–10, 16–21, 200–206.

[17] Bruce A. Campbell, "Patterns of Change in the Partisan Loyalties of Native Southerners: 1952–1972," *Journal of Politics* 39:3 (August 1977): 737; Alan I. Abramowitz and Kyle L. Saunders, "Ideological Realignment in the U.S. Electorate," *Journal of Politics* 60:3 (August 1998): 647; Helmut Norpoth, "Under Way and Here to Stay: Party Realignment in the 1980s," *Public Opinion Quarterly* 52:3 (autumn 1997): 385.

[18] Larry M. Bartels, "Partisanship and Voting Behavior, 1952–1996," *American Journal of Political Science* 44:1 (January 2000): 35–50.

Democrats for the most part support the national Democratic Party's stand on issues, so they feel little pressure to split their ticket. One might expect ticket splitting to further decline as Republicans contest an even higher share of local offices in the future.

The debate over whether dealignment or realignment best describes changes in southern politics is closely related to the question of whether the South has experienced uniform or split-level partisan change. Scholars have long noted that Republican support appeared greater in federal contests than in state or local elections. Some speculated that the conservative nature of southern Democratic politicians led to a split-level alignment in which southerners continued to send conservative southern Democrats to their state capitals and Congress but oppose national Democratic nominees for president as overly liberal. The greater conservatism of southern Democrats compared to their northern brethren helps explain the slow pace of Republican gains.[19] However, the evidence increasingly suggests that the split-level nature of the realignment was temporary. Southern Democratic candidates increasingly took liberal stands on a variety of issues and became steadily less distinguishable from their northern colleagues. At the same time, Republicans made steady gains below the presidential level, belying the notion that southerners had a split-party identification.

Explaining Partisan Change in the South

Much of the southern politics literature has attempted to explain Republican growth in the South as part of a standard process of partisan change. Although different scholars may develop competing theories, most essentially argue that old issues gradually decline in relevance to the electorate and new, more salient issues arise to divide voters in new ways.[20] Political change in the South is part of the regular turning of the wheel in which a new issue seizes the electorate and propels changes in the political bases and strength of the parties. Recent GOP successes can thus be placed in

[19] Glaser 1996, 80–141; but see Patricia A. Hurley, "Partisan Representation, Realignment, and the Senate in the 1980s," *Journal of Politics* 53:1 (February 1991): 24. Hurley argues that the strong conservatism of the Republicans slowed realignment to the GOP in the 1980s.

[20] Carmines and Stimson 1989; Jeffrey M. Stonecash, *Class and Party in American Politics* Boulder, CO: Westview, 2000); Sundquist 1993, 269–97, 352–449; David Brady and Joseph Stewart Jr., "Congressional Party Realignment and Transformation of Public Policy in Three Realignment Eras," *American Journal of Political Science* 26:2 (May 1982): 333–60; Everett Carll Ladd, "The 1994 Congressional Elections: The Postindustrial Realignment Continues," *Political Science Quarterly* 110:1 (spring 1995): 19; Peter F. Nardulli, "The Concept of a Critical Realignment, Electoral Behavior, and Political Change," *American Political Science Review* 89:1 (March 1995): 18–19.

the context of past upheavals in party fortunes, such as the demise of the Whigs and the rise of the Republicans in the 1850s and 1860s. Carmines and Stimson essentially take this approach in their highly influential study of racial issues and American politics.[21] Indeed, they believe that their study of racial issues is an example of "issue evolution," an approach they present as an alternative to traditional realignment theory.

These attempts by scholars to situate southern political change in the context of a general theory of partisan change centered around issues are both laudable and understandable but ultimately misguided. Southern political developments over the past several decades should not be viewed merely as a routine process of partisan change but as the long-term result of the South's democratization. Institutional changes, culminating in the Voting Rights Act of 1965, dramatically expanded the franchise and thus changed the landscape of southern politics. Nevertheless, Carmines and Stimson give short shrift to these changes. They mention them to explain the salience of racial issues but do not explain how the South's institutional legacy continued to shape politics beyond bringing new issues to the fore.

Issues certainly played a major role in promoting gradual Republican growth among white southerners over the course of several decades and the rapid completion of the long-term shift of black voters to the Democrats in the mid-1960s. However, one ignores the role of old and new institutions and the operation of strategic Democratic elites who already held power in this changed context at the peril of missing key factors that shaped the development of southern politics. Exploring elites and institutions as well as the historical context facilitates a better understanding of the role of various issues in southern politics over the past several decades. Indeed, an examination of the historical context helps explain that (1) though race explains why African Americans became nearly unanimously Democratic in the mid-1960s, (2) racial issues were not the predominant factor in promoting Republican growth among southern whites despite the great public importance of race in the 1960s and (3) southern GOP growth must be viewed as the result of a democratization process rather than part of the normal vicissitudes of party fortunes within an established democratic system. Because of the importance of the historical context, especially surrounding racial issues, the next section gives a brief overview of the historical role of race in the South.

The Historical Role of Race in the South

As is well-known, the American South was highly undemocratic at the dawn of the twentieth century. As Reconstruction drew to a close, white

---

[21] Carmines and Stimson 1989.

supremacist Democrats used state institutions and other means to establish and maintain the dominance of their party. In *The Shaping of Southern Politics*, J. Morgan Kousser explains that the establishment of the one-party Democratic South under conservative Bourbon leadership did not result from the unified support of even white southerners. The establishment of overwhelming Democratic dominance resulted directly from successful efforts to exclude most non-Democrats, black and white, from the franchise and thus from political power.[22]

A variety of means were used by the conservative Democratic barons to accomplish the exclusion of most non-Democrats and establish the permanent dominance of their party, race, and class. Three groups were the primary targets of the Bourbon Democrats. Wealthy white southerners viewed African-American political equality as unnatural and efforts to assert black political power even tentatively as a great insult to their status as leaders of the South. Equally important, African Americans identified their freedom with the Republican Party. Blacks naturally identified with the party of Emancipation and an overwhelming share of African Americans steadfastly supported the GOP. Continuing black support for the Republicans during Reconstruction was not at all surprising when one contrasts that vocal support for black rights offered by many Republicans, particularly fervent Radicals like Representative Thaddeus Stevens and Senator Charles Sumner, with the outright opposition to black political equality and support for Jim Crow by most Democrats. The few insincere, patronizing, and transparent attempts by Democratic politicians to solicit black votes failed. African Americans acted to support their political interests by voting Republican.

Bourbon Democrats similarly were nonplussed by the prospect of voting by poor whites as support by the lower classes for Populist or Republican candidates might challenge their economic and political dominance. Governments acting in the interests of landless whites and yeoman farmers might abolish the regressive taxation system under which white plantation owners often paid a far lower share in taxes than poorer whites who did not own vast estates and barely scratched out a living. Native white Unionists, who had often suffered greatly for their support of the Union during the Civil War, were pejoratively labeled "scalawags" by their opponents as part of the effort to suppress opposition to the Democrats. Similarly, though most northern immigrants moved south for ide-

[22] Alexander Keyssar, *The Right to Vote: The Contested History of Democracy in the United States* (New York: Basic Books, 2000); J. Morgan Kousser, *The Shaping of Southern Politics: Suffrage Restriction and the Establishment of the One-Party South, 1880–1910* (New Haven: Yale University Press, 1974); Michael Perman, *Struggle for Mastery: Disfranchisement in the South, 1888–1908* (Chapel Hill: University of North Carolina Press, 2001).

alistic reasons, they were broadly tarred with the epithet "carpetbagger" in order to stigmatize them. Some northern immigrants wanted to bring economic development and prosperity to the region, while others wanted to aid black southerners by establishing educational institutions for freedmen.[23] These goals were anathema to Bourbon Democrats who worked steadily to marginalize those northern immigrants whom they could not co-opt into supporting the Democratic Party and their goals.

White conservatives paraded the threat of government under the evil triumvirate of blacks, "scalawags," and "carpetbaggers" to gain support for black disfranchisement. Democracy, even for whites, was doomed in the South by the unwillingness of most whites to acknowledge the right of blacks to basic political rights. Proponents of disfranchisement nevertheless had to tread gingerly. The Fifteenth Amendment, ratified in 1870, flatly states, "The right of citizens of the United States to vote shall not be denied or abridged by the United States or by any State on account of race, color, or previous condition of servitude." In addition to possibly inviting judicial action, southerners hesitated to ban blacks directly from voting because they also feared intervention by a federal government under Republican control. Northern Republicans had a strong incentive to protect their southern wing as some southern support was critical to the national Republican majority prior to 1896.[24] Southern jurisdictions consequently used nonracial means that had the far from coincidental effect of eliminating black access to the ballot. A variety of means, including literacy tests, poll taxes, registration laws, fraud, and violence, were used to disfranchise African Americans. As the education of blacks under slavery was illegal, the literacy gap between blacks and whites was quite large.

Corrupt Democrats in majority-black counties often successfully gained control of the election machinery and counted black votes as having been cast for the Democrats regardless of how blacks voted or if they voted at all. Fraud was particularly rampant in Louisiana, where parishes with overwhelming black Republican majorities managed to somehow record humongous majorities for Democratic candidates. Manipulation of the black vote by corrupt white politicians in majority-black counties was critical to the maintenance of statewide Democratic control in Alabama prior to the adoption of a new state constitution in 1901 designed to assure Democratic supremacy. Mississippi and South Carolina Democrats happily used violence to assure the election of their preferred candi-

[23] Eric Foner, *Reconstruction: America's Unfinished Revolution, 1863–1877* (New York: Harper and Row, 1988), 291–307.

[24] Richard M. Valelly, "National Parties and Racial Disenfranchisement," in Paul E. Peterson, ed., *Classifying by Race* (Princeton: Princeton University Press, 1995), 188–216.

dates.[25] Violence against blacks carried little stigma in the Reconstruction South. Indeed, white women actually competed to bring pies to white men imprisoned for murder under the federal Ku Klux Klan Act.[26]

The use of nonracial means to accomplish black disfranchisement meant that many less-affluent whites also lost access to the suffrage. This outcome was intended on the part of the conservative whites who led the disfranchisement movement as they believed that the "wrong sort" of whites were just as unfit to govern as blacks. The representatives of heavily white areas that contained few affluent plantations were often aware of the potential impact of disfranchisement laws on their constituents and the likely consequences for their own political future. They and their constituents consequently opposed black disfranchisement at a higher rate than did white representatives from the heavily black plantation counties of the "Black Belt" (named for the rich soil, not the people) or worked to water down its potential effect on white voting.[27] More farsighted white Populists and Republicans realized that they had little chance of commanding a majority in the region without black support.

Bourbons strategically maneuvered to undercut whites opposed to suffrage and to buy off their support with measures designed to limit the impact of disfranchisement measures on poor whites. The oft-misunderstood grandfather clause was the classic example of this sort of measure. Contrary to popular understanding, grandfather clauses were actually designed to enfranchise rather than disfranchise voters. Grandfather clauses permitted voters who were disfranchised by other laws to vote if their grandfather could vote. The grandfather clause ingeniously created a loophole through which white voters, but not newly freed blacks, could hope to jump to evade disfranchisement. The clause succeeded brilliantly in attracting white support to the disfranchisement cause but failed miserably, or spectacularly from the perspective of wealthy Bourbons, at maintaining white levels of enfranchisement. Illiterate whites were usually embarrassed by their illiteracy and too proud or too fearful of public humiliation to take advantage of the clause in order to register.[28]

State constitutional conventions in the 1890s helped consolidate Democratic control and made the exclusion of blacks a part of each state's organic law. These new state constitutions reduced the need for statutes or corruption to exclude African Americans or protect Democratic dominance and set the pattern for southern politics until the Civil Rights

---

[25] W.E.B. DuBois, *Black Reconstruction in America, 1860–1880* (New York: Simon and Schuster, 1935), 670–708; Foner 1988, 442; Kousser 1974, 26, 54–56, 152–54; Perman 2001.

[26] Lou Falkner Williams, *The Great South Carolina Ku Klux Klan Trials, 1871–1872* (Athens: University of Georgia Press, 1996).

[27] Kousser 1974, 88–91, 97–99, 166–68, 175–78; Perman 2001.

[28] Kousser 1974, 58–60; Perman 2001.

Movement. Populists occasionally challenged the dominance of conservative Democrats but with ephemeral success. The one-party system made it easy for Democrats elected as populists who supported progressive measures to gradually shift over their careers into racial demagoguery or economic conservatism. South Carolina Governor and Senator "Pitchfork" Ben Tillman, for example, began his career as a tribune of the white masses but ended as a stalwart conservative backed by the Bourbons. Neither set of positions conflicted with his consistent advocacy of white supremacy. It may appear miraculous to those who best remember him as a segregationist candidate for president in 1948 and a staunch conservative in the U.S. Senate, but Strom Thurmond was elected governor of South Carolina as a progressive Democrat in 1946.[29]

The Longs of Louisiana probably had greater success than any other southern populists in enacting their program. Their "share the wealth" program of providing schoolbooks to children and building roads while attacking large corporations proved tremendously popular with the white masses. Occasionally the Longs even publicly recognized race baiting as deleterious to the interests of poor whites because it served to distract from governmental solutions to problems that conflicted with the interests of the wealthy elite. However, the long-term success of the Longs was undercut by the corruption of their administrations and the inevitable reaction that repeatedly led to the election of thrifty white anti-Long conservatives as reformers.[30]

In sum, the political dominance of the Democrats prior to the Civil Rights Movement resulted not from overarching dominance among the voting-age population but from institutional mechanisms designed to exclude Democratic opponents from the franchise and minimize their impact on southern politics. The fight for a broad franchise was a long struggle that took over several decades in the courts, in Congress, and on the streets. Legal activists struggled to convince federal judges to overturn discriminatory state laws and state constitutional provisions for violating federal law and the federal constitution. They won a major victory as early as 1944 when the Supreme Court declared in *Smith v. Allwright* that the Democratic primary was "state action" and banned the white primary. During the Civil Rights Movement, activists working in southern communities worked to register blacks and mobilize support for black enfranchisement. Their heroic efforts made possible the passage of a strong federal voting rights law by Congress in 1965.

While the Fifteenth Amendment and past legislation had theoretically

[29] Jack Bass and Marilyn W. Thompson, *Ol' Strom: An Unauthorized Biography of Strom Thurmond* (Atlanta: Longstreet Press, 1988), 79–88; V. O. Key Jr., *Southern Politics in State and Nation* (New York: Vintage, 1949), 142–43, 147–50, 302–10.

[30] Key 1949, 156–82.

enshrined protections against racial discrimination in voting into law, the Voting Rights Act of 1965 was the first legislation to contain sufficient provisions for enforcement. Section 5 of the Act barred "covered jurisdictions," generally the worst offenders in the South, from enacting any new law governing voting without preclearance from either the U.S. Attorney General or the D.C. District Court. This provision prevented southern states from enacting new laws designed to disfranchise African Americans after the overturning of old ones by either federal legislation or federal judges. Additionally, Section 2 of the Act authorized private lawsuits to enforce voting rights, and Sections 6 and 7 allowed the U.S. Attorney General to send federal registrars to covered jurisdictions if a sufficient number of complaints of voting rights violations were received. The Supreme Court upheld the central provisions of the Voting Rights Act of 1965 in *South Carolina v. Katzenbach* (1966). Rapid increases in African-American voter registration followed implementation of the Act. White registration also substantially increased.

In short, the Civil Rights Movement was more than a successful social movement for minority rights. It was also central to a process that must properly be labeled as one of *democratization*. The long-term hyperdominance of the Democrats was highly unnatural. The Civil Rights Movement, itself a product of broad social and economic processes,[31] shattered the core institutions that maintained the undemocratic status quo. The end of the complete dominance of southern politics by the Democrats and their shifting of policy positions on race were the natural consequences of the great expansion of the franchise not only among blacks but among whites as well.

The Civil Rights Movement nevertheless left much of the electoral system intact. While it destroyed some institutions, such as barriers to voter registration, it maintained others, like primary elections. Indeed, Section 5 of the Voting Rights Act made it difficult to change these institutions by requiring federal preclearance for changes to any voting practice or procedure. In contrast to more dramatic revolutions, the Civil Rights Movement did not remove much of the old elite from public office. Existing officials continued to occupy their offices and could wield substantial resources to maintain them even in the face of an expanded franchise. Unlike the political upheavals prior to the Civil War, the Civil Rights Movement did not result in the collapse or replacement of either of the two major national parties. In the immediate aftermath of the passage of both the Civil Rights Act of 1964 and the Voting Rights Act of 1965,

---

[31] Doug McAdam, *Political Process and the Development of Black Insurgency, 1930–1970* (Chicago: University of Chicago Press, 1982).

most southern whites retained their Democratic party identification. It took time for the changes wrought by the expanded franchise to percolate through the political system and result in a more vibrant, democratic politics.

The following sections outline how elites, institutions, racial context, and various issues shaped the growth of the southern GOP. Democratization created changes that eventually reshaped all of these factors. Elites had to respond to an expanded electorate. The Civil Rights Movement destroyed some institutions even as it maintained others and created new ones. The racial context of southern politics greatly changed as African Americans gained the right to vote and, more recently, Latinos expanded their southern presence outside of south Texas. Perhaps most important, the destruction of the old system allowed southern voters to focus on new issues. Racial issues did not disappear, but the demise of the old anti-democratic system and the passage of federal civil rights legislation eliminated the ability of elites to appeal to voters based on the maintenance of a dead white supremacist electoral system. It also made it more difficult for elites to suppress other issues in the name of maintaining white solidarity in order to preserve a legal system that no longer existed.

Elites, institutions, issues, and the racial context do not operate separately from one another. Although each of the following sections (and then chapters in the book) focuses primarily on one of these factors, they tend to interact to produce important partisan changes in southern politics. Consequently, information about one factor will inevitably jump into another section that focuses on the other. I have attempted to place these sorts of discussions of multiple factors in the section or chapter where it makes the most sense to raise the issue.

Political Elites and Partisan Change

Political scientists have long noted the important role that strategic elites play in politics. In his now classic work, *Congress: The Electoral Connection*, David Mayhew argues that the desire to win reelection is central to members of Congress and must remain the primary goal of most representatives as success in reelection is necessary to achieving all other goals. He further explains that Congress is uniquely designed to further these reelection goals.[32] Gary Jacobson and Samuel Kernell detail how strategic actors both respond to electoral pressures and greatly influence electoral outcomes in their pathbreaking work, *Strategy and Choice in Congressional Elections*. According to Jacobson and Kernell, strong candidates act stra-

---

[32] David R. Mayhew, *Congress: The Electoral Connection* (New Haven: Yale University Press, 1974).

tegically by seeking election when their chances of victory are high and foregoing contests during times of weaker opportunity. The decision by strong candidates to seek election greatly influences whether incumbents win reelection and a party gains or loses seats in congressional elections. In later work Jacobson argues that the impact of national trends on electoral outcomes is increasingly dependent on the responses of strategic elites to these trends, rather than the impact of the trends on voting behavior. Additional works have confirmed the applicability of Jacobson and Kernell's basic thesis to senatorial, gubernatorial, and state legislative elections.[33]

Carmines and Stimson were among the first scholars to attempt to expand the impact of elites beyond their action in an individual election by integrating the role of elites into a theory of systematic partisan change. Carmines and Stimson pay attention to elites in their role as policymakers and setters of the issue agenda. The rise of differences between the parties on new issues may spur changes in the partisan preferences of voters. In particular, they contend that the growing gap between the Democrats and Republicans on racial issues, underlined by the 1964 contest between Johnson and Goldwater for the presidency, spurred further Republican growth as the issue gained support for the GOP among white racial conservatives even as African Americans became hugely supportive of the Democrats.[34] Edsall and Edsall similarly argue that the racially conservative stance of Ronald Reagan attracted many white voters to the Republican banner in his runs for the presidency in 1976, 1980, and 1984 even as black voters were alienated by his racial conservatism.[35]

Carmines and Stimson cleverly show that changes in the relative positions of the two parties on issues can result from electoral happenstance as well as political opportunism. The defeat of liberal Republicans by liberal Democrats in 1958 in the North and the defeat of conservative Democrats by conservative Republicans in the South had the impact of moving the congressional Democratic Party to the left and the congressional Republican Party to the right on racial issues. On the other hand,

[33] Gary C. Jacobson and Samuel Kernell, *Strategy and Choice in Congressional Elections*, 2nd ed. (New Haven: Yale University Press, 1983); Jacobson 2001, 92–93; Jonathan S. Krasno, *Challengers, Competition, and Reelection: Comparing Senate and House Elections* (New Haven: Yale University Press, 1994); David Lublin, "Quality, Not Quantity: Strategic Politicians in U.S. Senate Elections, 1952–1990," *Journal of Politics* 56 (1994): 228–41; Gary F. Moncrief, Peverill Squire, and Malcolm E. Jewell, *Who Runs for the Legislature?* (Upper Saddle River, NJ: Prentice-Hall, 2000).

[34] Carmines and Stimson 1989, 37–84.

[35] Thomas Byrne Edsall and Mary D. Edsall, *Chain Reaction: The Impact of Race, Rights, and Taxes on American Politics* (New York: Norton, 1991), 148–214.

strategic elites often intentionally try out new issues and modify existing ones in their never-ending battle for public support.[36]

Despite the marked advance of Carmines and Stimson's work in explaining the role of political elites in promoting partisan change, more needs to be done to incorporate the key insights of Jacobson and Kernell. Equally important, one needs to consider the unique role of political elites in states where the franchise has been radically expanded. Specifically, I intend to show the following.

Former Democratic Monopoly Slowed Republican Gains. In order for democratic politics to function well, voters must have a choice among candidates and parties. As V. O. Key nicely explains, the old southern system of restricting all choice to within the Democratic primary did not function well.[37] The absence of consistent factions with opposing ideas did not allow voters to hold politicians accountable for their actions. While voters in most liberal democracies can choose from more than two parties at the polls, voters require at least two parties and two sets of candidates if they are to have the chance to select between competing programs or to at least reward or punish the incumbents for their performance in office.

As the franchise expanded and the South became more democratic, the overwhelmingly dominant Democrats faced difficult times as they needed to please an increasingly diverse set of voters with conflicting priorities. However, their status as the dominant party gave them enormous advantages in undertaking the challenges posed by the greatly changed political arena. Democratic officeholders generally did not form a unified structure of candidates seeking collectively to hold on to power. However, the weakness of Democratic Party organizations allowed Democratic candidates to adopt a variety of issue positions without fear of reprisal from any central party authority. At the same time, all Democratic Party candidates continued to benefit from the overwhelming identification of the region's voters with the Democrats. The absence of a strong central party authority further did not prevent the formation of strong networks among Democratic officeholders and other elites. Put in this light, it hardly seems surprising that the versatile Democrats should be able to maintain their dominance of southern politics in the wake of the relatively evolutionary changes wrought by the Civil Rights Movement on the southern political system.

Candidate recruitment is critical to party success in the American system. The dominance of the single-member district system for elections

---

[36] Carmines and Stimson 1989, 6–7, 14–19, 59–72.
[37] Key 1949, 142–50, 299–310.

and the plethora of political offices requires an aspiring major party to recruit a battery of candidates if it is to appear credible. The decision by strategic high-quality candidates to seek election under the banner of one party rather than another may stymie or accelerate partisan change. The ability of a new or rising party to attract any candidate, let alone a high-quality candidate with a good chance of success, is critical to a party's growth. After all, a party cannot win elections in which it does not run candidates.

The focus of much of the literature on partisan change in federal elections results in neglect of Republican problems in recruiting any candidates in many local and state legislative contests. As chapter 3 explains, a lack of candidates impeded GOP efforts to expand their base of office-holders in the region for many years. Democrats had such dominance of offices at every level of government that recruiting candidates with previous experience in public office was difficult for the GOP. Potential Republican candidates for legislative bodies knew they would form a very small and often powerless minority among a sea of Democratic legislators—hardly a temptation for any aspiring politician.[38] Even candidates for executive positions faced the challenge of operating within a network of Democratic officeholders. Chapter 3 explores these issues and how the incumbency advantage helped maintain Democratic dominance by discouraging Republican opposition.

Racial and Economic Contexts Shape Elite Recruitment. In undemocratic states with a single party, the path to power is relatively straightforward: join the ruling party. The stunted political system of the pre–Civil Rights Movement South did not offer aspiring politicians much more of a choice. The dominance of the Democrats made the choice of political party obvious for individuals hoping to advance.

Democratization expands viable political opportunities beyond a single party and makes the decision to join the Democratic Party less obvious. Strategic elites must act more cagily in a more open, democratic political system, weighing the advantages of joining one party over another. The opening of the South's political system to non-Democratic competitors created new opportunities. However, the opportunities presented by GOP membership vary widely around the region. After all, the southern electorate is now more diverse, but it is hardly uniform and the potential for Republican candidates to win office may vary considerably.

As part of its exploration of the role of racial context, chapter 5 examines how strategic elites respond to the varying electoral dynamics in different parts of the South to the benefit of the Republicans in some

[38] Sundquist 1983, 285–87, 373.

areas but to their detriment in others. Republicans have difficulty attracting candidates and winning elections in areas with high numbers of African-American voters, as blacks vote heavily Democratic. Running for office is a difficult, uphill battle at best. Strategic candidates will not want to seek election as Republicans in areas where the presence of sizable numbers of black voters means that the GOP label reduces the viability of their candidacy.

Race is not the only demographic context to influence elite recruitment. Debates over economic issues, especially the role of government in promoting employment and social welfare, shaped debates between Democrats and Republicans outside the South since the New Deal. Low-income voters tended to value social welfare programs and give support to the Democrats while high-income voters resented being taxed to pay for this government-provided safety net. As the GOP began to achieve some success in the South, southern politics began to reflect this now traditional divide over economic issues as well. Chapter 6 demonstrates that Republicans have had greater success in recruiting candidates in heavily white, high-income areas as part of its discussion of the continuing power of economic issues. Democrats have increasingly found it difficult to attract candidates in these areas in recent years as Republican dominance has grown.

Elite Positions on Social Issues Slowed Realignment in Rural Areas. Elite responses to the pressures posed by new issues raised in a more democratic South shape where the GOP makes gains and where it does not. After all, a party cannot win office where it does not have candidates. However, elites can also shape the speed and the scope of partisan change through the issues positions they take. When local political elites of different parties react to new issues by taking similar positions, change should likely slow as voters have little reason to alter their past party preferences.

Black and Black detail how the racial conservatism of many white Democratic candidates in the 1960s and 1970s derailed prospects for any rapid partisan shift centered on racial issues.[39] Similarly, rural Democrats slowed the ability of Republicans to attract voters based on social issues through the adoption of highly conservative positions on social issues. In most parts of the rural South, there is usually little gap between Demo-

[39] Earl Black and Merle Black, *The Rise of the Southern Republicans* (Cambridge, MA: Harvard University Press, 2002), 152–73. See also Stanley P. Berard, *Southern Democrats in the U.S. House of Representatives* (Norman: University of Oklahoma Press, 2001), 118–42, for more evidence on the continuing conservatism of southern Democrats in the 1970s and 1980s.

cratic and Republican partisans or local officials on social issues because the liberal position is highly unpopular and would be political suicide for the ambitious politician—or even one who merely desires to continue to hold office. Members of neither party favor gun control in rural areas where hunting remains popular. Similarly, school prayer continued in many rural schools with the blessings of Democrats and Republicans alike even after the Supreme Court declared it violated constitutional requirements on the separation of church and state. Few abortion clinics exist in rural areas. In contrast, urban southern Democrats were more likely to adopt socially liberal positions due to pressures from more liberal urban Democrats. The gap in party positions in urban areas allowed the GOP to appeal to urban social conservatives in a way that was not possible in rural areas.

The lack of a difference between Republicans and Democrats on social issues in rural areas worked to the advantage of Democrats and stalled partisan change toward the Republicans in the rural South. Why should socially conservative Democrats leave their party when Democrats are no more liberal on social issues than Republicans? Democrats, however, could not forever forestall change related to social issues in rural areas. Prodded by urban and suburban liberals, Democratic candidates running for statewide and federal office have gradually taken more liberal positions on social issues. As part of its exploration of rising social issues, chapter 6 explains how awareness of the partisan gap on social issues at the elite level gradually seeped into rural areas. Even though local rural Democrats largely maintained their traditional conservatism, the greater liberalism of state and national Democrats aided Republican candidacies among rural voters.

Institutions and Partisan Change

If the presence of a broad swath of Democratic elites impeded Republican efforts to gain political traction in the post–Civil Rights Movement environment, institutions assured that Democratic elites could not stave off substantial Republican gains indefinitely. As outlined above, Democratic rule during the Jim Crow era was not a natural outgrowth of the region's politics. In the wake of Reconstruction, southern Democratic elites adopted a variety of institutions that eliminated black participation and undercut anti-Democratic parties, like the Republicans and Populists.[40] Scholars have further highlighted how racist white politicians used their control of southern political institutions to prevent blacks from

---

[40] DuBois 1935, 572–75, 630, 694; John Hope Franklin, *Reconstruction after the Civil War* (Chicago: University of Chicago Press, 1961), 194–227; Keyssar 2000; Kousser 1974; Perman 2001. *Struggle for Mastery: Disfranchisement in the South, 1888–1908* (Chapel Hill: University of North Carolina Press 2001).

gaining an effective voice even after the Voting Rights Act of 1965 assured African Americans access to the ballot. In many states, political leaders gerrymandered the boundaries of congressional and state legislative districts so that African Americans would not form a voting majority able to elect blacks to either the state or the national legislature.[41]

As part of the effort to undermine institutionalized racism, Congress and the federal judiciary, continually prodded by activists, attacked and eliminated many institutions that were part of the edifice that maintained white supremacy. However, institutions perceived as nonracial even if they were established for racial reasons, like primary elections, continued to operate in the changed post-Movement political climate. It is easy to overlook the crucial role of institutions because many of them were developed long ago and are an accepted part of the political landscape. While many scholarly works examine the partisan impact of one institution or another,[42] less attention has been paid to the systematic role of institutions in propelling forward Republican southern gains over the past forty years. Old institutions like the primary often operate in new ways that advantage the Republicans.

New institutional rules designed to protect the gains of the Civil Rights Movement also influenced southern politics. The Voting Rights Act as interpreted and enforced during the 1990s redistricting round not only protected existing majority-minority districts but forced the creation of substantial numbers of new ones. The systematic creation of numerous new majority-minority constituencies for local, state, and federal legislative bodies advantaged Republicans as well as minority Democrats.

Scholars who focus exclusively on issues or candidates ignore key forces that shaped partisan change in the South. In examining the wide-ranging game of politics, it is crucial to remember that the rules help dictate winners and losers. After all, this is why supporters and opponents of the Civil Rights Movement put so much effort into fighting over the nature of the rules. Southern congressional delegations would not have so vehemently opposed the Voting Rights Act of 1965 if they had not believed that it would undermine their positions. Dr. Martin Luther King Jr.

---

[41] Chandler Davidson and Bernard Grofman, eds., *Quiet Revolution in the South: The Impact of the Voting Rights Act, 1965–1990* (Princeton: Princeton University Press, 1994); J. Morgan Kousser, *Colorblind Injustice: Minority Voting Rights and the Undoing of the Second Reconstruction* (Chapel Hill: University of North Carolina Press, 1999); Frank R. Parker, *Black Votes Count: Black Empowerment in Mississippi after 1965* (Chapel Hill: University of North Carolina Press, 1990).

[42] Jay Barth, "The Impact of Election Timing on Republican Trickle-Down in the South," in Robert P. Steed, Lawrence W. Moreland, and Tod A. Baker, eds., *Southern Parties and Elections: Studies in Regional Political Change* (Tuscaloosa: University of Alabama Press, 1997); David Lublin and D. Stephen Voss, "Racial Redistricting and Realignment in Southern State Legislatures," *American Journal of Political Science* 44 (October 2000): 792–810.

would not have declared, "Give us the ballot—we will transform the South," if he had not held similar beliefs about the importance of rules governing access to the franchise and to politics more generally.[43] In this work, primarily in chapter 4, I show that institutional rules aided the southern realignment in the following ways.

Primary Elections Accelerate Republican Gains.   Southern states established primary elections both as a method to exclude blacks and settle factional disputes within the Democratic Party. As an internal party affair, primary elections historically could legally exclude blacks. The use of elections to settle nomination contests helped legitimize the nominee and prevent defections to an opposing party by the loser. In the one-party South, the Democratic primary was the critical election as it selected the nominee of the party who was almost invariably destined to win the general election.

The Supreme Court declared that the Democratic primary was "state action" and banned the white primary in *Smith v. Allwright* in 1944. The Voting Rights Act of 1965 led to a major influx of new black and white voters who were attracted to the Democratic Party, and its primary, because of the liberalism of the national party, the party's traditional social and political dominance, and because the Democratic primary remained the contest that really settled the election. Why join the Republicans when the action was with the Democrats?

White conservatives and moderates saw their dominance within the party diluted by the entry of African Americans, but they remained dominant within the party—at first. However, as some white conservatives, excited by the conservatism of Republicans like Barry Goldwater and Ronald Reagan, began to abandon the Democrats for the Republicans, it became easier for liberals and harder for conservatives to win Democratic nominations. This spurred further defections by white conservative candidates, who saw their chances of winning Democratic nominations decline, and white conservative voters, who grew dissatisfied as the party nominated increasingly moderate or liberal candidates. Like a rock gathering speed as it rolls down a hill, the cycle constantly repeated and reinforced itself until white liberals and racial minorities dominated Democratic primaries.[44]

Racial Redistricting Aided Republican Growth.   The Supreme Court attacked anti-black racial gerrymandering in *Allen v. State Board of Elections*

---

[43] Martin Luther King Jr. and James Melvin Washington, eds., *A Testament of Hope: The Essential Writings and Speeches of Marting Luther King, Jr.* (San Francisco: Harper, 1991), 197–99.

[44] Sundquist 1983, 375.

in 1969. However, it was the Court's 1986 decision in *Thornburg v. Gingles*, after Congress amended the Voting Rights Act in 1982, that really paved the way for an aggressive effort by African Americans and Latinos to force localities and states to create majority-minority districts for local, state, and federal elections.

The regular round of redistricting following the 1990 Census led to the creation of numerous new African-American and Latino majority districts and the election of many new minority congressional representatives and state legislators. Many southern states elected their first black representatives to the U.S. House since Reconstruction. However, the concentration of minority Democrats, especially African Americans, in majority-minority districts undercut the Democratic base in adjoining districts and aided the Republicans. Moreover, it provided an incentive for whites to run as Republicans as the number of districts favorable to white Democrats declined.

The Supreme Court attacked districts with bizarre boundaries designed to aid the election of minorities as "racial gerrymanders" that violated the Equal Protection Clause beginning with their decision in *Shaw v. Reno* (1993). States and localities still have an obligation to draw majority-minority districts where they can draw reasonably compact districts and racial bloc voting prevents the election of minority candidates. Some majority-minority districts have nevertheless been eliminated in the wake of *Shaw* and jurisdictions have become more resistant to demands to create or protect majority-minority districts. Over the long term, this shift will probably aid Democrats.

The Initiative Process and Term Limits Opened Doors for Republicans. The presence of incumbent Democrats formed a barrier to Republican gains, especially in local and state legislative contests. Incumbents have resources that discourage strong candidates from opposing them and make them difficult to defeat even if they attract a challenger. By forcing Democratic incumbents to retire, term limits expanded political opportunities for Republicans. As state legislators resemble other people in their loathing of unemployment, term limits never would have passed without successful use of the initiative process. Term limits have not passed in any southern state where voters lack the right to initiate new laws by placing them on the ballot.

Racial Issues, Racial Context, and Partisan Change

Scholars have fiercely debated the role of various issues, especially race, in promoting southern Republican growth. Many scholars argue that race played the dominant role in polarizing southern voting behavior. Once Democrats abandoned the historic commitment of their party to white supremacy in favor of liberal positions on racial issues, African Americans unified in the Democratic Party. At the same time, conservative positions on racial issues adopted by Republicans attracted white voters to the GOP. According to this argument, southern whites supported the Democratic Party prior to the Civil Rights Movement because southern Democrats protected white supremacy and the national Democrats avoided interfering with the South's racial hierarchy. The disenchantment of white southerners with the national Democratic Party began with Truman's push to integrate the armed forces in 1948. Many southern Democrats bolted from the party in that year in order to lend support to Strom Thurmond's States Rights Democrats, though they returned to the party after the election. On the other hand, Truman's stand markedly increased African-American support for the Democrats.[45] White anger with Democrats crystallized with President Lyndon Johnson's aggressive promotion of the Civil Rights Act of 1964 and the Voting Rights Act of 1965.

The Republicans became an attractive alternative for southern whites due to Barry Goldwater's outspoken opposition to the Civil Rights Act of 1964 and the support given his 1964 presidential campaign by many conservative southern Democrats. Since 1964, Republican candidates have wooed southern white voters through their advocacy of more racially conservative policies than those of their Democratic opponents. At the same time, Democratic candidates support racially liberal policies, like affirmative action and minority set-asides. Alienated by the racial conservatism of Republicans and attracted by the racial liberalism of Democrats, most southern blacks back the Democrats. This solid support for the Democrats by black voters only further serves to identify the Democrats with African Americans in the mind of southern white voters and increase their support for the GOP.[46]

This story forms a compelling historical narrative. And one would be foolish to argue that racial issues were not central to political debates in the 1960s. However, the importance of race during this critical transition period does not inherently mean that it became the central source of political division in the period that followed. Focusing on the consequences of democratization for southern politics as well as the operation

---

[45] Nancy J. Weiss, *Farewell to the Party of Lincoln* (Princeton: Princeton University Press, 1983), 295.

[46] Earl Black and Merle Black, *Politics and Society in the South* (Cambridge, MA: Harvard University Press, 1987), 235–36; Earl Black and Merle Black, *The Vital South: How Presidents Are Elected* (Cambridge, MA: Harvard University Press, 1992), 141–75; Thomas Byrne Edsall and Mary D. Edsall, *Chain Reacton: The Impact of Race, Rights, and Taxes on American Politics* (New York: Norton, 1992).

of democratic politics today helps provide a stronger understanding of the extent to which race influences southern politics today.

Maintaining white supremacy was the central motivating principle of the Jim Crow southern political system. Other issues might be debated, but only if they did not threaten the racial status quo. Southern congressional delegations worked to advance southern interests on a number of fronts, but their primary goal was to protect the South against federal interference in the continuation of the "southern way of life"—that ever-so-polite euphemism for black political and economic subordination. Southern congressional delegations constantly monitored federal legislation for any threat to the southern system of white supremacy.[47]

The Civil Rights Movement brought the injustice of this racist, undemocratic system to national attention and forced the federal government to take action against it. However, the centrality of civil rights issues to political debates in the 1960s does not mean that it remained central. After all, the forceful implementation of federal legislation combined with the desire of many southerners, black and white, to move forward and beyond the South's racist past changed key aspects of public life in the South. The Civil Rights Act of 1964 forced the integration of public accommodations and brought down the signs labeling facilities for "white" and "colored" that served as visible public symbols of Jim Crow. The Voting Rights Act of 1965 permanently ended the exclusion of African Americans from the franchise.

In short, the Civil Rights Movement shattered the institutions that were critical to maintaining both white supremacy and Democratic dominance in the South. Once the back of white supremacy had been broken, Democrats could no longer argue that failure by whites to support the party constituted a racial betrayal that could lead to the end of white supremacy and black political power. The core institutions of white supremacy had already been defeated and efforts to maintain it constituted an increasingly rearguard action. Moreover, the national Democratic Party was aggressively moving to attract black voters. The successes of the Civil Rights Movement actually freed whites to consider other political questions besides race precisely because the battle for the existing system had been so conclusively lost. One of the wonderful political results of the changes of the 1960s is that it allowed southerners to focus on issues besides the racial organization of their society.

Even if race remained of primary concern to voters in the racially charged atmosphere of the 1960s and early 1970s, the GOP found it nearly impossible to achieve many gains by aggressively emphasizing racial conservatism. In the wake of the events of the 1960s, most southern

[47] Key 1949, 370–73; Black and Black 2002, 42–55.

Democratic officials continued to eschew liberal positions on racial issues in favor of conservative or moderate ones in order to protect their white conservative base. As Black and Black explain, Republican candidates found it difficult to gain any traction running on racial issues against southern Democrats during this period.[48]

The Republican decision to write off the black vote just as black vote increased dramatically was also costly to the GOP. Blacks usually backed even relatively conservative Democrats as the lesser of two evils and because of the identification of the national Democrats with racial liberalism. However, African Americans were quick to back Republican candidates, like Governors Winthrop Rockefeller in Arkansas and Linwood Holton in Virginia, whose support for racial liberalism contrasted favorably with the racial conservatism of their Democratic opponents in the eyes of black voters.

The demise of the old system combined with the lack of major differences between Democratic and GOP candidates on racial issues finally forced white southerners to begin the process of curtailing their overarching obsession with protecting white supremacy and debate other issues that animated politics elsewhere. Moreover, once African Americans began voting in large numbers, Democratic candidates had extremely strong incentives to turn the focus away from race even as they quietly abandoned conservative positions on racial issues. Democrats who took unacceptably conservative positions on racial issues risked alienating black voters who made up a growing share of the Democratic primary electorate. Many white Democrats also needed black Democratic support to secure a majority in the general election. On the other hand, overly liberal positions might alienate moderate and conservative whites, so Democrats had powerful motivation to focus on nonracial issues in order to maintain their biracial coalition of blacks and whites.[49]

Race nevertheless has not disappeared from southern politics, though often for very different reasons than in the past. The share of blacks in the population, referred to here by the shorthand of "racial context," plays an important role in multiple ways. In the past, racial context mattered because white voters who lived in areas with many blacks feared the end of white supremacy most keenly and provided more aggressive political support for the racial and political status quo. Whites who inhabit regions with many blacks may still retain a greater sensitivity to racial questions. However, any backlash against the presence of blacks is outweighed by the influence of black voters in these areas. Today, racial context influences the geography of elections by inhibiting GOP success

---

[48] Black and Black 2002, 138–204.
[49] Ibid., 174–202; Glaser 1996, 80–141.

in areas with sizable black populations due to overwhelming support for Democrats among African Americans. Chapter 5 explores how racial context matters in the post–Civil Rights Movement South and shows the following.

Racial Issues Matter More for Blacks Than Whites. Even without the South's history of black oppression, the minority status of blacks would be likely to make racial issues more sensitive for blacks than whites. The starkly different stands of the two major parties on racial issues further raises the salience of racial issues in the minds of African Americans. Goldwater strongly identified the Republicans with opposition to the Civil Rights Act of 1964, a position that was utterly unacceptable in the eyes of black voters. Republicans remain unacceptable to black voters because of their continued opposition to racially liberal policies and the identification of their party with southern symbols, like the Confederate flag, that reek of racism to many African-American southerners. Even for blacks attracted to the Republicans because of their positions on nonracial issues, the continued partisan divide over racial issues renders the Republicans largely unacceptable. Black support for the GOP remains very low throughout the region as a result.

Racial issues no longer matter as much for white southerners. As the majority, whites do not share black historical memories of oppression or fear becoming a racially oppressed minority. Some whites nevertheless resent the increased status of African Americans and policies, like affirmative action, designed to make up for past oppression. Support for the racially conservative party, the Republicans, naturally increases as a result. However, racial issues are now only one type of issue competing for the attention of white voters. The demise of the old system has allowed whites to focus on issues other than race. Nevertheless, even if whites' voting behavior is not primarily explained by their beliefs on racial issues, racial context can still exert great influence on Republican success because of near uniform support for the Democrats among black voters.

Racial Context Constrains Republican Gains. African Americans' near unanimous support of Democratic candidates assures that racial context has an enormous impact on the geography of Republican gains. The presence of large numbers of black voters makes it easier for Democrats and harder for Republicans to win election. As the black share of the population increases, Democratic candidates need a smaller share of the white vote to win a majority. Republicans find it exceedingly difficult to win contests in areas with a black majority or a sizable black minority. Equally important, the GOP finds it hard to attract white candidates in these areas. As the discussion on elites in chapter 3 explains, ambitious politicians do not like to identify with the losers. In areas with a black majority or strong black minority, it makes sense for strategic politicians to seek election as Democrats as this is the dominant party. Moreover, even if a savvy white candidate manages to win election as a Republican in such an area, he or she remains vulnerable to the threat that a challenger may combine a unified black vote for the Democrats with a small share of the white vote and win.

White Backlash Is a Relatively Minor Factor. Studies of white voting behavior in the South prior to the passage of the Voting Rights Act of 1965 often showed that whites living in areas with sizable black populations were more likely to support racially conservative candidates. Theories suggest that blacks present more of a threat to white political control in black areas, spurring greater white conservatism. More recent studies sometimes confirm that these findings apply to politics today, though others dispute them.[50] I find little evidence of continuing white backlash. The expression of black electoral power matters more for southern politics than any negative reaction among white voters to that power.

Racial, Economic, and Social Issues and Partisan Change

The absence of issue cleavages that was the legacy of the pre–civil rights political system benefited the Democrats as they could continue their role as a "big tent" party designed to contain all major strands of southern public opinion. The more that partisan elites differentiated the two parties, and the more that voters identified these changes, the more that the Republicans were liable to benefit as people would have a reason to leave the Democrats and join the Republicans. The identification of

[50] Charles Bullock III, "Congressional Voting and the Mobilization of a Black Electorate in the South," *Journal of Politics* 43 (1981): 662–82; Mark A. Fossett and K. Jill Kiecolt, "The Relative Size of Minority Populations and White Racial Attitudes," *Social Science Quarterly* 70 (1989): 820–35; Michael W. Giles and Melanie A. Buckner, "David Duke and Black Threat: An Old Hypothesis Revisited," *Journal of Politics* 55 (1993): 702–13; Michael W. Giles and Kaenan Hertz, "Racial Threat and Partisan Identification," *American Political Science Review* 88 (June 1994): 317–26; Mary Herring, "Legislative Responsiveness to Black Constituents in Three Deep South States," *Journal of Politics* 52 (1990): 740–58; Robert Huckfeldt and Carol Weitzel Kohfeld, *Race and the Decline of Class in American Politics* (Urbana: University of Illinois Press, 1989); David Lublin, *The Paradox of Representation: Racial Gerrymandering and Minority Interests in Congress* (Princeton: Princeton University Press, 1997), 87–89; Donald R. Matthews and James W. Prothro, "Social and Economic Factors and Negro Voter Registration in the South," *American Political Science Review* 57 (1963): 24–44; D. Stephen Voss, "Beyond Racial Threat: Failure of an Old Hypothesis in the New South," *Journal of Politics* 58 (November 1996): 1156–70; Kenny Whitby and Franklin D. Gilliam, "A Longitudinal Analysis of Competing Explanations for the Transformation of Southern Congressional Politics," *Journal of Politics* 53 (1991): 504–18.

the Republicans with the conservative position further aided the GOP among most white voters.

Not all scholars adhere to the view that racial issues have been the primary cause of Republican gains among southern whites. Some scholars claim that the role of race in explaining southern politics in the post–Civil Rights Movement era has been overestimated. Rather than arguing for the primacy of race, they contend that the traditional New Deal cleavage over economic and social welfare issues extended to the South once the disfranchisement of blacks ended and southern politics began to resemble the conventional two-party framework. This analysis suggests that Republicans gained support primarily from voters who either benefited from the GOP's support for lower taxes or opposed the expansion of government and social welfare programs on philosophical grounds. GOP support grew not due to its advocacy of racial conservatism but to the middle and upper classes' support of economic conservatism.[51] The growing prosperity of the region further aided the GOP as it increased the attractiveness of economic conservatism.

More recent scholarship points to rising social issues as spurring greater identification with the Republicans among southerners.[52] Social issues encompass a range of issues outside the traditional debate over either racial or economic issues. Many discussions of social issues focus almost exclusively on abortion rights because it is a highly emotional issue for advocates on both sides of the intense debate surrounding this topic, but other contentious social issues include school prayer, gun control, gay rights, and pornography. Some suggest that the rising prominence of social issues in public debate and the identification of the GOP with the conservative position on each issue have encouraged white southerners, conservative on most social issues, to leave the Democrats, a party increasingly identified with social liberalism, for the Republicans.

Of course, racial, economic, and social issue theories of partisan change are not mutually exclusive.[53] Even if the democratization of southern politics has reduced the importance of racial issues, they may remain of great importance for a subset of whites. Racial issues may work in a complementary fashion with economic and social issues to spur voters who support conservative policies on more than one type of issue to

[51] Alan I. Abromowitz, "Issue Evolution Reconsidered: Racial Attitudes and Partisanship in the U.S. Electorate," *American Journal of Political Science* 38 (February 1994): 1–24; Richard Nadeau and Harold W. Stanley, "Class Polarization in Partisanship among Native Southern Whites, 1952–90," *American Journal of Political Science* 37 (August 1993): 900–919.

[52] Greg D. Adams, "Abortion: Evidence of an Issue Evolution," *American Journal of Political Science* 41 (July 1997): 718–37.

[53] Black and Black 1987; Nadeau and Stanley 1993.

support the Republicans instead of the Democrats. Alternatively, racial issues may explain why some low-income voters support the GOP even if most low-income voters give their votes to the Democrats as the party that defends social welfare programs. I argue that the role of racial, economic, and social issues in promoting GOP gains has often been misunderstood and make the following arguments in chapter 6.

Economic Issues Best Explain Partisan Change but Are Now Declining in Relative Importance. Contrary to racial theories of partisan change, economic issues most quickly began to differentiate Republicans and Democrats after passage of the Voting Rights Act of 1965. During the 1964 presidential campaign, Goldwater did as much, and possibly more, to identify the Republicans with economic conservatism, the political cause closest to his heart, as with racial conservatism. For several decades, economic issues almost exclusively explained why some white voters identified with the Republicans rather than Democrats as well as the voting behavior of white southerners. At the same time, differences between southern Democrats and southern Republicans over economic issues began to grow within the halls of Congress. Southern Democratic support for liberal social welfare policies grew while southern Republicans led the movement of opposition to such policies within their party. The increasing differentiation of the two parties meant that the GOP was more attractive to economic conservatives as time passed. The rapidly increasing prosperity of the South worked in parallel to increase the appeal of the Republican message on economic issues as time passed.

Race may indirectly play a role in the rise of economic issues as the influx of black voters spurred southern Democrats to adopt more liberal positions on these issues. At the same time, economic liberalism was less likely to split their biracial support coalition in the same manner as a focus on racial issues. The importance of economic issues in terms of their predictive power over southern white partisanship and voting behavior has not declined over time. However, other issues have begun to rise in importance.

Racial and Social Issues Are Rising in Importance. Most racial theories of partisan change point to 1964 as the critical year that polarized the electorate over the issue of race. However, the analysis presented in chapter 5 suggests that race did not begin to play a major factor in explaining white partisanship until the mid-1980s. The average southern white Democrat was not more liberal than the average southern white Republican on racial issues until after 1980. Despite the recent salience of racial issues, there appears to be some continuity with the past. The areas that provide the most ardent support for Republicans today are the same areas that supported Strom Thurmond—who ran on an anti–civil rights platform—in 1948. Since the mid-1980s, the influence of race has continued to grow.

The social issues gathered force even later. The average southern white Democrat was actually slightly more likely to be pro-life than the average southern white Republican until after Ronald Reagan emphasized abortion during his victorious 1980 campaign for the presidency. Abortion increasingly differentiated Democratic and Republican politicians and voters after 1992. Today, racial, economic, and social issues all play a roughly equal role in explaining southern white voting behavior, though economic issues remain the most powerful for now.

Outline of the Book

Authors of books on southern politics have often taken a historical or state-by-state approach to their subject. The region's seemingly obsessive interest in its past, particularly the Civil War, certainly encourages this approach. The difficulty of the region in grappling with long-term, often seemingly intractable problems surrounding race and economic development further spurs students of southern politics to take the long view. At the same time, the real variation in the politics among southern states encourages systematic, comparative study of the politics of each state. The region's many colorful political figures tempt the author to take this approach if only not to forego opportunities to retell the stories of the region's politics that make the subject so interesting to many of us who follow it closely.

Both of these approaches have merit. However, this work follows a different path in its organization around different themes related to the focus on democratization. By bringing together a discussion of how institutions, elites, and issues interact in a one-party region where access to the franchise has recently been greatly expanded, this work hopefully contributes to the literature on southern politics by providing a more integrative approach. Though the chapters rarely follow a historical outline or systematically detail the operation of factors in individual states, I nevertheless hope that this work remains attentive to both history and geographic variation. As this chapter has already explained, I believe that knowledge about institutional structures and elite networks created in the past is critical to understanding the development of southern politics today. Moreover, focusing on broad patterns should provide a deeper understanding of why politics in one southern state differs from that of another.

Before turning to themes of elites, institutions, and issues, chapter 2 describes the rate of Republican gains at the local, state, and national level. Chapter 3 examines GOP difficulties in recruiting candidates to challenge the impressive Democratic pool of incumbent officials. The massive dominance of the Democrats combined with the dearth of potential and actual challengers to these officials alone goes a long way toward explaining the slow development of the GOP. Chapter 4 explains why southern political institutions interacting with the expanded franchise nevertheless made it possible for the Republicans to eventually successfully challenge Democratic control of the region. Chapter 5 explores how racial context conditioned the scope of Republican success. When African Americans compose a sizable share of the electorate, Republican growth is usually inhibited due to strong black support for the Democrats. Chapter 6 assesses the relative importance of racial, economic, and social issues in promoting Republican growth among white voters. Additionally, the chapter shows how the responsiveness of strategic elites to demographics and issues, conditioned by the operation of key institutions like primary elections and redistricting, aided the Republicans in some areas but made it more difficult for the GOP to make advances in others. Chapter 7 concludes with an examination of the outlook for the future and the prospects of both parties in the South.

CHAPTER TWO

The Pace of Republican Gains

MOST STUDIES OF PARTISAN CHANGE focus on federal and gubernatorial elections.[1] Survey and electoral data from these elections are more readily available than local election results, so this approach is highly practical. However, partisan change is often conceived as a broad process related to shifts in partisanship that affect which party wins elections at all levels of government. On the other hand, some scholars argue that partisan change can occur as split-level phenomena with a party making major gains at one level of government but experiencing few gains at another.[2] Examining partisan change at several levels of government is consequently ideal. In order to determine the depth of Republican gains in the South, this chapter examines Republican success in winning votes and election to a very broad range of local, state, and federal offices. By examining offices ranging from county coroner up to president of the United States, one can gauge the extent and timing of Republican growth in the South much more firmly.

As inspection of the data will show, movement toward the Republicans has been an uneven, gradual process. Periods of steady growth were occasionally punctuated by a year of remarkable Republican gains. Alternatively, the GOP sometimes experienced years of stagnation and even reversals. The Watergate scandal and nomination by Democrats of southerner Jimmy Carter delayed Republican growth in the 1970s. Despite the election in 1980 of regionally popular Republican President Ronald Reagan, the Republicans made their most impressive gains in the 1990s. Negative reaction against an unpopular Democratic President Clinton, particularly in 1994, did more to promote the GOP than even popular President Reagan could accomplish. In particular, the gap between GOP success in presidential and nonpresidential elections closed rapidly during the mid-1990s. However, Democrats still tenaciously maintain their hold over most nonfederal and non-statewide offices. The long-term growth in Republican organizations combined with the suc-

---

[1] Black and Black 1987, 1992; Carmines and Stimson 1989; Alexander P. Lamis, *The Two-Party South*, expanded ed. (New York: Oxford University Press, 1988); Alexander P. Lamis, ed., *Southern Politics in the 1990s* (Baton Rouge: Louisiana State University Press, 1999); Phillips 1969; Sundquist 1983.

[2] Speel 1998, 14–15, 65, 181–83, 197–98, 200–203.

cess of President George W. Bush in attracting southern support greatly weakened Democratic control over even these offices by 2002.

Federal Elections

Presidential Elections

Figure 2.1 presents the regional share of the vote won by Democrats since 1944. Perhaps it is especially critical to note that the decline of the so-called Solid South is hardly a recent phenomenon. The fall in support for Democratic presidential nominees occurred long before the passage of either the Civil Rights Act of 1964 or the Voting Rights Act of 1965. Nineteen forty-four was the last year that Democrats received over 70 percent of the regional vote. The movement of the national Democratic Party in the direction of a more racially liberal platform under the leadership of President Truman in 1948 immediately caused a decline in the Democratic share of the vote from nearly three-quarters to around one-half of the southern electorate.

Of course, the pre-1965 figures represent the anemic southern electorate typical of the pre–Civil Rights Movement South. Prior to the passage of the federal Voting Rights Act of 1965, most blacks were excluded by disfranchisement laws, such as literacy tests, understanding clauses, and poll taxes. Violence and economic intimidation further limited black participation at the polls.[3] Disfranchisement laws also kept many whites away from the polls, especially poorer ones, though whites rarely faced the same barriers to participation as did African Americans. The decline in support for the Democratic presidential nominees after 1944 thus reflects changes primarily among those whites that participated in elections. Black support for the Democrats increased greatly from 1944 through 1964,[4] and black levels of participation increased even though a majority of African Americans still could not participate in 1964.[5] Consequently, the change of overall support for the Democrats during this period probably underestimates the shift in white opinion.

The Democratic share of the regional vote oscillated up and down in the late 1960s and 1970s in response to the presence of regional candidates and the nature of the Democratic nominee. George Wallace grabbed Democratic votes as a regional candidate in 1968 and the Democratic vote share plunged to 31 percent. The Democratic share of the vote dropped further to 29 percent in 1972 as Richard Nixon successfully

---

[3] Kousser 1974; Perman 2001; Keyssar 2000.

[4] Weiss 1983.

[5] James E. Alt, "The Impact of the Voting Rights Act on Black and White Voter Registration in the South," in Davidson and Grofman 1994, 351–77.

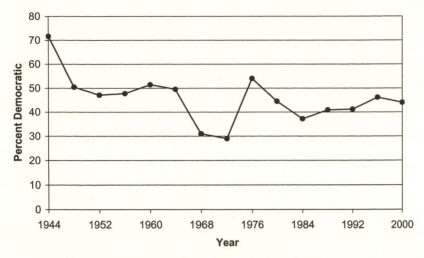

Figure 2.1. Percent Democratic of Southern presidential vote.
Note: The percentages reported here are the percent Democratic of the total presidential vote throughout the South, defined as the eleven former Confederate states.
Sources: *Presidential Elections 1789–1996* (Congressional Quarterly, 1997); Michael Barone, Richard E. Cohen, and Grant Ujifusa, *The Almanac of American Politics 2002* (National Journal, 2002).

followed his "southern strategy" designed to attract racial conservatives and the Democrats nominated antiwar liberal George McGovern.[6] On the other hand, former Georgia Governor Jimmy Carter won 54 percent of the region's vote against northerner Gerald Ford in the wake of Watergate in 1976.

After these severe gyrations, the Democratic regional vote share in presidential elections stabilized in a range from 37 to 46 percent after 1976. Excluding home-state candidates, a majority was recorded for the Democratic nominee in any southern state only once since 1980 (Clinton in Louisiana in 1996). During the same period, no Democratic nominee received less than 35 percent of the vote in any other southern state. While Jimmy Carter relied on his southern base to win election, Democratic presidential candidates now usually carry southern states only when they could win the election without a single southern electoral vote. The South, however, is not nearly as solid for the Republicans as it once was for the Democrats. The failure of the Republicans to

---

[6] Augustus B. Cochran III, *Democracy Heading South: National Politics in the Shadow of Dixie* (Lawrence: University Press of Kansas, 2001), 93–94; Edsall and Edsall 1992, 74–115; Phillips 1969.

achieve such overwhelming hegemony reflects that the majority party no longer retains its power through anti-democratic exclusionary means as the Democrats did in the past.[7] Democrats have a core base of African-American and liberal, or at least progressive, white supporters who together compose more than one-third of the electorate in all southern states.[8]

Congressional Elections

Figures 2.2 and 2.3 show the percentage of southern House and Senate seats won by the Democrats since 1960. Major Republican gains appear to be a recent phenomenon based on the crude evidence from these graphs. The Democrats quickly lost their near total stranglehold of southern congressional seats after the rapid expansion of the southern electorate due to the Voting Rights Act of 1965. However, they continued to win over two-thirds of House and Senate seats until 1980.

The Democrats still consistently won around two-thirds of House seats after 1980. Comparing the rate of turnover in the U.S. House unfavorably with the Supreme Soviet, Republican leaders often blamed the incumbency advantage for their steady lack of success. Incumbents usually fare better than challengers in congressional elections. As the majority party, the Democrats benefited from the incumbency advantage more often than did the Republicans. However, retirements assured that seats held by incumbents gradually became open even if no incumbents suffered defeat, so the incumbency advantage does not explain the GOP's failure to make major southern gains between 1970 and 1990.

Political scientists have offered other more convincing explanations for the continued Democratic success in congressional elections in the 1980s despite the party's dismal performance in presidential elections. Gary Jacobson argues that the weakness of candidates recruited by the Republicans in open-seat contests explains much of the chronic failure of the Republicans to win significant numbers of new seats. Democrats were much more likely to run candidates with prior experience in elective office than the Republicans in open-seat contests. As stronger candidates, they won more elections and preserved the Democratic advantage in House seats even as incumbents retired.[9]

James Glaser similarly argues that the different nature of Democratic

---

[7] Kousser 1974.

[8] Black and Black 1987, 138–44, 186–94, 241; Katherine Tate, *From Protest to Politics: The New Black Voters in American Elections* (New York and Cambridge, MA: Russell-Sage Foundation and Harvard University Press, 1994).

[9] Jacobson 1990.

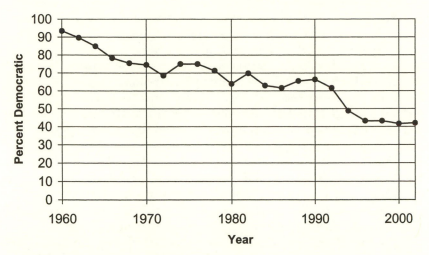

Figure 2.2. Percent Democratic of Southern U.S. Representatives.
Note: The percentages reported here are the percent Democratic after the election.
Sources: *Congressional Elections 1946–1996* (Congressional Quarterly, 1998); Michael Barone, Richard E. Cohen, and Grant Ujifusa, *The Almanac of American Politics 2002* (National Journal, 2002).

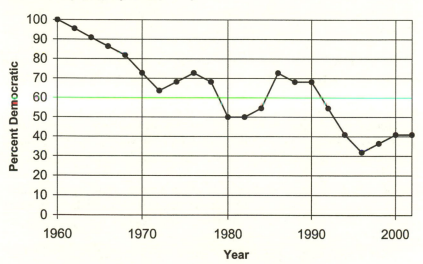

Figure 2.3. Percent Democratic of Southern U.S. Senators.
Note: The percentages reported here are the percent Democratic after the election.
Sources: *Congressional Elections 1946–1996* (Congressional Quarterly, 1998); Michael Barone, Richard E. Cohen, and Grant Ujifusa, *The Almanac of American Politics 2002* (National Journal, 2002).

and Republican southern congressional candidates is the key to explaining the endurance of Democratic dominance. Like Jacobson, Glaser acknowledges the superior experience of Democratic candidates. However, he also contends that their ideology played a significant role. Unlike at the national level, Democrats often nominated moderate to conservative candidates for congressional office. This relative conservatism made it difficult for Republicans to paint Democrats as liberals during campaigns and encouraged GOP candidates to take relatively extreme conservative positions in order to appear more conservative than their Democratic opponents. Unlike for the Democrats, this heightened conservatism often caused problems for GOP congressional candidates. Nominating candidates who were more conservative than popular conservative Republican Presidents Reagan and Bush made it easy for Democratic candidates to paint their Republican opponents as extremists.[10]

Black and Black argue that southern Democrats were especially conservative during the period immediately following the Civil Rights Movement. By the 1980s, most southern House Democrats compiled more moderate, but not liberal, records. Southern Democrats could no longer vote a strict conservative line due to the need to accommodate black voters at home and northern Democrats in Washington. African-American support was a crucial component of the biracial coalitions that southern Democrats increasingly relied on for reelection. Black support was especially crucial in the primaries that selected the Democratic nominee due to split partisanship of whites and the overwhelming Democratic partisanship of blacks. Moreover, changes in Democratic Caucus rules allowed the party's dominant liberal wing to prevent southerners perceived as too conservative from holding powerful committee chairmanships.[11] At the same time, southern Democrats were quite careful not to vote lockstep with their northern colleagues, particularly on social questions that resonated powerfully with southern voters. While national Democratic candidates in the 1980s opposed the death penalty, southern Democratic congressional candidates almost invariably strongly supported the death penalty as part of their strong stand against crime. Stances likes these made it difficult for Republican candidates to paint southern Democratic candidates as northern liberals with southern accents and paved the way for their reelection.[12]

Glaser additionally explains how Democratic congressional candidates successfully used these popular Republican presidents as foils. Democrats

---

[10] Glaser 1996.

[11] Black and Black 2002: 174–81; Steven S. Smith, *Call to Order: Floor Politics in the House and Senate* (Washington, DC: The Brookings Institution, 1989).

[12] Black and Black 2002, 181–85.

promised to work with the Republican presidents. At the same time, they campaigned against conservative excesses, such as cuts in the extremely popular Social Security program. Moreover, Democratic candidates promised to fight hard to bring home benefits for the districts, arguing that their membership in the majority party would aid their effort to win a "fair share" of federal money for the district. Republican congressional nominees found it hard to distance themselves from unpopular aspects of the program of their party's president. GOP efforts to mobilize whites around racial issues usually backfired. Democrats often avoided discussing racial issues that might divide their biracial coalition but used the Republican attacks to mobilize black voters.[13]

The 1980 senatorial elections were a well-documented debacle for Democratic candidates and form a notable exception to the general pattern of congressional Democrats successfully weathering the treacherous seas of Republican presidential success.[14] The Democratic loss of four southern seats raised the GOP share of the region's seats from 32 to 50 percent. However, if these losses indicated a permanent shift in the partisanship of the electorate, the Democrats should have continued to lose Senate seats over the course of three elections. Only one-third of the Senate faces election every two years, so it takes three elections for all Senate seats to come up for election. If the swing against the Democrats was part of a lasting trend, the GOP should have picked up seats in the last two elections of the six-year senatorial election cycle as well as the first one. However, the Democrats experienced no net losses in 1982 or 1984. Tellingly, the Democrats triumphantly gained more seats in 1986 (when the senators elected in 1980 faced reelection) than they had lost in 1980 and retook control of the Senate. This pattern suggests that the 1980 election was a deviation from the normal pattern rather than the beginning of a permanent shift to the GOP.

House Democrats bounced back from their 1980 losses even more quickly. All House seats come up for election every two years, so the Democrats did not have to wait six years to take on the new Republicans elected in 1980. The Democratic share of the South's House seats fell from 71 percent in 1978 to 63 percent in 1980, but rose to 70 percent in 1982. However, though they continued to dominate southern congressional delegations throughout the 1980s, the Democrats were never again able to garner as high a level of seats as in 1982. During the remainder of the 1980s, the Democratic share of southern U.S. House seats remained stable, ranging from 62 to 66 percent.

The 1990s exhibited a strikingly different pattern in both House and

[13] Glaser 1996, 43–66.
[14] Black and Black 1987, 276–91; Glaser 1996; Lamis 1988.

Senate. Democrats lost seats in both houses in 1992, 1994, and 1996. The consistent heavy losses in three straight senatorial elections are directly at odds with the pattern of the 1980s and indicate a long-term shift against the Democrats. The percentage of Senate seats held by Democrats dropped from 68 in 1990 to 55 in 1992. In the Republican glory year of 1994, the Democratic share plunged to 41 percent, giving the GOP the majority of southern Senate seats for the first time since Reconstruction. The Democrats did not hit bottom until the third election in the cycle, after which they held only 32 percent of the region's seats.

Democratic losses in the U.S. House concentrated in the 1994 elections, though the Democrats managed to lose seats in 1992 and 1996 as well. The Democratic share of seats fell from 66 percent in 1990 to 62 percent in 1992 even as they won southern electoral votes for the first time since 1980. As chapter 4 explains in much greater detail, these losses were not too severe considering that the concentration of Democratic voters in new majority-minority districts likely cost the party seats. As in the Senate, the 1994 elections cost House Democrats control of a majority of the region's House seats; the Democratic seat share fell to 49 percent. Democrats represented only 43 percent of southern congressional districts after the 1996 elections.

The congressional Democratic Party now appears to have at least temporarily stabilized its position. Democrats endured no further net losses in either the House or the Senate in 1998. In 2000, the Democrats lost one House seat but gained one Senate seat. The 2002 elections brought the Republicans gains at the national level but left their share of southern House and Senate seats unchanged despite the strong popularity of President George W. Bush throughout the region. While the Democrats are undoubtedly relieved that the hemorrhage of seats has ceased for now, they must be even more perturbed that their formerly dominant party now holds only a minority of the region's seats.

STATE ELECTIONS

Gubernatorial Elections

Democrats retained a stranglehold on southern statehouses until 1967. The passage of the Voting Rights Act in 1965 signaled the failure of the southern Democratic Party as a bulwark for white supremacy and caused the entry of large numbers of new black and white voters into the electorate. Both factors helped erode the previously near monolithic Democratic control of southern state politics. The Republicans gained a foothold when they captured the governor's office in both Arkansas and Florida in 1966. As figure 2.4 shows, Democrats nevertheless continued

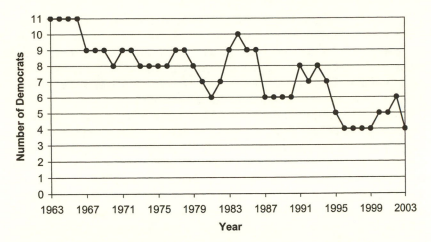

Figure 2.4. Number of Democratic Southern governors.
Note: The numbers reported here are the number of Democrats after the election held in that year.
Sources: *Gubernatorial Elections 1787–1997* (Congressional Quarterly, 1998); Michael Barone, Richard E. Cohen, and Grant Ujifusa, *The Almanac of American Politics 2002* (National Journal, 2002).

to dominate gubernatorial elections even though they were no longer able to shut out the GOP completely from the highest state executive office.

The Republicans held only two or three of the eleven governors' offices between 1967 and 1979—a gain over the past but a record that clearly demonstrated the GOP's minority status. These numbers somewhat mask the increase in the GOP base of support during the 1960s. Prior to the Civil Rights Movement, the general election only occasionally provided a serious challenge for the Democratic gubernatorial nominee. As late as the period between 1959 and 1962, Democrats received over 70 percent of the vote in a majority of southern gubernatorial contests. Democrats won under 60 percent of the vote in only three of the thirteen contests held during this period. Republicans showed far greater strength in the 1963–79 period despite winning less than one-quarter of gubernatorial contests. Democrats won more than 70 percent of the vote in only one-fourth of all contests. The GOP held the Democrats to less than 60 percent of the vote in nearly one-half of gubernatorial elections.

Democrats may have seen their status as masters of the region's statehouses challenged in more vibrant contests than occurred in the past. However, they nevertheless continued to win most of these contests, increasingly by adapting to the changed political circumstances of the post–Civil Rights Movement South. The power of African-American votes increasingly spurred Democrats to take less hostile stances toward civil rights and black concerns more generally. At the same time, Democrats took moderate and even conservative positions on a variety of other issues to maintain their acceptability to white voters.

Jimmy Carter, elected governor of Georgia for one term in 1970, encapsulated the uneasy political transition made by many southern Democrats. During his successful bid in 1970, Carter struck a populist tone, designed to appeal to less wealthy Georgians of both races, but especially whites who had voted for George Wallace for president in 1968. He attacked his opponent as a tool of the "big-money boys." While not making overt racial appeals, Carter attacked busing and promised to invite George Wallace to Georgia if elected. However, once elected, Carter adopted a relatively progressive agenda and directly embraced the new racial order when he proclaimed in his inaugural speech that "the time for racial discrimination is over."[15] In a further display of racial symbolism, he hung a portrait of Dr. Martin Luther King Jr. in the Georgia Capitol. Later successful Democratic gubernatorial campaigns generally featured less of an abrupt shift from campaigning to governing as white southern Democrats grew more comfortable appealing to blacks and more dependent on black votes. At the same time, they generally pursued a similar strategy of pursuing nonracial moderately populist or progressive policies designed to appeal to a broad swath of the electorate. Carter's racial moderation enabled him to run successfully for the presidency in 1976—an achievement beyond the reach of the segregationist southern Democrats who dated from before the new political approach pioneered by politicians like Carter.

Republicans often owed their breakthrough victories in gubernatorial elections to flukes and deep divisions among the Democrats. In 1974, James Edwards became the first Republican to win the South Carolina's governor's mansion after the winner of the Democratic nomination was deemed ineligible under state law and replaced by the runner-up. Alabama Republican Guy Hunt had expected to serve as his party's sacrificial lamb in 1986. However, Hunt won after the state Democratic executive committee disqualified the relatively conservative winner of the Democratic primary runoff and substituted the more liberal runner-up as the nominee.[16] In both South Carolina and Alabama, the replacement of the

---

[15] Jack Bass and Walter DeVries, *The Transformation of Southern Politics* (New York: Basic Books, 1976), 144–48; Lamis 1988, 96–99.

[16] Michael Barone and Grant Ujifusa, *The Almanac of American Politics 1988* (New York: National Journal, 1987), 2–3.

primary winner caused divisions among Democrats. Many of the supporters of the original Democratic primary winner crossed over to support the Republican nominee in the general election.

Early Republican successes were not always an indication of a shift in conservative support to the GOP. In several cases, the Republican nominee was actually more liberal than the Democratic candidate. In Arkansas, Republican Winthorp Rockefeller, an opponent of segregation, defeated racist Democrat Orval Faubus in the gubernatorial elections of 1966 and 1968 with under 55 percent of the vote. While Rockefeller opposed segregation, Faubus had infamously attempted to block black children from attending Little Rock's Central High School. Rockefeller combined traditional Republican support in the Ozark counties of northwestern Arkansas with the heavily black Mississippi Delta counties in the eastern part of the state to win election twice. In both of his successful campaigns, Rockefeller was unusually lucky in his opposition. Rockefeller lost in a landslide in 1970 when progressive Dale Bumpers defeated Faubus for the Democratic nomination.

Virginia Republican Linwood Holton became the first GOP governor of the Old Dominion in 1969 with a coalition almost identical to Rockefeller's. Liberal State Senator Henry Howell Jr.'s loss of the Democratic nomination to moderate William Battle disillusioned urban blacks and liberal whites. Holton combined their support with votes from Appalachian Republicans to win the governor's office with 52.5 percent of the vote.[17] Holton opposed "massive resistance" to civil rights laws during his campaign. While in office, he appointed the first African American to the governor's staff and personally took his daughter to an overwhelmingly black school at the height of the integration crisis in Richmond.[18]

Republicans came closer to achieving parity with Democrats on a consistent basis in gubernatorial elections during the Reagan and Bush administrations. Even if they did not win election, Republican candidates showed themselves to be competitive, serious candidates in nearly every contest. Democrats won more than 70 percent of the vote in only one election between 1980 and 1991; they gained 60 percent or more in less than one-third of races during this same period. However, Republican gains in votes did not always translate into victories during this period. They won slightly less than one-third of all gubernatorial elections; the GOP occupied the governor's mansion of only one or two southern states from 1983 to 1986. On the other hand, they held a then record high of five from 1987 until 1991.

Nevertheless, typical southern governors tended to be moderate Dem-

[17] Lamis 1988, 121–22, 150–51.
[18] Bass and DeVries 1976, 358–59.

ocrats rather than the occasional Republicans during this period. In Arkansas, progressive Dale Bumpers was followed by two more governors in a similar mold: David Pryor and Bill Clinton. Bumpers, Pryor, and Clinton dominated Arkansas politics for several decades. Like Bumpers, Pryor won election to the U.S. Senate after serving two terms as governor. Bill Clinton won his first term as governor in 1978. Although he narrowly lost his bid for a third term in 1982, the "comeback kid" won back the governor's mansion by vanquishing the incumbent in 1984. While serving an amazing fifth term as governor, Clinton won the first of his two presidential terms in 1992 and became the first president ever to hail from Arkansas.

Moderate Democrats held the keys to the executive mansion in most other parts of the South as well. As in Arkansas, racist conservative Democrats in Mississippi eventually gave way to a succession of moderate Democrats who focused on nonracial progressive issues like education as part of their effort to develop the economy, raise living standards, and maintain their biracial electoral coalition. Racist demagogues, like Ross Barnett and John Bell Williams, best known for their ineffective, hysterical voting-winning efforts to stop integration, were replaced by a succession of moderate "New South" Democrats like William Winter, Bill Allain, and Ray Mabus. Like Clinton, they made improving education a major focus of their gubernatorial administrations.

Governors Jim Hunt of North Carolina, Dick Riley of South Carolina, and Bob Graham of Florida were also typical of the period. All served two full terms during the late 1970s and early 1980s. Unlike Graham, who parlayed his success as governor into a long U.S. Senate career, Hunt lost a bitter battle for the U.S. Senate to incumbent Jesse Helms in 1984. However, Hunt returned to win two more terms as governor in 1992 and 1996. Dick Riley never sought elective office again but served as secretary of education during the Clinton administration.

As in the U.S. Congress, 1994 was a watershed year for the Republicans in gubernatorial elections. After the dust had settled from the electoral earthquake, Republicans occupied the governor's office in a majority of southern states for the first time. Examining all of the gubernatorial elections held during the Clinton administration suggests that the Republican victories of 1994 are part of an enduring growth in GOP support, rather than a temporary backlash against the Democrats. Republicans won 57 percent of the 23 elections held between 1992 and 2000. Democrats did not win more than 60 percent of the vote in a single contest; they exceeded 55 percent in a paltry three elections. No signs remain of the former Democratic hyperdominance of gubernatorial elections throughout the South. However, Mark Warner's 2001 victory in Virginia temporarily gave Democrats a majority of southern statehouses for the first time since 1994. Democrats are no longer the dominant party in gubernatorial elections, but they usually remain competitive and the GOP cannot take victory for granted.

Republicans who manage to attract religious social conservatives without alienating more traditional business conservatives seem to have the best chance of both winning and holding on to office. South Carolina Governor Carroll Campbell became one of the pioneers of this formula. Campbell, a developer with close ties to religious conservatives, won a close election in 1986. While in office, he reformed the structure of state government and continued the education reforms of his Democratic predecessor, Dick Riley. At the same time, he pursued an anti-tax and socially conservative agenda. By 1990, no strong Democrat would challenge him and Campbell demolished a black state senator with nearly three-quarters of the vote. Texan George W. Bush followed a similar strategy in pursuing his gubernatorial ambitions. In 1994, Bush united his party to defeat Democratic icon Ann Richards for reelection. Even his toughest critics applauded Bush's education reforms, which he pursued at the same time as his otherwise staunchly conservative agenda.[19] Bush became the first Texas governor ever to win a second consecutive four-year term and the first since 1974 to receive more than 55 percent of the vote when he coasted to reelection with over two-thirds of the vote in 1998 before winning the presidency, albeit with fewer votes than his opponent, in 2000.

Republicans who appeared too extreme even for the broadly conservative southern electorates found it more difficult to gain or hold office. In particular, GOP candidates who appealed strongly to the religious right but alienated the portion of more traditional conservatives who are socially liberal generally had less political success. In contrast to his brother in Texas, Jeb Bush positioned himself as a more radical conservative in his 1994 gubernatorial bid. While George W. Bush defeated one incumbent in Texas, Jeb Bush narrowly lost to another in Florida. In 1998, Jeb Bush retooled his campaign message on the model of his brother as a more compassionate conservative and won election on his second attempt. Despite Democratic desire to take revenge for the fierce battle over Florida's electoral votes in 2000, Bush ended up easily dispatching his Democratic opponent in 2002.

Fob James of Alabama and David Beasley of South Carolina, both beloved of religious conservatives, won very narrow victories during the banner Republican year of 1994. However, they both lost reelection in 1998 after alienating key sections of their base. James spent much of his

---

[19] Molly Ivins and Lou Dubose, *Shrub: The Short but Happy Political Life of George W. Bush* (New York: Vintage, 2000).

term in futile efforts to protect school prayer, including urging schools to defy federal court orders.[20] After facing a strong primary challenge from a business conservative, James received only 42 percent of the vote against Democrat Don Siegelman. Like popular Georgia Democratic Governor Zell Miller, Siegelman advocated using a state lottery to finance increased education spending. South Carolina Democrat Jim Hodges advocated a similar plan in his successful campaign to unseat incumbent David Beasley. Beasley alienated sections of his religious conservative base by dropping his opposition to the lottery one month before the election. His earlier perplexing lies about his high school record as a track star and appearance at a motorcycle rally similarly caused concerns about his reliability among religious conservatives. Beasley had already further angered another conservative constituency by abandoning a 1994 campaign promise to protect the flying of the Confederate flag from the state Capitol dome. In an election with an increased black turnout, Beasley lost with 45 percent of the vote.

However, Democrats found it difficult to maintain their grasp of southern statehouses in 2002 as the GOP recruited a stronger group of candidates and benefited from the strong popularity of President George W. Bush. In South Carolina, former U.S. Representative Mark Sanford defeated incumbent Jim Hodges by resuscitating the normally successful Republican coalition between business and religious white conservatives. U.S. Representative Bob Riley similarly defeated incumbent Don Siegelman in Alabama. Republicans were even more gleeful about their unexpected 2002 defeat of incumbent Georgia Governor Roy Barnes. State Senator Sonny Perdue's victory made him the first Republican governor of Georgia since Reconstruction. The only bright spot for the Democrats in southern gubernatorial elections in 2002 was the capture of the open Tennessee's governor's office, previously held by Republican Don Sundquist for two terms, by former Nashville Mayor Phil Bredesen's.

State Legislative Elections

The pattern of Republican gains in state legislative elections largely follows that for congressional and gubernatorial elections, except that Republican growth was comparatively delayed. State legislative gains are arguably more important for the GOP in the South than in other parts of the United States because the governors of southern states usually have fewer powers than elsewhere. Historically, most southern states did not allow governors to run for reelection so southern governors entered

[20] Michael Barone and Grant Ujifusa, *The Almanac of American Politics 2000* (New York: National Journal, 1999), 58.

office as lame ducks. Virginia still adheres to this tradition. North Carolina's governor only gained a veto in 1996. Legislators hold two of the three seats on the key budget committee in South Carolina. As Molly Ivins and Lou Dubose vividly describe in *Shrub*, their screed attacking then-Governor George W. Bush, the Texas governor's office remains small and executive power, as in other southern states, remains surprisingly fragmented.[21] Many southern states, like Texas, elect a pantheon of state executive officials besides the governor with their own powers. While governors may dominate the legislative process in some non-southern states, like Maryland, state legislators usually more than hold their own in executive-legislative battles in the South.

Prior to the mid 1960s, Republican state legislative caucuses could literally meet in the back seat of a taxicab in most southern states. Many state manuals from this period did not bother to record the party of state legislators because the idea that legislators might not be Democrats simply did not occur to the authors in this era of extreme Democratic dominance. Figure 2.5 shows that Republicans held under 10 percent of the region's state legislative seats prior to 1966. Table 2.1 further reveals that prior to 1966, Republicans composed more than 10 percent of the legislatures of only three southern states: North Carolina, Tennessee, and Virginia.[22]

An enduring strain of mountain Republicanism explains the relative strength of the Republican Party in these states. All three states contain sections of Appalachia that resisted secession and remained pro-Union during the Civil War, despite suffering greatly for their views. These mountain regions have remained unusually Republican since that time. The presence of few African-American residents made it easier for mountain regions to resist pressure to join the Democrats in order to protect white supremacy. Mountain support for the GOP remains particularly striking when one considers the continuing poverty of these areas

---

[21] Ivins and Dubose 2000.

[22] Table 2.1 focuses on state House elections rather than state Senate elections for several reasons. The election of many southern state senators to staggered terms, as in the U.S. Senate, makes it difficult to assess the impact of any one election. Unlike the U.S. Senate, all members of state Senates must face election together after the completion of redistricting at the beginning of each new decade. Finally, prior to the Supreme Court's attack on malapportionment in *Baker v. Carr*, *Wesberry v. Sanders*, and *Reynolds v. Sims*, state Senates were even more severely unrepresentative than state Houses. Following the model of the U.S. Senate, many states allotted every county a single senator, regardless of population. Populous counties were woefully underrepresented in the state Senate as a result. On the other hand, urban counties usually sent multiple representatives to state Houses, even if they received a much smaller share than strict adherence to population would have required. One should nevertheless note that state Senate results tended to closely parallel state House results.

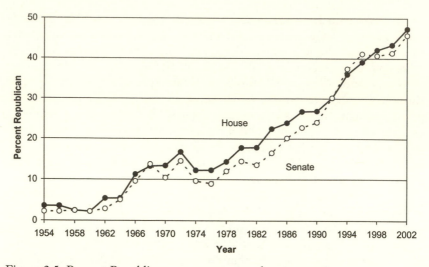

Figure 2.5. Percent Republican state senators and representatives.
Note: The percentages reported here are the percent Republican after the election.
Sources: Data for 1952–92 gathered from Charles D. Hadley and Lewis Bowman, eds., *Southern State Party Organizations and Activists* (Praeger, 1995); data for 1994–2000 state House elections compiled by author from official state election returns; data for 1994–2002 state Senate and 2002 state House elections from the National Conference of State Legislatures.

and the general identification of the Democratic Party with the poor since the New Deal. Similarly situated West Virginians have overwhelmingly become Democrats. The continuing opposition of mountain regions to the Democratic elites, who invariably dominated politics within southern states, probably explains the maintenance of their identification with the GOP. Despite its own racial problems,[23] West Virginia has never had a sizable African-American population so political alliances did not remain frozen around the race issue.

Republicans made steady gains in the region after 1964 through 1972. The GOP share of southern state House seats increased from 5 to 17 percent during this period; their share of state Senate seats similarly increased from 5 to 15 percent. Table 2.1 shows that Republican state House gains were not spread evenly around the region. The GOP continued to hold almost no seats in four states: Alabama, Arkansas, Louisiana, and Mississippi. Republicans, however, made impressive gains elsewhere in the South. After the 1972 elections, Republicans composed around one-third of the state Houses of Florida and North Carolina, and

[23] Henry Louis Gates Jr., *Colored People: A Memoir* (New York: Vintage, 1995).

TABLE 2.1
Percent Republican State House Seats by State

	A. Pre-Voting Rights Act, 1954–64							B. After Voting Rights but before Reagan, 1966–78						
	54	56	58	60	62	64		66	68	70	72	74	76	78
AL	0	0	0	0	2	2	AL	0	0	2	2	0	2	4
AR	2	2	0	0	1	1	AR	2	4	2	1	2	5	6
FL	6	6	3	3	5	9	FL	22	35	32	35	28	28	26
GA	2	2	2	0	1	3	GA	11	13	11	16	13	13	11
LA	0	0	0	0	0	2	LA	2	0	1	4	4	4	9
MS	0	0	0	0	0	0	MS	2	0	1	2	3	3	3
NC	8	8	3	2	18	12	NC	22	24	20	29	8	5	12
SC	0	0	0	0	0	0	SC	14	4	9	17	14	10	13
TN	18	19	17	15	21	24	TN	39	50	43	49	35	32	38
TX	0	0	0	0	5	1	TX	2	5	7	11	11	13	15
VA	7	6	5	8	11	11	VA	11	15	24	20	17	21	25

	C. Reagan and after, 1980–2002											
	80	82	84	86	88	90	92	94	96	98	2000	2002
AL	4	8	12	15	16	21	22	28	28	34	35	39
AR	7	7	9	9	11	9	10	12	14	24	30	30
FL	33	30	36	38	39	38	41	48	50	61	64	67
GA	13	13	14	15	20	14	29	36	41	43	41	41
LA	10	11	13	14	16	16	15	15	26	26	31	32
MS	3	4	5	7	7	16	20	20	30	30	27	27
NC	20	15	32	30	38	33	35	56	51	45	48	51
SC	14	16	22	26	30	33	40	48	52	55	56	59
TN	39	38	37	38	40	43	36	40	38	40	41	45
TX	23	24	35	37	38	37	38	41	45	48	48	59
VA	33	34	33	35	39	39	41	46	46	50	52	65

Note: The numbers reported here are the percentage of Republican state House members after the elections held in that year.

Sources: Data for 1952–92 gathered from Charles D. Hadley and Lewis Bowman, eds., *Southern State Party Organizations and Activists* (Westport, CT: Praeger, 1995); data for 1992–2002 compiled by author from official state election returns; data for 2002 from the National Conference of State Legislature.

one-half of the Tennessee House. In terms of seats gained, rather than simply the share of seats, Florida and Tennessee Republicans impressively gained over one-quarter of the membership of their entire state Houses over the decade. Republican candidates in North Carolina and South Carolina increased their share of seats by 17 percent. Georgia, Texas, and Virginia Republicans lagged behind the leaders but still won at least 9 percent more of the seats in their state Houses.

Reaction by some white southerners against the Civil Rights Movement combined with Goldwater's linkage of the Republicans to opposition to federal intervention to overturn the racial status quo account for some of these early GOP gains. However, the deep identification of state Democratic parties and candidates with racial conservatism undermined any potential racial appeal by Republican state legislative candidates. While Lyndon Johnson had indelibly linked national Democrats with racial liberalism, state and local Democrats at this point largely remained free from the same taint that condemned Johnson in the eyes of many southern whites.

The reapportionment revolution undoubtedly aided GOP state legislative candidates. Just as *Baker* and *Reynolds* forced states to end the system of allotting one state senator to each county, they similarly required states to more fairly apportion the seats in their state Houses. Suburban areas, often the most egregiously underrepresented in southern state Houses, gained seats and so did the Republicans.[24] Rural areas, the heartland of the traditional southern Democratic Party, suffered the most.

The disastrous impact of Watergate on U.S. House Republicans is well-known. Political observers attached the sobriquet "Watergate babies" to Democrats elected to the U.S. House in 1974 because of the scandal and the bumper crop of Democrats elected as a consequence. Although less attention has been paid to the effect of Watergate on Republican prospects in southern state legislative contests, likely because of the normal media and scholarly focus on the federal legislature, the impact was equally devastating. Republicans did not manage to elect the same number of southern state representatives elected in 1972 until Ronald Reagan's election as president in 1980. The Republican share of southern state senators did not surpass the level held in 1972 until Reagan's landslide reelection in 1984.

Republicans have never suffered any actual net losses of state House seats in the South since the Watergate setback. Instead, as the trend in figure 2.5 shows, steady attrition from Democratic ranks has been the general rule. Close examination of the general pattern, however, reveals that the Democrats managed to attenuate their losses on three occasions. The nomination of popular southerner Jimmy Carter in 1976 made it difficult for Republicans to recover quickly from their 1974 losses. Severe economic recession during a Republican presidency reduced the popularity of the GOP in 1982. Relatively mild economic problems combined with the length of Republican tenure in the presidency probably contributed to GOP stagnation in 1990.

Democrats managed to actually increase their share of seats on three occasions since Watergate: 1976, 1982, and 1998. However, the gains

---

[24] Richard C. Cortner, *The Apportionment Cases* (Knoxville: University of Tennessee Press, 1970); Charles W. Eagles, *Democracy Delayed: Congressional Reapportionment and the Urban-Rural Conflict in the 1920s* (Athens: University of Georgia Press, 1990).

were always relatively small—less than 1 percent of the total number of seats—and did not seriously undermine the general trend of Republican advances in state Senate elections. Republican gains in state Senate elections consistently lagged behind their state House gains between 1970 and 1990. For most of these two decades, Republicans held 2–4 percent fewer state Senate seats than state House seats, though the gap between the two branches temporarily grew to nearly 6 percent in 1984. Since 1992, the share of Republican state senators has more closely matched the proportion of Republican state representatives.

The post-Watergate era has also been punctuated by two periods of major increases in GOP state legislators. Reagan triumphantly won re-election in 1984 with 60 percent or more of the vote in every southern state except Tennessee. At the same time, GOP state representatives successfully increased their share of the region's seats by an impressive 4.6 percent over their share in 1982. Most of these gains occurred in state House districts with few black residents in urban areas. As chapter 5's exploration of racial context will show, the presence of few black voters, who overwhelmingly support Democrats, makes it easier for the Republicans to attract candidates and then to win the general election. Urban areas tend to contain more high-income residents, attracted to the GOP's conservative message on economic issues. Immigrants to the South have also concentrated in urban areas. As non-southerners, these immigrants were never inculcated with the anti-Republican prejudices of the Solid South and were more open to voting Republican than native southerners. To the extent that immigrants to the region were Democrats, they tended to be liberals rather than southern conservative Democrats. They encouraged urban Democratic candidates to adopt liberal positions that spurred more southerners to vote Republican. Both of these themes are explored in greater depth in chapter 6.

Republican state legislative gains were even more spectacular in 1994 as they garnered nearly 6 percent more of the region's state House seats and 7 percent more of the region's state Senate seats. Deeply disappointed in President Clinton, a southerner who turned out more liberal than expected, white southerners not only voted out their Democratic members of Congress but many Democratic state legislators. The 1994 elections raised the total GOP share of southern state legislators above one-third for the first time in the twentieth century. By this time, Republicans began to make gains in rural areas of the South that had previously seemed more impervious to Republican appeals. As chapter 6 outlines, increased Democratic identification with liberal positions on social issues like abortion and school prayer may explain the newfound difficulties faced by Democratic candidates. After the 2000 elections, Republicans held 43 percent of the region's state House seats.

As before, gains were not steady or uniform in all southern states. The Republicans controlled the state Houses of Florida, South Carolina, and Virginia after the 2001 elections. In Florida and Virginia, Republicans impressively held over 60 percent of the seats. During the heated dispute over Florida's electoral votes in the 2000 presidential election, Republican state legislative leaders threatened to directly select Republican electors if the Florida Supreme Court's decision resulted in a Gore victory. Vehement opposition from Democratic legislators posed little threat to Republican plans. If Republican legislators in Florida can remain united, they have the votes to run roughshod over their Democratic colleagues whenever they choose.

Republicans have not been as successful everywhere. In 2002, Republicans held only 27 to 39 percent of state House seats in Alabama, Louisiana, and Mississippi (see table 2.1). Mississippi Republicans actually lost seats in the 1999 elections as the state narrowly elected its first Democratic governor since 1987. As Republicans have fared best in heavily white, urbanized areas, it is not altogether surprising that these relatively rural states with large black populations have relatively few Republicans in their state legislatures.

Tennessee represents an exception to the usual pattern with clear GOP strength over a much longer period than most other southern states. Despite this early start, the GOP has stagnated in Tennessee at the state legislative level. As a close examination of table 2.1 uncovers, Democrats have consistently held approximately 60 percent of the seats in the Tennessee House between 1978 and 2000. Despite successfully capturing both U.S. Senate seats and the governorship during the 1990s, Republicans had difficulty achieving further inroads in the state House, though they did capture 45 percent of state House seats in 2002. While the late 1990s constituted a high-water mark for state legislative Republicans in every other southern state, the halcyon days for the Tennessee GOP were in 1968 and 1972, when they controlled approximately one-half of state House seats.

Arkansas Republicans seemed permanently stuck with a desultory share of seats until the GOP jumped from 14 to 24 percent of seats in 1998 (see table 2.1). A tradition of populism, relatively low incomes, and the election of a Democratic president from Arkansas in 1992 and 1996 helped maintain Democratic hegemony longer than in other southern states. As chapter 4 explains, term limits produced an extraordinary number of open seats, more vulnerable to Republican candidates than seats held by incumbents, in 1998. Corruption scandals resulting in the resignation of Democratic Governor Jim Guy Tucker also obviously helped the GOP. Republicans celebrated the election of their first U.S. Senator in Arkansas in 1996 and their first governor in 1998. However, Republicans remained stuck at 30 percent of seats after the 2002 state House elections.

North Carolina remains the only state where Democrats were able to retake a state House after losing it. Democrats suffered a meltdown in 1994 when the Republican share of seats rose from 35 to 56 percent. Careful examination of table 2.1 shows that this was the largest swing in percentage terms between the two parties in any southern state House in any two-year period except for the North Carolina GOP's stunning drop from 29 to 8 percent of seats in 1974. North Carolina's use of multimember districts may account for these unusually large shifts in partisan fortunes. A swing of party control of one district can result in a gain or a loss of as many as three seats for a party. Tar Heel Democrats managed to roll back GOP gains in 1996 and 1998, retaking the majority with 55 percent of the seats in the latter year. However, Republicans gained seats in 2000, leaving them only a few seats short of a majority. The GOP narrowly recaptured majority status in the 2002 state House.

Republican state legislative gains in 2002 were not limited to North Carolina. Major gains combined with Democratic defections gave Georgia Republicans control of the Georgia Senate despite aggressive Democratic efforts to secure their majority through redistricting. Democratic control of the redistricting process proved more effective in thwarting Republican efforts to convert votes into seats on the House side. Georgia Republicans still hold only 41 percent of state House seats though they have won a majority of votes in all state House elections since 1996.[25] Florida and Virginia Republicans were as aggressive as Georgia Democrats in promoting their party's electoral interests through redistricting. Virginia passed a partisan plan as payback for the partisan Democratic plan passed in 1990.[26] In 2001, the number of Republicans in the Virginia House soared to 64 out of 100. Florida Republicans similarly utilized their unified control of state government to pass a pro-Republican plan that increased the share of state House Republicans from 64 to 67 percent.

LOCAL ELECTIONS

Republican inroads in county elections started late compared to federal or state contests. Table 2.2 shows the percentage of selected county of-

[25] Personal Communication, Professor Charles E. Bullock, University of Georgia. Confirmed by examining analyzing election results on the Georgia Secretary of State's web site at: http://www.sos.state.ga.us. The GOP received 51% of the two-party vote in 1996, 53% in 1998, and 52% in 2000. The Democrats ran candidates in 77% of state House seats in 1996, 71% in 1998, and 74% in 2000. The Republicans ran candidates in 65% of state House seats in 1996, 70% in 1998, and 57% in 2000. Democrats consistently ran more candidates than the Republicans.

[26] I should point out that I served as a consultant to Virginia Democrats attempting to overturn the redistricting plan passed by Republicans. I wrote an expert report and testified on the compactness of the state legislative districts.

TABLE 2.2
Percentage Republican Winners of County Offices by State and Year

Virginia

	Clerk	Treasurer	Revenue Com.	Sheriff	Comm. Attorney
1981–83		9	9	13	12
1985–87		11	10	15	10
1987–91	13				
1989–91		12	9	18	15
1993–95		16	15	17	23
1995–99	18				
1997–99		18	20	20	26

Florida

	Tax Collector	Sup. of Elections	Clerk	Property Appraiser	Sheriff
1980	7	7	7	12	20
1984	5	9	12	19	20
1988	12	18	21	23	28
1992	11	17	21	30	34
1996	16	20	30	32	36

Texas

	District Clerk	County Clerk	County Judge	Tax Assessor	Sheriff
1980	5	3	6	3	9
1984	11	5	16	6	11
1988	8	6	11	8	14
1992	16	16	29	16	21
1996	21	24	34	22	37

North Carolina

	Clerk	Sheriff		Register of Deeds
1982	10	18	1982–84	9
1986	14	20	1986–88	17
1990	15	24	1990–92	21
1994	18	31	1994–96	22
1998	20	32		

South Carolina

	Probate Judge	Clerk	Auditor	Treasurer	Coroner	Sheriff
1980–82	4	0	4	2	7	2
1984–86	4	2	7	4	9	11
1988–90	13	2	18	11	20	24
1992–94	15	9	25	20	26	24
1996–98	26	20	32	34	33	30
2000–02	17	30	30	33	35	39

Georgia

	Probate Judge	Tax Com.	Coroner	Clerk	Sheriff
1980	2	2	1	2	4
1984	2	3	3	4	5
1988	2	3	1	4	7
1992	4	4	4	5	6
1996	7	9	10	11	14
2000	11	13	14	14	20

Arkansas

	Clerk	Assessor	Treasurer	Sheriff	Coroner	Judge
1980	3	3	1	4	4	3
1984	1	1	4	3	6	3
1988	1	1	4	3	6	3
1992	1	1	4	1	5	4
1996	1	1	4	3	8	5
2000	1	4	4	5	7	9

Louisiana

	Assessor	Clerk	Sheriff	Coroner
1979	0	2	0	7
1983	0	0	2	21
1987	3	3	2	15
1991	0	5	5	26
1995	0	5	7	47
1999	11	13	17	43

Mississippi

	Circuit Clerk	Tax Assessor	Coroner	Chancery Clerk	Sheriff	Sup. of Education	County Attorney
1983	4	3	1	1	1	1	2
1987	0	3	0	0	1	0	3
1991	1	1	1	5	4	2	5
1995	4	6	9	7	8	12	13
1999	5	6	9	10	10	13	15

Note: The numbers reported here are the percentage of Republican officials after the elections held in that year. See chapter 3 for more information on the composition of the local elections data set.

Sources: Data compiled by author from official election returns and state manuals and directories of officials. In some cases, telephone calls were made to local officials to confirm the party affiliation of officials.

fices held by Republicans over time for the nine southern states for which data is available (see chapter 3 for more information on the local elections data set). As late as 1980, county officials were rarely Republican in most southern states.

At the beginning of the 1980s, regional differences within the South helped explain which states had more Republican officials than others. In general, Republicans experienced greater success in electing officials in the Peripheral South than in the Deep South. Black and Black define the Deep South as comprising Alabama, Georgia, Louisiana, Mississippi, and South Carolina. The Peripheral South includes the remaining former Confederate states: Arkansas, Florida, North Carolina, Tennessee, Texas, and Virginia.[27] Table 2.2 indicates that Republicans occupied 3 percent or fewer of offices in all Deep South states examined here in the early 1980s. However, in the Peripheral South states of Florida, North Carolina, and Virginia, between 11 and 13 percent of local officials were Republicans. As in state legislative elections, mountain Republicanism likely explains the early election of significant numbers of Republican officials in North Carolina and Virginia. Florida's enormous non-southern population similarly accelerated the election of Republicans in the Sunshine State at the local and state legislative levels.[28] Arkansas and Texas lagged compared to other Peripheral South states as only 3 and 5 percent, respectively, of local officials in these two states were Republicans.

Rates of growth in Republican strength at the local level after 1980 varied considerably from state to state as figure 2.6 reveals for three selected southern states: Arkansas, Louisiana, and South Carolina. The Republican revolution appears to have bypassed President Clinton's home state of Arkansas. Alternatively, impressive growth propelled South Carolina Republicans into over one-third of offices by 1998 even though they had won almost none in 1980. Steady growth improved the GOP's standing in other states as well. While not as rapid as in South Carolina, gradual progress left the Republicans with substantially more offices in states like Louisiana, Florida, North Carolina, and Virginia. Texas also fits this pattern, except that Republican growth temporarily paused for one election when Democrat Ann Richards captured the governor's of-

---

[27] Black and Black 1987, 14. The definition of the South itself is much debated; see John Shelton Reed, "The South. What Is It? Where Is It?" in Paul D. Escott and David R. Goldfield, eds., *The South for New Southerners* (Chapel Hill: University of North Carolina Press, 1991), 18–41. I adhere to the traditional definition of the eleven former Confederate states in this book, though other compelling definitions are frequently invoked by others. When debating this question in my southern politics class, one of my former students, a Greenville, South Carolina, native, came up with one of my personal favorites. He claimed that southern-ness was something that radiated out from South Carolina.

[28] Black and Black 1987, 16–19.

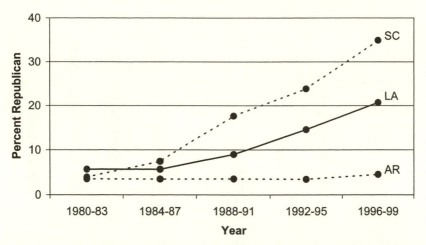

Figure 2.6. Percent Republican county officials in Arkansas, Louisiana, and South Carolina.
Note: Each data point reflects the percent Republican officials of all of the county officials included the data set (see table 2.2 for a list) after the elections held during that period.
Source: Data compiled by author.

fice for one term in 1990. In contrast, several states, like Georgia and Mississippi, experienced little growth in officeholding by Republicans at the local level until the mid or late 1990s. In Mississippi, the GOP went from winning only 3 percent of offices in 1991 to 8 percent in 1995 and 10 percent in 1999.

The data on Republican success in winning county offices presented in table 2.2 and figure 2.6 overstate the dominance of the Democrats. Republicans have tended to win in heavily populated urban and suburban counties. Democrats may win far more offices than the GOP, but many of these victories occur in small, low-population, rural counties. As a result, the percentage of offices won by the Republicans is smaller than the percentage of people who live in counties with GOP officials. Figure 2.7 compares the percentage of counties with Republican sheriffs and the percentage of people who live in counties with Republican sheriffs during the 1993–96 period. In most states, the percentage of people who live in counties with Republican sheriffs exceeds the percentage of counties with Republican sheriffs by at least 10 percent. In Georgia, for example, the percentage of people living in counties with Republican sheriffs is 17 percent higher than the share of counties with Republican sheriffs. Even more impressively, for the selection of counties in Florida and Texas for which data are available, 49 and 70 percent, respectively, of all

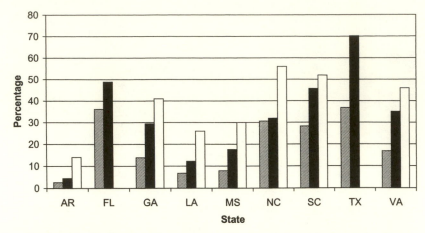

Figure 2.7. Comparison of the percentages of GOP sheriffs, GOP state representatives, and population of counties with GOP sheriffs, 1993–96.
Note: All numbers reflect the results of the elections held between 1993 and
1996. The percentage of GOP sheriffs is the percentage Republican of all sheriffs
in the state. The percentage of population of counties with GOP sheriffs is the
percentage of people living in counties with Republican sheriffs.
Sources: Population data from the U.S. Census. Election results compiled by
author.

people live in counties with Republican sheriffs. (The data for Florida
includes 52, or 78 percent, of the state's 67 counties; the data for Texas
includes 38 counties in east Texas, the culturally southern portion of the
Lone Star State. Data from other states include virtually all counties,
except the Louisiana data exclude Orleans Parish. There is no data from
either Alabama or Tennessee.)[29] The GOP is not quite as weak as it appears at first glance. Republicans may hold only a minority of county
offices, but they win most often where it counts.

At the same time, one should be careful not to exaggerate the extent of
Republican success at the local level. In Arkansas, Louisiana, and North
Carolina, the percentage of people residing in counties with Republican
sheriffs exceeds the percentage of counties with Republicans sheriffs by 5
percent or less. The general absence of Republican sheriffs explains the
low differential for the first two states. In North Carolina, unlike in other
southern states, most Republican sheriffs won in rural counties. A majority of the North Carolina counties that elected Republican sheriffs in

[29] See chapter 3 for more information about the local elections data set.

1994 lay west of the state's major population concentrations in the traditionally Republican mountain counties.

Moreover, even in the other states, comparatively fewer southerners inhabit counties with Republican officials than districts with Republican state representatives. For the seven states for which data is available from virtually all counties, the percentage of Republican members of the state House exceeded the percentage of people living in counties with Republican sheriffs (see figure 2.7). Excepting South Carolina, the share of each state's citizens living in counties with GOP sheriffs fell short of the percentage living in districts with Republican legislators by at least 10 percent. In North Carolina, the exceptional success of the GOP in the 1994 state legislative elections resulted in a yawning gap of 24 percent between the share of Republican state House members and people living in counties with GOP sheriffs. Even after taking into account the concentration of Republican officials in high-population counties, Republicans racked up gains more slowly at the local level.

Finally, as table 2.2 indicates, Republicans tended to win a higher share of elections for sheriff than for other county offices in most southern states. Comparing GOP success rates in elections for state representative and sheriff makes sense because sheriff is the only county office elected in every southern state. However, this comparison probably overestimates the overall Republican rate of winning local offices due to the relatively high rates of Republican success in elections for sheriff compared to other local offices.

Republicans not only fare better in sheriff's elections; the GOP generally wins a greater share of all offices associated with fighting crime. Besides sheriffs, coroners and prosecutors are especially likely to serve as Republicans. In Mississippi and Virginia, more county attorneys and commonwealth's attorneys win election as Republicans than to any other county office in their respective states. Examining table 2.2 closely reveals that the gap between the share of crime-fighting and non-crime-fighting offices held by Republicans is not usually enormous in absolute terms. After the 1999 elections, Republicans formed 15 percent of county attorneys, 10 percent of sheriffs, and 9 percent of coroners in Mississippi. In contrast, the GOP claimed only 5 percent of circuit clerks and 6 percent of tax assessors, though Republicans did hold 10 percent of chancery clerkships. In Virginia, 26 percent of commonwealth attorneys were Republicans after the 1999 elections. Republicans made up only 18 percent of clerks and treasurers, though members of the GOP also formed 20 percent of the revenue commissioners—the same share of sheriffs' offices occupied by Republicans in the Old Dominion.

The national image of the Republicans as tougher on crime may encourage voters to elect Republicans to these offices related to the critical local function of combating crime. Alternatively, these offices may be more attractive to strong Republican candidates than other offices precisely because of their focus on fighting crime. As chapter 3 elaborates, attracting candidates is critical to winning county elections. The GOP may win a greater share of these offices due to candidate strength rather than simple voter support.

Republicans also win a higher share of county offices with particularly strong executive power. The county judge is the king of county politics in Texas, and Republicans have a greater share of county judge office than any other office except sheriff. Table 2.2 indicates that over one-third of sheriff and county judge positions were occupied by Republicans after the 1996 and 1998 elections, though they held under one-quarter of the positions for district clerk, county clerk, and tax assessor. In a similar fashion, after the office of county attorney, Mississippi Republicans fare best in contests for the executive office of superintendent of education. Again, it is unclear if voters perceive Republicans as stronger executives than Democrats or if these offices attract stronger Republican candidates. One should keep in mind that Democrats still held 87 percent of superintendent offices after the 1999 elections (see table 2.2), so the gap between Republican success in federal and local elections remains huge in Mississippi even for executive offices.

Top-Down Republican Gains?

Republicans appear to fare better in elections as one moves up the political food chain. The GOP has been dominant in southern presidential contests for several decades. In 1994, Republicans won a majority of the region's seats in both houses of the U.S. Congress for the first time ever. At about the same time, the GOP won control of a majority of the southern governors' offices. However, Republican gains in state legislative elections have consistently lagged behind their successes in gubernatorial or congressional elections. In 1994, the same year that the GOP captured more congressional seats than the Democrats for the first time, Republicans won only 36 percent of the region's state House seats. The GOP continued to make gains throughout the remainder of the 1990s. However, even after the 2002 elections, the Republicans still fell short of a majority with 47 percent of the region's seats. As the previous section described, the Republicans lag even further behind in local elections.

This pattern of Republican success in races first for national office, then for state office, and then for local office has led many observers, like Aistrup and Bullock, to argue that the South is undergoing a "top-down" realignment.[30] Only after achieving success at the top of the ticket do Republicans begin to make gains in elections for less prestigious offices. These findings were especially notable because they contradict the traditional hypothesis of success at the local level preceding gains in elections for higher offices. Due to their greater name recognition and experience in campaigns, candidates who have previously won a lower office are almost always the stronger candidates for higher office than political novices.[31]

Explanations for this top-down pattern vary widely. Aistrup argues that the absence of local Republican organizations prevented the GOP from capitalizing on support for GOP presidential nominees.[32] Several scholars, including Aistrup and Bullock, have speculated that the size of the jurisdiction explains why GOP candidates fare better in elections for higher office.[33] More populous jurisdictions are likely divided over more issues and more diverse than smaller, more homogenous constituencies. Greater diversity and less unanimity of opinion may provide greater opportunities for a new, rising political party.

Others argue that local Democrats find it easier to distance themselves from the regionally unpopular policies of national Democrats the more removed they are from federal office. Local and state legislative Democratic candidates can campaign as conservatives untainted by any association with northern liberal colleagues of the same party, so they fare better in electoral contests than Democrats running in congressional or presidential elections.[34] Democratic presidential nominees in 1968, 1972, 1984, and 1988 were the stereotypical, much loathed, northern liberal. Over time, the policy differences between northern and southern wings of the Democratic congressional party have narrowed greatly,[35] so south-

---

[30] Joseph A. Aistrup, *The Southern Strategy Revisited: Republican Top-Down Advancement in the South* (Lexington: University Press of Kentucky, 1996); Bullock 1988, "Creeping Realignment in the South"; Charles S. Bullock, "Regional Realignment from an Officeholding Perspective," *Journal of Politics* 50 (1988): 553–74.

[31] Jacobson 2001, 36–40, 158; Jacobson and Kernell 1983; Montcrief, Squire, and Jewell 2000.

[32] Aistrup 1996; John H. Aldrich and John D. Griffin, "Blind (to) Ambition: The Emergence of a Competitive Party System in the American South, 1948–1998," unpublished manuscript (2001), 3; Key 1949.

[33] Aistrup 1996; Bullock 1988, "Creeping Realignment in the South"; Bullock 1988, "Regional Realignment from an Officeholding Perspective"; John R. Hibbing and John R. Alford, "Constituency Population and Representation in the U.S. Senate," *Legislative Studies Quarterly* 15 (1990): 581–98.

[34] Black and Black 2002, 152–67; Glaser 1996, 80–121, 127–41.

[35] Black and Black 2002, 80, 376–79; John H. Aldrich and David W. Rohde, "The Consequences of Party Organization in the House: The Role of the Majority and Minority Parties in Conditional Party Government" in *Polarized Politics: Congress and the President in a*

ern Democratic congressional candidates find it more and more difficult to convince southern voters that they are genuinely more conservative than Democrats from outside the region.

Recently, Aldrich and Griffin have argued against top-down theories of partisan change. Their statistical models show that Republican success in contests for lower offices actually preceded GOP success in campaigns for higher offices. Success at the lower level predicts future success at higher levels, but the reverse is not true.[36] Aldrich and Griffin's analysis supports the conventional explanation that a party develops a cadre of experienced and well-known officials at the local levels before scaling the higher offices. The perplexing question remains, however, how to reconcile these findings with the facts on the ground as Republicans consistently won a greater share of higher offices before lower offices.

Aistrup's top-down theory may contradict Aldrich and Griffin's bottom-up theory less than appears at first glance even if the two theories are not totally reconcilable. As argued by Aistrup, Republicans scored at the presidential level long before the GOP developed grassroots organizations or elected many lower-level officials. In parallel fashion, Republicans had greater success in gubernatorial and senatorial elections prior to their breakthroughs in local and state legislative elections that would indicate grassroots strength. GOP candidates in these elections were often helped by Democratic infighting or a deeply flawed Democratic nominee. In contrast, the failure of the Republicans to recruit candidates for many local and state legislative contests also played a role in the relative success of GOP nominees for higher office.

Aistrup would likely believe that the absence of candidates for lower-level offices merely proves his claim that Republican growth followed a top-down pattern. However, one should not neglect that Aistrup also contends that the lack of good candidates prevented the GOP from fully capitalizing on the popularity of Republican presidential candidates. Aistrup thus does not really reject at least a key portion of the spirit of

---

Partisan Era, ed. Jon R. Bond and Richard Fleisher (Washington, DC: Congressional Quarterly, 2000), 33–34; Richard Fleisher, "Explaining Change in the Roll-Call Voting Behavior of Southern Democrats," *Journal of Politics* 55 (May 1993): 327–41; Richard Fleisher and Jon R. Bond, "Congress and the President in a Partisan Era" in *Polarized Politics: Congress and the President in a Partisan Era*, ed. Jon R. Bond and Richard Fleisher (Washington, DC: Congressional Quarterly, 2000), 5; Richard Fleisher and Jon R. Bond, "Partisanship and the President's Quest for Votes on the Floor of Congress," in *Polarized Politics: Congress and the President in a Partisan Era*, ed. Jon R. Bond and Richard Fleisher (Washington, DC: Congressional Quarterly, 2000), 164, 184; Lublin 1997, 68–69; Jacobson 2001, 245–49; Keith T. Poole and Howard Rosenthal, *Congress: A Political-Economic History of Roll-Call Voting* (New York: Oxford University Press, 1997); David W. Rohde, *Parties and Leaders in the Postreform House* (Chicago: University of Chicago Press, 1994).

[36] Aldrich and Griffin 2001.

Aldrich and Griffin's claims: that success at the lower levels begets further success at higher levels. This conclusion suggests that Republicans should have achieved greater and more consistent successes in elections for higher office as they began to attract more experienced candidates—candidates who had already won elections for lower offices.

A cursory examination of the prior experience of Republican senators and governors provides evidence consistent with this more nuanced reading of Aistrup's claims. After the decisive 1980 defeat of Democrat Jimmy Carter, a native southerner, by Republican Ronald Reagan, Republicans held 10 of the region's 22 U.S. Senate seats and 5 of the 11 governorships. Nearly three-quarters of these Republicans elected to statewide office had never previously won another elected office. This inexperience cost the Republicans painfully when these officials sought reelection. None of the four Republican senators narrowly elected on Reagan's coattails in 1980s returned to the Senate after the 1986 elections. Three of the four Republican governors with no prior electoral experience were also defeated for reelection. Unlike more experienced incumbents, many inexperienced Republican officials apparently did not know how to use their office to their political advantage.

Republicans began to make steadier gains and ceased to suffer from such dramatic attrition of their incumbents once they recruited stronger candidates. Approximately 80 percent of the GOP senators and governors who held office after both the 1990 and 2000 elections had held some prior electoral office before seeking their current position. Over 70 percent of the senators and governors serving after both the 1990 and 2000 elections with prior experience in elected office had previously held either another elected statewide office or served in the U.S. House. Democrats have not found it nearly as easy to defeat these more seasoned Republican senators and governors as their greener predecessors. As Aldrich and Griffin claim, the presence of experienced candidates provided a firmer basis for long-term success.

The data clearly show that Republicans consistently won a greater share of offices at the top of the office ladder. Republican candidates began to break through and win a selection of higher offices despite their lack of experience. The appeal of the Republican national message and the luck of opposing flawed Democratic candidates allowed selected Republican candidates to win high offices despite their inexperience. However, greater success at the lower level also made expanded success at the higher level possible. The recruitment of high quality candidates also appears to have made it more likely that these candidates would additionally possess the skills necessary to avoid defeat when facing reelection.

CONCLUSION

For the most part, Republican southern gains have been gradual. The enactment of the Voting Rights Act of 1965 and the consequent expansion of the southern electorate quickly ended the highly (small-d) undemocratic hyperdominance of the (big-D) Democrats. Democrats continued to hold the vast majority of southern offices, but Republicans held a minority. Additionally, many elections became genuinely competitive in the general election—a major change from the Solid South era.

Democrats remained secure in their majority status below the presidential level until the 1990s. The occupancy of many offices by Democratic incumbents discouraged strong Republican challengers. Especially in state legislative and county elections, incumbents often face no challenger in the general election. The strength of Democrats in open-seat contests also inhibited Republican growth. Northern liberal Democratic presidential nominees may have had great difficulty in attracting southern support, but wily moderate southern Democrats continued to run winning campaigns.

Republicans nevertheless made steady, if often slow, growth in their share of offices even if they failed to gain a majority of offices. Events alternatively aided and hindered Republican efforts to win more offices. Watergate naturally helped Democratic efforts to fight GOP advances. On the other hand, the unpopularity of Democratic President Jimmy Carter hurt the Democrats despite his southern connections. These events, however, largely served to punctuate a long-term trend favoring the GOP.

The deep unpopularity of the Clinton administration appears to have played a critical role in helping the Republicans win a majority of congressional offices as well as several state legislative chambers in the mid-1990s. However, it would be a mistake to view the Republican majority as simply the result of tidal wave that overcame the previously impregnable Democrats. Long-term efforts provided the foundation upon which Republicans were able to build when political opportunity struck. In many ways, these gains were the culmination of a long-term process started decades earlier.

At the same time, one should not assume that the partisan change was a completely top-down process with Republican success at the presidential level trickling down to the local level. Republican victories at the local level may have helped produce greater gains at the state and national level even if Republicans achieved majority status at the national level first. Victories for local offices also provided a pool of more experienced candidates, which facilitated greater, less temporary Republican gains than were possible with the earlier shallow pool of GOP talent. If a party fails to recruit good candidates, its chances of winning and then holding on to office decrease markedly.

The next chapter explores the role of strategic elites in propelling or slowing Republican growth in greater detail. More specifically, the chapter details the ability of the GOP to recruit candidates for various elected offices over time. It also explains how the incumbency advantage put the brakes on Republican success in many elections by deterring potential Republican candidates from seeking office. Later chapters will further explore how both the demographic context and various issues further shaped whether potential Republican candidates chose to seek office or give Democrats a pass.

CHAPTER THREE

Strategic Elites and Partisan Choice

THE PREVIOUS CHAPTER SHOWED that Republican southern gains occurred at a very gradual pace over several decades. Despite the influx of new voters, black and white, in the 1960s, the Republicans scored only a few successes in the period following the Voting Rights Act. Republicans faced problems not only winning elections but finding candidates to run in them. The lack of party organization and an inability to attract candidates plagued southern Republicans. The party's lack of roots or power in the region made it difficult for the GOP to recruit any candidates, let alone experienced ones, for many offices.[1]

Strategic elites play a critical role in slowing or promoting Republican gains through both their choice of a party label and their decision to fight an election or give the race a pass.[2] Candidates for local and state legislative office run unopposed in a high percentage of contests.[3] Aspirants for office usually prefer winning election unopposed, or at least with relatively weak opposition, and are naturally more likely to gravitate to the party label that offers them the best chance of an easy election. The party chosen by successful candidates for low-level southern offices is crucial to a party's long-term success as these offices generate highly experienced potential candidates for statewide and federal office. Until recently, Republicans did not contest a significant minority of congressional seats and left a majority of state legislative Democrats without major-party opposition. Even at the end of the 1980s, Republicans still did not attract candidates for over 80 percent of county offices in the South.

Studies of congressional elections suggest that the incumbency advan-

---

[1] Tod A. Baker, Charles D. Hadley, Robert P. Steed, and Lawrence W. Moreland, eds., *Political Parties in the Southern States: Party Activists in Partisan Coalitions* (New York: Praeger, 1990); Lawrence W. Moreland and Robert P. Steed, eds., *The 1996 Presidential Election in the South: Southern Party Systems in the 1990s* (New York: Praeger, 1997); Robert P. Steed, John A. Clark, Lewis Bowman, and Charles D. Hadley, *Party Organizations and Activism in the American South* (Tuscaloosa: University of Alabama Press 1998); Robert P. Steed, Lawrence W. Moreland, and Tod A. Baker, eds., *The Disappearing South? Studies in Regional Change and Continuity* (Tuscaloosa: University of Alabama Press, 1990); Robert P. Steed, Lawrence W. Moreland, and Tod A. Baker, eds., *Southern Parties and Elections: Studies in Regional Political Change* (Tuscaloosa: University of Alabama Press, 1997).

[2] Jacobson 2001, 36–40; Jacobson and Kernell 1983.

[3] Montcrief, Squire, and Jewell 2001, 9–13.

tage has not made incumbents more likely to win reelection than in the past.[4] However, the incumbency advantage has become increasingly important in southern local and state legislative contests. The incumbency advantage manifests itself in county and state legislative elections primarily by discouraging challengers from running. As the occupants of the vast majority of offices until recently, Democrats have benefited from the incumbency advantage to a far greater extent than Republicans. Although the incumbency advantage has aided Democrats in staving off Republican growth, sufficient numbers of seats come open in each election for the Republicans to make major gains over the course of a few elections despite the incumbency advantage. Even if they had won only 40 to 50 percent of open seats, Republicans would have made major gains over the course of a decade in both congressional and local contests.[5] Recent Republican successes at all levels of government mean that the incumbency advantage increasingly helps Republicans protect their gains against Democratic opponents.

WHY FOCUS ON LOCAL AND STATE LEGISLATIVE CONTESTS?

Many important studies of partisan change in the South have focused on either gubernatorial or federal elections.[6] This section explains why it is important to examine often ignored elections for state legislative and county offices. State and local politics further deserve attention because state and local governments are making a greater share of critical decisions as federal Republicans successfully push for renewed federalism or the devolution of power away from the federal government. Scholars additionally need to examine partisan shifts below the congressional level in order to explain why partisan change has occurred more slowly as one moves down the ballot. This chapter details how local and state politics shed new light on how strategic behavior by elites and voters has propelled, or thwarted, Republican gains in the South. As Republican strength has grown slowest at the local level, gains in county elections indicate a real solidity and depth in the southern GOP lacking in the past despite statewide victories.

An Indicator of Partisanship

To the extent that partisan change is the product of a shift in the partisanship of individuals from the Democrats to the Republicans, it should

---

[4] Jacobson 2001, 21–30.

[5] See table 3.5, later in this chapter, for a breakdown of southern county offices by incumbency status weighted by county population.

[6] Black and Black 1987, 2002; Carmines and Stimson 1989; Sundquist 1993.

influence not only national or statewide offices but elections to the more humble state legislative and county offices. Though many municipal and school board officials are elected on a nonpartisan basis, most county officials win election in partisan contests. Outside of Virginia, the vast majority of county officials run and win as Democrats or Republicans.[7] Voters who think of themselves as Republicans should support Republican candidates for local office at particularly high rates. Little information is usually available on these races; they are rarely covered in any sort of depth by the television news media and local candidates usually cannot afford to pay for many, if any, television commercials. Even local newspapers tend to give relatively scant attention to local or state legislative races compared to statewide or national electoral contests. For these reasons, it is exactly these sorts of down-ballot contests for which party identification may serve most valuably as a cue. Voters may be aware of an issue position held by gubernatorial or senatorial candidates, but they usually have little basis other than party on which to form a judgment on candidates for local office.

Two factors may undermine the relevance of partisanship at the local level. First, voters may have different party identifications for local and national officials. Robert Speel argues that formerly Republican New England voters now possess different party identifications at the federal and state levels. They are now largely Democratic in presidential elections but more willing to vote for Republicans at the local and state level because New England Republicans are usually more moderate than Republican presidential nominees.[8] Similarly, some argue that the South has also experienced a split-level realignment.[9] Southerners may vote Republican in presidential elections but support Democrats at a higher rate at the local level because local Democrats are more conservative than national Democratic presidential nominees.

While such voting behavior is utterly rational, there is little evidence that many voters consciously split partisanship between the federal and state level. Moreover, any break in partisanship should be strongest between presidential and all other contests as presidential nominees are the

---

[7] See chapter 4 for a greater discussion of why Virginia has more independent officials. Even in Virginia, most county officials are affiliated with the Democrats or Republicans, though a sizeable minority are independents. Most municipal officials run on a nonpartisan ballot throughout the region.

[8] Speel 1998, 14–17, 59–62, 100–101.

[9] Philip E. Converse, "On the Possibility of a Major Political Realignment in the South," in Angus Campbell, Warren E. Miller, Philip E. Converse, and Donald E. Stokes, *Elections and the Political Order* (New York: John Wiley, 1966); Charles D. Hadley, "Dual Partisan Identification in the South," *Journal of Politics* 47:1 (February 1985): 254–68.

only candidates selected from outside the state. Yet there is clear evidence that southern support for the Republicans has risen in a variety of contests besides presidential elections. Instead of solely examining the partisanship of voters, it makes more sense to focus on how the choice of candidates offered voters influences the outcomes. Southern voters, especially southern whites, may be more prone to supporting the Republicans in national than local elections, but this split in voting behavior results from differences in the candidate offerings. Speel ultimately concludes that it is the relatively moderate ideology of northern Republicans that drives northern voters to support them at higher rates than national Republicans. He does not argue that voters focus on different issues or somehow have different ideologies when approaching state versus national elections.

Personal knowledge of local candidates may also override partisanship in small counties and state legislative districts. Studies of congressional elections show that voters are more likely to vote for a candidate when they have some knowledge about the candidate before entering the voting booth.[10] Meeting a candidate, which is not so unlikely in small counties and state legislative districts, makes one even more likely to vote for a candidate regardless of partisanship. State legislative size, however, has remained fixed over the last twenty years in all eleven southern states, so voters are increasingly unlikely to have personal contact with their state legislator. In the average southern state, the size of a state House district increased from just over 37,000 to just under 62,000 between 1970 and 2000—an increase of 57 percent. Districts in Florida and Texas now contain over 130,000 residents, and districts in all southern states except Arkansas, Mississippi, and South Carolina contain over 40,000 people.[11] Counties in metropolitan areas that contain most of a state's population are also unlikely to be sufficiently small for residents to have personal knowledge of candidates for county office. Even in counties or districts that are small enough for candidates to know a large chunk of the electorate, one suspects that savvy local candidates would opt for the party of most of their neighbors rather than attempt to override the natural partisan inclination of the community through personal connections. Another equally well-known local potential candidate might otherwise choose to run as the candidate of the more popular party.

[10] Jacobson 2001, 123–25.

[11] Based on U.S. census population projects for 2000 and assuming that the number of state House districts in states remains unchanged, the average number of residents (1000s) per state House district in each state is: Alabama 42, Arkansas 26, Florida 127, Georgia 44, Louisiana 42, Mississippi 23, North Carolina 65, South Carolina 31, Tennessee 57, Texas 134, and Virginia 70.

Strategic Behavior by Elites

Local and state legislative elections provide an excellent context in which to develop and further extend ideas about the role of political elites in the electoral process. As the previous discussion suggests, the behavior of potential candidates often plays a crucial role in influencing voting behavior and electoral outcomes. Political scientists have long recognized the importance of actions by political elites. In their pathbreaking work on congressional elections, Gary Jacobson and Samuel Kernell argue that high-quality candidates, defined as candidates with previous experience in elected office, receive a higher share of the vote than candidates without previous electoral success.[12] This elite group of candidates pays great attention to political context when deciding whether to seek election, and their decisions influence their party's vote share. More recently, Jacobson has argued that the impact of national political and economic factors, such as an unpopular president or a poor economy, on congressional outcomes is increasingly mediated by the responsiveness of this elite tier of potential candidates to these trends. Voters do not increase their support for one party over the other directly because of national political tides. Instead, a party runs stronger candidates in response to these tides and voters change their voting behavior in response to the altered set of candidate choices.[13]

Jonathan Krasno has confirmed the essence of Jacobson's argument as applied to U.S. Senate elections. Krasno neatly demonstrates that the competitiveness of Senate races as compared to House races does not mean that the processes that govern senatorial contests are inherently different.[14] As in House contests, elite decisions play a crucial role in determining the outcome of Senate races. Senate incumbents draw stronger challengers than House incumbents, likely because there are fewer members of the Senate and senatorial terms are six years instead of two. Due to the presence of stronger challengers, Senate incumbents must fight harder to retain their seats than the average House incumbent. The responsiveness of elites to political incentives once again plays an important role in determining the electoral outcome. Ironically, it is the similar nature of the electoral processes that explains why a greater share of senators than representatives are defeated for reelection.

David Canon gives center stage to elite decisions in his study of the impact of racial redistricting on African-American representation. According to Canon and his coauthors, the supply and distribution of can-

[12] Jacobson and Kernell 1983.
[13] Jacobson 2001, 153–59, 183; Lublin 1994, 232–34.
[14] Krasno 1994, 13–15, 72–102, 124–27.

didates determines the race and ideology of the Democratic nominee, who almost inevitably wins the general election in black-majority districts. The presence of a credible white candidate, for example, may take away votes from a black moderate and thus assure the election of a black liberal. On the other hand, if no prominent white candidate runs, black moderates can defeat black liberals by forming a winning electoral coalition of white and black moderate voters.[15]

Political elites merit even greater attention in local and state legislative elections than in the congressional contests that have been the focus of most studies of elite actions. Local and state legislative officials form a critical pool of high-quality potential candidates for statewide and federal office. A party that elects few candidates at the local level will lack experienced candidates for the U.S. House.[16] Unfortunately, these contests are often ignored due to the lack of data. Surveys on these sorts of elections are almost never publicly available. Even gathering data on the outcome of local contests is usually incredibly difficult.

The relative lack of study of elites at the local and state legislative level is a pity because political elites at this level often have the unique opportunity of running under a political party's label for the first time. Local and state legislative races are often the first partisan contests in which the candidates have participated, so candidates are not only seeking election but effectively selecting their public partisan persona. These candidates often have no track record, or only a very limited one, as members of a political party. Even if they held municipal office prior to seeking county or state legislative office, they most likely served as a nonpartisan official.

In contrast, switching parties may be more hazardous for experienced candidates for higher office who have served as officials in the past. Before switching parties, these candidates must carefully assess whether they are sacrificing too great a share of their network of supporters and allies both among voters and their colleagues. Candidates for higher office who do change parties must either act on high principle or believe that the potential gains outweigh the risks. Walter Jones Jr., who served in the North Carolina House as a progressive Democrat, is one of the more successful party switchers. In 1992 Jones sought, but did not win, his party's nomination to the First Congressional District, previously held by his father but reconfigured as majority black prior to the elec-

---

[15] David T. Canon, *Race, Redistricting, and Representation: The Unintended Consequences of Black Majority Districts* (Chicago: University of Chicago Press, 1990), 93–142; David T. Canon, Matthew M. Schousen, and Patrick J. Sellers, "The Supply-Side of Congressional Redistricting: Race and Strategic Politicians, 1972–1992," *Journal of Politics* 58 (1996): 837–53.

[16] Jacobson 2001, 76, 183–85.

tion.[17] Claiming "my old party has changed,"[18] Jones then switched parties and won election in 1994 as a Republican from the neighboring Third District. One cannot help but wonder if Jones would have experienced his Damascene conversion to the Republicans if he had won the First District in 1992.

The selection of a political party label has important consequences for potential candidates. Politically savvy elites are aware of the consequence of their party choice. Few politicians who aspire to hold office, rather than merely campaign for their ideas, choose third-party labels because they do not wish to consign themselves to political oblivion. Candidates will naturally gravitate toward the party that offers them a greater chance of success. In many ways, it is really not very different from choosing to affiliate a product with a brand name. Why arrange to sell your cookies as Mrs. Fields if people in your area prefer Famous Amos? Similarly, why call yourself a Republican when more people shop Democratic?

Choosing a party label based on its prospective aid to your campaign makes especially good sense for many county offices. Campaigns for many of these offices are usually devoid of ideological content due to the nature of the office. It is difficult to campaign as a liberal or a conservative for offices such as county clerk or county coroner. Is there a liberal way of conducting an autopsy or a conservative way of filing official papers? While crime is often a partisan or ideological issue at the state or national level, it is more difficult to make it an ideological issue in campaigns for sheriff. Virtually all candidates for sheriff wisely promise to combat crime aggressively in their area. Pro-crime candidates for sheriffs are few and far between and do not seem to get very far in their political careers.

Decisions by political elites play an especially vital role in local and state legislative contests because the party label that a high-quality candidate selects may determine the outcome of the election. As the section on candidate recruitment illustrates, major-party candidates for local and state legislative office win without opposition from the other major party at a far higher rate than congressional candidates. The ability to attract elites to its banner is thus a crucial component of a party's success. Relatedly, the success of Democratic incumbents in discouraging Republican challengers has helped prolong Democratic dominance of local politics in the South.

---

[17] Jones won the first primary with 38% of the vote but failed to pass the 40% threshold required to avoid a runoff under North Carolina law. African-American Eva Clayton won the runoff with 55% of the vote.

[18] Michael Barone and Grant Ujifusa, *Almanac of American Politics 1998* (Washington, DC: National Journal, 1997), 1064.

The Local Elections Database

In order to examine partisan change and elite recruitment at the local level, I constructed a database containing the results of elections held from 1979 through 1999 for partisan county offices. Information was gathered on partisan offices, rather than on nonpartisan offices, in an endeavor to maintain the focus on shifts in partisanship. The database includes only countywide offices because the county has long been considered the central political unit below the state level in the South.[19] Additionally, the U.S. Census contains a wealth of county demographic data that is almost impossible to obtain for offices elected from districts within counties or across counties as county councils and state legislatures often draw districts without regard to census boundaries.

Many southern states disperse power within counties by requiring counties to elect a wide variety of local officials. The database includes elections to county offices in eight southern states held between 1979 and 1999. Typical offices included in the data set are sheriff, coroner, clerk, and tax assessor. The selection and number of offices gathered from each state depended largely on the number of elected offices and the availability of data. While the data set includes information on seven distinct offices in Mississippi, it contains information on only three offices in North Carolina.[20] The database includes information for virtually every county in Georgia, Louisiana, Mississippi, North Carolina, South Carolina, and Virginia. The Louisiana data excludes Orleans Parish (New Orleans) because Orleans elects a somewhat different array of local officials than the rest of the Pelican State and elects them on a different timetable than the rest of Louisiana.[21] (Louisiana has traditionally used the term "parish" rather than "county" to describe its subunits due to its origin as a French colony.) The Virginia data include information on both counties and independent cities as independent cities are not controlled by county governments. Indeed, independent cities have more local powers than county governments and several counties have incor-

---

[19] Key 1949; Voss 1996.

[20] The data for Mississippi also include information on an eighth countywide office, tax collector, and the county supervisors. The office of tax collector was excluded from the analysis because most counties merged the office with tax assessor by the end of the period under study. County supervisors are elected from five districts, called beats, in all Mississippi counties.

[21] Orleans Parish elects its local officials in the same year as the midterm congressional election while all other parishes elect their officials in the odd-numbered year before the presidential election. Unlike other parishes, Orleans Parish elects several assessors by district rather than one assessor at large. New Orleans, coterminous with Orleans Parish, elects a mayor who has no real equivalent in other parishes.

porated as independent cities in order to gain these additional governmental prerogatives. The data from Texas and Florida were gathered from a sample of 38 counties in east Texas, the most culturally southern part of the Lone Star State, and 52 counties around Florida. The counties included from these two states are the counties from which it was possible to obtain data among all counties in Florida and the 100 counties surveyed in east Texas. Data from Alabama and Tennessee proved impossible to obtain for a sufficient number of counties.[22]

CANDIDATE RECRUITMENT

That a political party must field candidates in order to win elections is so obvious that it would seemingly not require mention. Under the winner-take-all system of elections used for virtually all elections at all levels of government in the United States, failure to field a candidate cedes the race to the opposition. Potential candidates, particularly high-quality candidates, are unsurprisingly reluctant to run under the banner of a party that rarely achieves success. Third parties elect few officials not only because people are reluctant to cast ballots for a "spoiler" in a winner-take-all electoral system but because these parties have great difficulty recruiting candidates. For example, despite the stunning success of Ross Perot in winning nearly 20 percent of the vote in his 1992 presidential bid (and much higher in many regions of the country), relatively few

---

[22] Information was solicited by telephone and mail (or fax) to all counties in Florida and over 100 counties in east Texas. The sample includes all counties that responded to requests for information. Unlike in Louisiana, Mississippi, North Carolina, South Carolina, and Virginia, data on local election outcomes are not available from a central source in the state capital in Florida or Texas.

Information was solicited by mail from Alabama and Tennessee, but counties responded at a very low rate to these requests. Alabama was the first state solicited for data; the requests to Alabama counties included a burdensome request for precinct election results that was not sent to counties in other states due to the non-response to this request on the part of Alabama officials. Discouragingly, many Alabama counties proved unwilling to provide even the most basic information on local election outcomes when requested in follow-up telephone calls. On the other hand, the Offices of the Secretary of State in both Alabama and Tennessee were unusually and repeatedly helpful in providing data on all elections for which they had records.

The Arkansas Secretary of State publishes information about the names and parties of past winners of county office around the state; see Sharon Priest, *Historical Report of the Arkansas Secretary of State 1998*. However, county election results were unavailable. Data on Arkansas is included in discussion of the party of county officials in chapter 2 (see table 2.2) but excluded here as it is unknown whether Republicans fielded a candidate when a non-Republican was elected.

The Louisiana data extend back to 1979. However, the North Carolina data do not extend beyond 1996; efforts to collect the results from 1998 were unsuccessful.

candidates for other offices chose to run under the Reform banner and the Reform Party elected almost no officials to public office.

Perhaps more shockingly, although many people want to hold elected office, the two major political parties face similar difficulties in attracting candidates for office. The Democrats and the Republicans regularly fail to field full slates for all congressional or state legislative seats as well as many local offices. The lack of a full slate reflects more than just a strategic decision not to run candidates for hopeless seats. The long-term inability to recruit candidates for office plagued the Republican effort to elect more officials to many offices until recently. Republicans had such problems recruiting candidates that for many years they could not even win majority control of southern state Houses even if they won every single race that they contested. Potential Republican candidates either chose not to run or decided that it would be politically advantageous to run as Democrats, long the region's hyperdominant political force. The Democratic monopoly on nearly all the levels of power provided another incentive to adhere to the region's dominant party. Joining the small minority caucus in a legislative body rarely provides many opportunities to exercise power.

Republican Contestation of Southern Elections

U.S. SENATE ELECTIONS

Figure 3.1 displays the percentage of U.S. Senate seats contested by the Republicans from 1960 to 2002. The staggered election of senators to six-year terms partly accounts for the erratic nature of the trend line in the figure. Different numbers and combinations of southern states elected senators every two years.[23] The figure nevertheless hints at the responsiveness of potential senatorial candidates to national trends. When the Democrats nominated northern liberal George McGovern in 1972, the Republicans successfully recruited candidates for all U.S. seats up for election for the first time since the ratification in 1913 of the Seventeenth Amendment to the Constitution requiring the direct election of senators. Republican recruitment success dropped to 71 percent in 1974 in the aftermath of the Watergate scandal and plunged further to 60 percent in 1976 when the Democrats nominated Georgian Jimmy Carter, who carried the South for the Democrats for the first time since 1964. The election of a packet of obscure and inexperienced Republican

[23] Five southern states (Florida, Mississippi, Texas, Tennessee, and Virginia) elect Class 1 senators. All eleven southern states, except Florida, elect Class 2 senators. Seven states (all except Mississippi, Tennessee, Texas, and Virginia) elect Class 3 senators. Class 1 senators were up for election most recently in 2000 while the terms for Class 2 and Class 3 senators expired in 2002 and 1998, respectively.

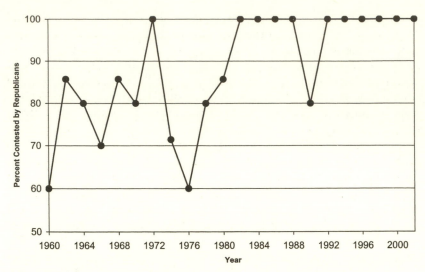

Figure 3.1. Percent Southern U.S. Senate seats contested by Republicans.
Note: Each data point shows the percentage of Senate seats contested by the
Republicans out of all seats regularly up for election; special elections are ex-
cluded. As senators have a term of six years and all states elect two senators, each
state was included in the calculation for only two of three sequential data points.
Only every third data point includes the same subset of the southern states.
Sources: *Congressional Elections 1946–1996* (Congressional Quarterly, 1998); Mi-
chael Barone, Richard E. Cohen, and Grant Ujifusa, *The Almanac of American
Politics 2002* (National Journal, 2002).

senators on President Reagan's coattails in 1980 encouraged the Republicans to field a full slate of senatorial candidates in 1982. The regular
success of Republican senatorial candidates since 1980 has encouraged
the Republicans to leave almost no Democrats unopposed since 1982.
Republicans lost only four of the fifteen elections for open U.S. Senate
seats in the South held between 1988 and 2002.[24]

Examining the share of seats with Republican candidates over the
complete cycle of three senatorial elections over six years provides a
more long-term view of Republican contestation. Throughout the 1960s,

[24] Popular former Virginia Governor Chuck Robb easily picked up the seat held by retiring Republican Paul Trible in 1988. Max Cleland won a narrow plurality to hold on to the
seat vacated by Georgian Sam Nunn in 1996. Blanche Lambert Lincoln won the Arkansas
seat vacated by Democrat Dale Bumpers in Arkansas in 1998. Mary Landrieu successfully
defended the Louisiana seat vacated by retiring Democrat J. Bennett Johnston in 1996,
though the outcome was disputed and ultimately decided the U.S. Senate itself. In 2000,
Ben Nelson picked up the vacant Florida seat previously held by Republican Connie Mack.
Former Georgia Governor Zell Miller won a special election to replace the late Paul Cov-
erdell in 2000. Technically, this was not an open seat as Miller had been appointed to fill
the vacancy.

the Republicans nominated candidates for around three-quarters of U.S. Senate seats: 73 percent in 1960–64 and 77 percent in 1966–70. In the early 1970s, the percentage of senatorial seats contested by the GOP edged above 80 percent for the first time (82 percent in 1972–76). Beginning in 1982, the Republicans left no seats unopposed except for two seats in 1990. These seats were held by Georgian Sam Nunn and Arkansan David Pryor, both highly popular incumbents. Republicans have consistently fought a higher percentage of U.S. Senate contests than U.S. House, state legislative, or local races since 1960. The importance of the office combined with the very small number of candidates required helps explain this gap in recruitment. The ability to recruit from a statewide pool of potential candidates, rather than from a single county or legislative district, also made it easier for the Republicans to oppose the Democrats in a relatively high share of senatorial contests.

U.S. HOUSE ELECTIONS

Figure 3.2 shows the percentage of U.S. House seats for which the Republicans and Democrats fielded candidates from 1962 through 2002. Through 1974, the Republicans regularly left one-third of all Democrats unopposed in presidential election years, and over 40 percent unopposed in midterm congressional elections. No wonder the GOP had little chance of winning a majority of the region's seats. The Republicans started contesting a higher share of southern House elections beginning in the mid-1970s but still left an average of one-quarter of seats without Republican candidates through 1990. In contrast, the GOP ran candidates for over 95 percent of all southern House seats from 1992–96. Indeed, they contested a greater share of seats than the Democrats and gained seats in all of these elections. However, the percentage of seats contested by Republicans dropped below 90 percent in 1998 to 2002, though the Republicans did not experience a net loss of seats and continued to contest more elections than the Democrats.

The percentage of House races contested by the Republicans was higher than for state legislative or local elections, but not senatorial contests, across the entire period studied. Gary Jacobson has focused on the critical role played by the availability of candidates with prior electoral experience in a party's crusade to win U.S. House seats. Candidates without prior experience running and holding office fare more poorly than other congressional candidates.[25] Recruiting these high-quality—or any—candidates is difficult if a party holds few or no local offices. As the next section demonstrates, the Republicans did not even contest a significant minority of county offices until quite recently.

[25] Jacobson 2001, 36–40, 153–59.

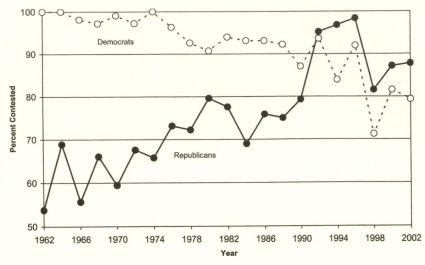

Figure 3.2. Percent Southern U.S. House seats contested by Democrats and Republicans.
Note: Each data point shows the percentage of southern U.S. House seats contested by either the Democrats or the Republicans; special elections are excluded.
Sources: *Congressional Elections 1946–1996* (Congressional Quarterly, 1998); Michael Barone, Richard E. Cohen, and Grant Ujifusa, *The Almanac of American Politics 2002* (National Journal, 2002).

The failure of the Republicans to fight over 80 percent of U.S. House elections until 1992 is perhaps not so surprising in light of their thin talent pool. However, as the discussion in chapter 2 of the top-down realignment of South outlines, each congressional district contains many local officials and state legislators and the Republicans need to find only one high-quality candidate per race. Low rates of contestation reflect the power of incumbency; Republicans contested all but a few open seats.

The growing strength of the Republicans and the thinning of the Democratic pool of candidates in selected areas of the South is reflected as well in figure 3.2. The Democrats contested over 95 percent of congressional seats until 1978. They failed to recruit a general election candidate for more than one in ten of U.S. House races for the first time in 1990. The Democrats have ceded an even greater share of House contests in more recent years. In the three elections held between 1998 and 2002, the Democrats conceded at least 18 percent of House races without a fight. Democrats left a stunning 29 percent of southern Republican House candidates unopposed in 1998—a rate last exceeded by the Republicans in 1984.

STATE HOUSE ELECTIONS

Republicans had markedly varied success in fielding candidates for elections to the state legislature. As table 3.1 shows, the percentage of seats contested by the GOP has generally increased over time in most southern states. Republicans did not contest a majority of state House seats in many southern states, mostly in the Deep South, until the 1990s. Republicans fought for a majority of districts for the first time in Alabama in 1990, Georgia in 1994, and Mississippi in 1995. Arkansas Republicans did not contest a majority of districts until term limits took effect in 1998. Louisiana Republicans have yet to contest a majority of state House districts. In South Carolina, Republicans impressively fought a majority of state House seats as early as 1970, 1972, and 1974. However, the South Carolina GOP's success at recruitment proved ephemeral as the party contested only around one-third of seats in the early 1980s. It was not until 1990 that the Republicans again ran in a majority of state House seats. Republicans could hardly have been expected to form a substantial minority, let alone a majority, throughout the region when they contested only a minority of seats in so many states.

On the other hand, Republicans became a serious force in state House elections at an earlier stage in portions of the Peripheral South. Excepting 1976, Republicans contested a majority of seats in each of the state House elections held in Tennessee between 1968 and 2002. Throughout this same period, Florida Republicans never allowed the Democrats to win a majority of seats by default; they always ran candidates in a majority of seats. Indeed, Sunshine State Republicans never contested less than two-thirds of seats after 1986 or less than three-quarters after 1996. After 1970, Republicans usually managed to attract candidates for a majority of seats for state House elections held in North Carolina, Texas, and Virginia. Republicans ran candidates in an even higher share of races by the end of the 1990s in all three states.

LOCAL ELECTIONS

Table 3.2 presents the percentage of the population living in counties in which the Republicans contested a selection of county offices in eight states around the South. Since some counties are home to many people while others have relatively few residents, the GOP may fight contests in only a minority of counties but these counties may contain a majority of the population. For example, the Republicans regularly contest elections in most counties in metropolitan Atlanta and other urban areas in Georgia but leave the Democrats unopposed in numerous small counties in rural south Georgia that are home to comparatively few Georgians. In order to avoid underestimating the impact of Republican gains at the

TABLE 3.1
Percent Southern State House Seats Contested by Republican Candidates

	68	69	70	71	72	73	74	75	76	77	78	79	80	81	82	83	84	85	86	87	88	89
AL			2				30				32				25				47			
AR	5		37		1		11		4		12		15		7		17		20		17	
FL	63		53		72		55		51		58		50		67		60		69		67	
GA	37		32		27		26		26		23		27		30		32		34		36	
LA	35							x				x				x				31		
MS				12				23				30				22				24		
NC			75		70		71		42		47		72		53		53					
SC	13		66		61		51		46		29		31		36		35		38		47	
TN	64		71		71		67		48		64		73		57		54		61		51	
TX	47		39		50		39		37		46		57		53		44		52		57	
VA		25		72		60		48		53		62		58		54		59		53		61

	90	91	92	93	94	95	96	97	98	99	2000	01	02
AL	55		59				73		x		70		
AR			x		39		42		51		46		
FL			x		73		77		77		83		77
GA	38		90		65		70		66				
LA		44				49				41			
MS		39				53				38			
NC	x		71		83		74		80		78		
SC	53		65		77		71		69		69		
TN	64		68		68		63		65		80		
TX	62		58		71		70		63		76		
VA		64		90		85		72		81			

Note: The table shows the percentage of state legislative seats with Republican candidates in each state for year in which there was a general election for the state House. Mississippi held elections in both 1991 and 1992 because the state did not complete the redistricting process until after the 1991 elections had already been held under the old map. x = missing data.

Sources: For all elections held from 1991 through 2002, and all elections held in Alabama, Georgia, Mississippi, South Carolina, and Tennessee, data compiled by author from official sources. For all elections held prior in 1992 in Arkansas, Florida, North Carolina, Texas, and Virginia, data compiled from the ICPSR Dataset 8907, "State Legislative Election Returns in the United States, 1968–1989," and from official sources.

county level, table 3.2 along with the other tables in this section present the share of the population living in counties with Republican candidates rather than the percentage of counties with Republican candidates.[26] In most cases, the share of people living in counties with Republican candidates and the number of counties with Republican candidates both increased over time.

Even though most people lived in counties with Republican candidates by 1999, Republicans rarely sought office in a majority of counties by this time. Indeed, Republicans sought office in only a very small percentage of counties in most states for virtually all offices until the late 1990s. Republicans cannot win where Republicans do not run, so the traditionally dominant Democrats continued to win a majority of local offices around the region without any major-party opposition. North Carolina and Virginia counties appear to be the major exception as the GOP contested county offices in a comparatively high percentage of counties even in the early 1980s.

Nevertheless, it is critical to realize that growing white identification with the GOP led to the Republicans' fielding candidates for local office more and more often in the populous counties home to most of the region's residents by the end of century. By 1998 the GOP sought office in counties home to an impressive 73 percent of the people of the counties sampled in east Texas. Around 60 percent of Florida, North Carolina, and South Carolina residents inhabited counties with Republican candidates for county office by the end of the 1990s. Georgia, Mississippi, and Virginia Republicans contested elections in counties where approximately one-half of each state's residents lived. However, only 39 percent of Louisianans lived in parishes with Republican candidates for county office by 1999.[27]

The Incumbency Advantage in Local Elections

Scholars of congressional elections conceive of the incumbency advantage as the difference in the vote share received by an incumbent candi-

---

[26] The share of the population living in counties with Republican candidates is equivalent to weighting the share of counties with Republican candidates by the population. The county population according to the U.S. Census served as the weight.

[27] The figure for Louisiana may actually overstate the level of Republican contestation because heavily Democratic Orleans Parish is excluded from the database. Republicans do not seem to contest many low-level offices elected by the entire parish. The GOP runs candidates more often for offices elected by district as they have strength in portions of the parish, presumably dominated by whites, even if they fare poorly in the parish as a whole. Republicans often run for mayor of New Orleans and make it to the runoff if the initial primary is sufficiently fractured, though they have not won election in the past three decades.

TABLE 3.2
Weighted Percentage of Southern County Offices Contested by Republicans

Virginia

Clerk			Treasurer	Revenue Com.	Sheriff	Comm. Attorney
		1981–83	25	27	52	43
		1985–87	32	30	47	31
1987–91	49	1989–91	40	31	64	32
		1993–95	39	41	55	53
1995–99	59	1997–99	47	45	53	43

Florida

	Tax Collector	Sup. of Elections	Clerk	Property Appraiser	Sheriff
1980	38	57	23	61	60
1984	50	50	27	73	52
1988	35	47	43	65	55
1992	74	51	49	73	75
1996	53	45	46	79	69

Texas

District Clerk			County Clerk	County Judge	Sheriff	Tax Assessor
1982	8	1980	20	45	49	13
1986	57	1984	47	69	41	30
1990	54	1988	50	65	77	57
1994	58	1992	62	71	73	62
1998	62	1996	66	72	89	78

North Carolina

	Clerk		Sheriff	Register of Deeds
1982	27	1982–84	58	24
1986	34	1986–88	66	47
1990	50	1990–92	76	43
1994	43	1994–96	72	60

South Carolina

	Clerk	Probate Judge	Auditor	Coroner	Treasurer	Sheriff
1980–82	14	18	13	47	21	40
1984–86	28	16	38	36	26	39
1988–90	29	50	52	51	43	57
1992–94	25	43	60	61	72	69
1996–98	56	60	63	67	69	66

Georgia

	Probate Judge	Clerk	Tax Commis.	Coroner	Sheriff
1980	9	31	30	26	27
1984	14	24	34	43	38
1988	18	25	38	46	29
1992	22	22	40	47	49
1996	28	50	44	54	73

Mississippi

	Circuit Clerk	Tax Assessor	County Attorney	Sup. of Education	Coroner	Chancery Clerk	Sheriff
1983	6	10	4	3	13	8	28
1987	12	9	4	4	7	11	21
1991	15	15	19	19	31	33	61
1995	27	28	18	38	43	33	67
1999	19	33	37	33	33	49	49

Louisiana

	Clerk	Assessor	Sheriff	Coroner
1983	27	14	19	17
1987	12	18	22	17
1991	36	22	42	36
1995	33	18	54	26
1999	36	46	44	32

Note: The percentages were weighted by county population from the 1980, 1990, or 2000 U.S. Census. For elections held in non-Census years, the population from the nearest census was used as the weight. The data set for Louisiana excludes Orleans Parish for all years because it elects different officials on a different schedule from the rest of the state. The Florida data set includes the 52 counties from around the state from which it was possible to obtain data. The Texas data set includes the 38 counties that responded to a request for election data made to 100 counties in east Texas, the culturally most southern part of the state. In Mississippi, approximately 15 counties do not elect a county attorney and 19 counties do not elect a superintendent of education.

Source: Data compiled by author.

date compared to the vote share that a non-incumbent candidate would have received running for the same seat. Paradoxically, the incumbency advantage in U.S. House elections has steadily increased since the 1950s but incumbents appear no safer today than fifty years ago. In other words, even though today's incumbents win at least 6 percent more of the vote, on average, than incumbents in the 1950s, their chances of holding their seats has not improved. The rising swing in vote share from election to election explains this perplexing contradiction. Although today's incumbents win more votes than their predecessors, the chance of a large vote swing against them has also grown. Incumbents who win 60 percent of the vote today consequently fail to win reelection at the same rate as incumbents who won 55 percent in the 1950s.[28]

The concept of the incumbency advantage should apply to other contests besides congressional elections. Candidates for local and state legislative offices likely hold similar advantages over their opponents as U.S. House candidates. Studies suggest that the greater name recognition by the electorate of incumbents as compared to challengers is a major source of the incumbency advantage. People do not like to vote for candidates whose name they cannot even recognize on a list.[29] Local and state legislative incumbents likely have an advantage in name recognition over challengers that is similar to that of House candidates.

Nevertheless, the approach to the incumbency advantage pioneered in studies of congressional elections appears unworkable when applied to local elections in the South without modification. First, conceptualizing the incumbency advantage in terms of vote share is of little help in examining uncontested elections. Second, the incumbency advantage actually has gradually become a more meaningful advantage in general elections as Republicans have become a more important electoral force in the South.

As we have already seen, the majority of candidates for county office win election without opposition. Substantial numbers of state legislative seats, often a majority, also go uncontested by one of the major parties in each election. Scholars who study congressional elections have faced this problem as well because not all U.S. House incumbents attract challengers. Some scholars simply ignore these seats when calculating the incumbency advantage. Gelman and King more ingeniously try to estimate the share of the vote that the incumbent would have received if the

---

[28] Andrew Gelman and Gary King, "Estimating the Incumbency Advantage without Bias," *American Journal of Political Science* 34 (1990): 1142–64; Jacobson 2001, 21–30; David R. Mayhew, "Congressional Elections: The Case of the Vanishing Marginals," *Polity* 6 (1974): 295–317.

[29] Jacobson 2001, 110–16.

incumbent had encountered a challenger instead of breezing back unopposed for another term.[30] While better than simply pretending the problem of unopposed candidates did not exist, this tactic may underestimate the incumbency advantage. Discouraging all major-party opposition surely indicates that an incumbent is stronger than an incumbent who attracts a challenger, even a weak one.[31]

For local elections, the most salient aspect of the incumbency advantage may be that incumbents are far less likely to attract an opponent. The impact of incumbency in a local or state legislative contest may be comparable to the shadow cast by a congressional incumbent's "war chest" of campaign funds over potential challengers. The financial advantage held by congressional incumbents often discourages serious competition, or any competition, from taking the plunge and challenging the incumbent.[32] One means of measuring the incumbency advantage in state legislative or local contests is to compare the rate that a party runs candidates for open seats as compared to challengers against opposite-party incumbents. As table 3.3 shows, Republicans consistently ran for open seats in county elections at a greater rate than for seats held by Democratic incumbents. Southerners living in counties with open seats in virtually all of the states studied here were usually at least twice as likely to have a Republican candidate for county office in the general election than southerners living in counties with Democratic incumbents.[33]

The difference is sizable in absolute terms as well. At the end of the 1990s, fewer than 16 percent of people living in counties in Louisiana, Mississippi South Carolina, and Virginia with incumbent Democrats seeking reelection had the opportunity to vote for a Republican challenger (see table 3.3). The situation was quite different in contests for open seats in all four states. Republican candidates sought election in

---

[30] Gelman and King 1990.

[31] Note that I am not claiming that all candidates who face no opposition are stronger than all candidates who attract a challenger. For example, Massachusetts Democrat John Olver glided to reelection unopposed in 1994 but won with only 53 percent of the vote in 1996. However, candidates without opposition are generally stronger than candidates who face an opponent.

[32] Janet M. Box-Steffensmeier, "A Dynamic Analysis of the Role of War Chests in Campaign Strategy," *American Journal of Political Science* 40 (May 1996): 352–71; David Epstein and Peter Zemsky, "Money Talks: Deterring Quality Challengers in Congressional Elections," *American Political Science Review* 89 (June 1995): 295–308.

[33] Unfortunately, the data set does not currently contain primary election data for states other than Louisiana. Under Louisiana's unique electoral system, all candidates, regardless of party, run in the primary. If no candidate receives a majority, the top two candidates compete in a runoff. The vast majority of local elections are settled in the primary. The federal judiciary has invalidated the Louisiana system for federal elections, but this change should not affect state and local contests.

TABLE 3.3
Weighted Percentage of Southern County Offices Contested by Republicans by Incumbency

	Georgia			Texas			Mississippi	
	D Incumbent	Open		D Incumbent	Open		D Incumbent	Open
1984	15	16	1984–86	25	50	1987	6	15
1988	7	27	1988–90	24	58	1991	21	39
1992	12	42	1992–94	19	81	1995	19	60
1996	22	69	1996–98	24	78	1999	15	48

	South Carolina			Louisiana			North Carolina	
	D Incumbent	Open		D Incumbent	Open		D Incumbent	Open
1980–82	15	39	1983	11	53	1986–88	42	51
1984–86	22	30	1987	15	19	1990–92	37	83
1988–90	27	67	1991	20	55	1994–96	38	77
1992–94	25	71	1995	18	46			
1996–98	16	79	1999	16	51			

	Florida			Virginia	
	D Incumbent	Open		D Incumbent	Open
1984	21	69	1985–87	21	51
1988	23	59	1989–91	28	69
1992	27	80	1993–95	36	46
1996	27	70	1997–99	13	70

Note: For the selection of county offices up for election available for each state (see table 3.2), the table shows the percentage of people living in a county with a Republican candidate out of all the county-level contests for which data was available. See table 3.2 for information on the weighting procedure and table 3.5 for the weighted percentage of seats by incumbency status.

Source: Data compiled by author.

counties home to around one-half of Louisianans and Mississippians and three-quarters of South Carolinians and Virginians under these more favorable circumstances.

Similarly, when a Democratic incumbent sought reelection, only around one-quarter of the citizens of Florida, Georgia, and Texas saw a Republican candidate listed on the ballot as the century drew to a close. However, over two-thirds could vote for the GOP in open-seat contests in all three of these states. Local elections were most hotly contested under any condition in North Carolina. Close to 40 percent of people living in counties with Democratic incumbents still had the opportunity to vote for a Republican through the period studied here—a much higher figure than in other states though still much lower than the proportion for counties with open seats.

Unlike in congressional elections, the incumbency advantage has grown not only in size but in importance over time. In most states the difference between the percentage of open seats with a Republican candidate and the percentage of seats held by a Democratic incumbent with a Republican challenger grew substantially in the 1990s. Republicans were not terribly likely to field candidates in either seats that were open or held by Democratic incumbents seeking reelection in some state during the 1980s. Open seats were less safe for Democrats, but Republicans still could not attract a candidate for most open seats. In Georgia, for example, 15 percent of people in counties with Democratic incumbents but 16 percent of people in counties with open seats had GOP candidates on the ballot in 1984—a gap between open and incumbent seats of only 1 percent (see table 3.3).

By the 1990s, Republicans no longer faced such strong barriers to candidate recruitment as more candidates decided that running as a Republican was a viable, or even preferable, option. As a result, the ability to discourage Republicans from running became a more valuable asset to Democratic incumbents. In 1996, 69 percent of Georgians living in counties with open seats could vote Republican. However, the GOP recruited challengers to Democratic incumbents in counties home to 22 percent of Georgians—a gap of 47 percent. This pattern was repeated in most states throughout the region, though the increase in the gap was not quite so dramatic outside of Georgia.

This change makes sense as an incumbency advantage has real meaning in general elections only in regions with genuine two-party competition, a development that was just beginning at the local level in many parts of the South in the 1980s but had blossomed by the 1990s. However, even though Republicans found it easier to attract candidates, these candidates were far less willing to challenge Democratic incumbents than run for open seats. In seats with Democratic incumbents, the percentage of people who could vote Republican often stagnated and sometimes even declined. This pattern likely at least partially reflects that the GOP increasingly already held seats in territory favorable to them or found it easier to encourage Democratic incumbents to retire in these areas.

The extent to which one party's incumbents succeed in discouraging opposition from the other major party varies substantially from state to state. Table 3.4 shows that both the size of the advantage and the party holding the advantage vary around the region. Most commonly, both Republicans and Democrats run candidates in counties home to over 60 percent of residents of open seats. On the other hand, under one-quarter of the residents of counties with an incumbent of one party encounter the name of a challenger of the other party on their ballot. This pattern appears to describe county elections in Georgia, South Carolina, Texas, and Virginia.

TABLE 3.4
Weighted Percentage of Southern County Offices Contested by Incumbency

	Contested by Democrats		Contested by Republicans	
	Republican Incumbent	Open Seat	Democratic Incumbent	Open Seat
Florida 1996	24	83	52	84
Georgia 1996	16	73	22	69
Louisiana 1999	32	89	17	51
Mississippi 1999	43	90	15	48
North Carolina 1994–96	65	98	38	77
South Carolina 1996–98	20	68	16	79
Texas 1996–98	17	69	24	78
Virginia 1997–99	24	61	14	69

Note: For the selection of county offices available for each state, the table reports the percentage of people living in a county contested by a candidate of the appropriate party out of all the counties for which data was available with the same incumbency status. County population data was from the 2000 U.S. Census. See table 3.2 for information on the weighting procedure and table 3.5 for the weighted percentage of seats by incumbency status.

Source: Data compiled by author.

In Florida, open seats were contested at nearly identical rates by both parties. Republican incumbents, however, did a much better job of discouraging opposition than Democratic incumbents. Floridians living in seats with Democratic incumbents could vote Republican around one-half of the time, but only one-fourth of people in seats with Republican incumbents could vote Democratic. Republicans appear to have a stronger incumbency advantage as they discourage more Democrats from even attempting a challenge.

In contrast, North Carolina Republicans contested both open seats and seats held by incumbents of the opposite party at a lower rate than Democrats. Democrats fielded candidates in nearly every open seat in the mid-1990s, but Republicans contested county elections in counties home to just over three-quarters of North Carolina residents living in open seats—a high rate of contestation compared to many states in the region but still much lower than that of the Democrats. Similarly, Democrats ran challengers to Republican incumbents in counties home to nearly two-thirds of North Carolinians in counties with GOP incumbents. Only 38 percent of the people living in counties with Democratic incumbents could vote for a Republican challenger—the second highest rate in the region but far below the comparable rate for Democrats. Even though

Democrats generally contest more seats than do Republicans, after weighting by the population of the county, the incumbency advantage may be roughly the same for each party. The gap between the weighted share of open and incumbent-held seats contested by Republicans is 39 percent; the same gap for seats contested by Democrats is 33 percent.

As in North Carolina, Republicans contest seats at lower rate than Democrats in both Louisiana and Mississippi. However, Republicans rates of contestation are much lower than in North Carolina in these two Deep South states. In Louisiana and Mississippi, only around 50 percent of the people living in open seats and 16 percent of the people living in seats with Democratic incumbents have the opportunity to vote for a Republican candidate. However, table 3.4 indicates that approximately 90 percent of the people living in open seats can vote for a Democrat. Democrats challenge Republican incumbents in Louisiana and Mississippi more often than Republicans challenge Democrats, though at a lower rate than in North Carolina.

One should be somewhat cautious in interpreting these results. Seats won by the Republicans are probably, on average, more politically favorable to the Republicans than the average collection of open seats. If the seats held by Republican incumbents were open, Democrats would thus probably contest them at a lower rate than open seats. The same goes for seats held by Democratic incumbents. However, analysis of the data indicates that a substantial incumbency advantage exists in local elections even after taking into account the partisan complexion of the county. After controlling for a county's partisanship, defined as the percentage of the vote received by President Clinton in 1996, the probability of a Republican seeking county office declined by 46 percent in the late 1990s if the seat was held by a Democratic incumbent. The Democrats, in turn, were 57 percent less likely to field a candidate when the seat was held by a Republican incumbent.[34]

---

[34] The estimates of the incumbency advantage were based on two separate logit analyses of local elections held from 1996 to 1999. The probability of a Democratic candidate being present in the election equals $1/(1 + \exp(Z_1))$, where $Z_1 = -.53 + 4.36$(proportion for Clinton in 1996)-2.59(Republican Incumbent). Only open seats and seats with a Republican incumbent are included in this analysis ($N = 933$). Similarly, the probability of a Republican candidate seeking office equals $1/(1 + \exp(Z_2))$, where $Z_2 = 2.48 - 3.79$(proportion for Clinton in 1996)-2.00(Democratic incumbent). Only open seats and seats with a Democratic incumbent were included in this analysis ($N = 2272$). Republican incumbent and Democratic incumbent are dummy variables coded 1 for seats with an incumbent of the respective party and 0 otherwise. All coefficients achieved statistical significance ($p < .01$). The size of the incumbency advantage is calculated by comparing the probability of a Republican (Democratic) candidate running when the Democratic (Republican) incumbency variable is set equal to 1 with the probability when the same variable was set equal to 0. These probabilities vary with the share of the vote received by President Clinton. The

TABLE 3.5
Weighted Percentage of Southern County Offices by Incumbency Status

	Georgia				Texas				Mississippi		
	D	R	Open		D	R	Open		D	R	Open
1984	67	6	25	1984–86	65	5	30	1987	67	2	31
1988	62	15	18	1988–90	48	29	24	1991	62	1	37
1992	55	11	30	1992–94	39	30	31	1995	63	6	30
1996	57	17	22	1996–98	30	52	18	1999	57	14	29

	South Carolina				Louisiana				North Carolina		
	D	R	Open		D	R	Open		D	R	Open
1980–82	68	6	25	1983	82	1	17	1986–88	61	8	31
1984–86	70	8	21	1987	75	5	18	1990–92	63	9	28
1988–90	59	10	31	1991	73	9	16	1994–96	58	20	22
1992–94	50	24	27	1995	71	13	16				
1996–98	39	40	21	1999	61	14	14				

	Florida				Virginia			
	D	R	Open		D	R	Open	Ind
1984	61	28	10	1981–83	57	21	2	20
1988	54	22	24	1985–87	48	16	18	18
1992	43	30	27	1989–91	43	11	29	17
1996	50	34	15	1993–95	39	21	24	16
				1997–99	33	30	19	18

Note: For the selection of county offices available for each state, the table shows the percentage of Democratic incumbents, Republican incumbents, and open seats over time weighted by county population. As primary election data was not available, a seat is defined as held by the incumbent if the incumbent was on the ballot in the general election for all states except Louisiana. In Louisiana, the seat is defined as held by an incumbent if the incumbent sought reelection in the primary. The table also shows the percentage of independent incumbents for Virginia. See table 3.2 for information on the weighting procedure.

Source: Data compiled by author.

Historically, the consequence of Democratic hyperdominance of southern politics was that the incumbency advantage has been terribly one-sided in local elections. Table 3.5 shows that as late as the early 1980s, there were far more Democratic than Republican incumbents in most southern states even after weighting by the population of the county. In the early 1980s, the typical resident of a southern state had a greater than 60 percent chance of living in a county with a Democratic

values of incumbency advantage reported in the text are for the 44% of the vote received by President Clinton across the entire region.

incumbent seeking reelection. Outside of Florida and Virginia, 8 percent or less of southerners lived in counties with Republican incumbent.

Republican gains since the early 1980s have eroded the Democratic advantage due to the incumbency advantage throughout the South. The GOP even eliminated the Democratic advantage in some states, though they made surprisingly small gains in others. The number of open seats has remained largely steady so Republican gains have come at the expense of Democrats. The most dramatic shift occurred in the sample of east Texas counties examined here (see table 3.5). In the mid-1980s, only one-twentieth of residents of these counties lived in counties with Republican incumbents seeking reelection. By the end of the 1990s, the share of people inhabiting counties with GOP incumbents rose to just over one-half. At the same time, the proportion living in counties with Democratic incumbents plummeted from nearly two-thirds to under one-third—a truly remarkable reversal of fortune for the two major parties.

In South Carolina and Virginia, after weighting by population, the GOP ran as many incumbents as the Democrats by the end of the century. Table 3.5 shows that South Carolina Democrats held almost the same yawning advantage as Texas Democrats in the mid-1980s with over two-thirds of South Carolinians living in counties with Democratic incumbents but under 10 percent residing in counties with Republican incumbents. In the wake of substantial Republican gains in the 1990s, each party's incumbents sought reelection in counties containing around 40 percent of the Palmetto State's population.

In Virginia, for reasons explained in the next chapter, an unusually large share of county elections were won by independents. From 1981 through 1999, the share of Virginians who had the opportunity to reelect a Democratic incumbent gradually declined from 57 percent to 33 percent. For much of the period, the decline in seats held by Democratic incumbents mainly resulted in a rise in open-seat elections. However, Republicans and Democrats both had the advantage of running incumbents in places containing around one-third of Virginians by 1999.

In the remaining six states, Democrats have shown a surprising degree of tenacity despite Republican successes in elections for higher office. Democrats continued to run incumbents in 50 percent or more of seats, while the Republicans made much more modest gains than in South Carolina, Texas, or Virginia (see table 3.5). The situation in Georgia was rather typical. The proportion of Georgians living in counties with Democratic incumbents seeking reelection gently declined from 67 percent to 57 percent between 1984 and 1996 while the proportion living in counties with Republican incumbents rose to only 17 percent. The only major departure from this pattern was in Florida. Republicans in Florida started the period studied here with the most impressive base of incumbents in the region: 28 percent of Floridians lived in counties with GOP incumbents seeking reelection in 1984. Unlike in other contests in Florida, the Republicans showed little ability to capitalize on this lead. Despite their head start, only 34 percent of Floridians lived in counties with Republican incumbents running for reelection in 1996.

One should remember that Republican gains often represent victories by a relatively small number of candidates in populous counties. As chapter 6 uncovers, Democrats tend to dominate politics in small, rural counties, but Republicans have made major inroads in the relatively few populous urban counties that contain the bulk of the South's population. The vast majority of southern local officials remain Democrats even if these officials were elected by a far smaller share of southerners than in the past.

Altogether, local election results indicate a high degree of longevity and continued vibrancy on the part of Democrats at the county level. Although Democratic incumbents occupied most local offices up for election between 1980 and 1999, sizable numbers of open seats were up in every election. The Republicans could have never defeated a Democratic incumbent and made more substantial gains. However, in a majority of states examined here, Republicans made relatively few inroads until toward the end of the period.

The scope of open-seat opportunities available to Republicans at the local level indicates that the top-down nature of the partisan shift toward the Republicans discussed in chapter 1 was not simply an artifact of immovable incumbents at the local level. Candidate recruitment at the local level was a greater problem. In the early 1980s, the GOP fielded so few candidates even in open-seat elections that a majority of southerners living in counties with open-seat contests in all of the states examined here could not vote for GOP candidates even if they were so inclined. Over time, Republicans managed to attract greater numbers of candidates. By the end of the 1990s, in the average state, 70 percent of people in counties with open-seat elections had the opportunity to vote Republican. A solid majority of southerners nevertheless lived in counties home to Democratic local officials in all of the states examined here except South Carolina, Texas, and Virginia. This continued Democratic success at the local level appears all the more striking when contrasted with Republican victories in national elections. By 2000, Republicans had won a majority of southern states in presidential elections for two decades and held a majority of the southern delegations to the U.S. House and the U.S. Senate for six years.

CONCLUSION

Strategic elites have long played a critical role in shaping the outcome of campaigns before a single ballot has been cast. The decision of an incumbent to run for reelection or to retire helps determine the competitiveness of the election—many incumbents for local and state legislative office do not face any challengers in the general election. At the same time, decisions by potential high-quality challengers to take on an incumbent or to pass on the contest in favor of other opportunities or simply to retain their existing office greatly influence elections. When a high-quality candidate decides not to challenge an incumbent, the incumbent and the incumbent's party can usually rest easy, knowing that the battle has already been won. Parties cannot win elections without good candidates.

These well-known theories about how elites influence election outcomes apply more broadly to condition systematically the pace and shape of partisan change. The GOP's inability to attract strong candidates long impeded Republican growth in the South. Even as new voters entered the electorate thanks to the Voting Rights Act and the passage of time, Republicans failed to have a shot at winning many contests. They did not recruit any candidates so they were not even in the game. The occupancy of most offices by incumbent Democrats explains much of the problem as the task of defeating an incumbent is more formidable than winning an open seat. Strong challengers like to run when they have a good chance of victory. At the same, Republicans passed on many contests for open seats, so incumbency alone does not explain delayed Republican success.

The growing ability of the Republicans to attract candidates helps explain why Democratic dominance greatly eroded by the end of the twentieth century. To better understand Republican growth, it is important to explain why Republicans had so much more success in recruiting candidates as time passed. As we will see, elites do not operate in a vacuum and are highly responsive to an environment conditioned by institutions, demographic context, and voter positions on issues. The next chapter begins to explore why elites were more and more attracted to the Republicans by explaining how political institutions increasingly funneled white conservatives into the Republican Party. In particular, primary elections and racial redistricting made sure that minorities and white liberals would gradually increase their hold over the Democratic Party and its nomination process. As minorities and white liberals became ever more dominant within the Democratic Party, its utility as a vehicle for white conservatives to pursue their political ambitions declined. Later chapters demonstrate that the electoral environment has also gradually become more favorable to Republicans. Nevertheless, many parts of the South still tilt toward the Democrats despite major changes in the party's composition and public stance on key economic, racial, and social questions.

CHAPTER FOUR

The Role of Institutions

ELITE DECISIONS GREATLY INFLUENCE election outcomes. More specifically, as chapter 3 explains, candidate recruitment is vital to a party's ability to contest elections. As we have already seen, Republican failure to attract candidates often prevented the Republicans from challenging Democratic dominance of southern politics. Parties cannot win elections if they cannot recruit candidates. Moreover, Democratic dominance of officeholding in the South gave the Democrats a huge advantage in terms of a talent pool over the Republicans. Even when both parties could attract candidates, the Democrats were more likely to recruit candidates with experience in running a campaign and holding office. Republican success in attracting candidates, especially in open-seat contests where the Democrats lack the incumbency advantage, was critical to their rise as a major political force.

Elites do not exist or operate in a political vacuum. Ambitious politicians are highly attuned to the political environment. Voter preferences obviously play a key role in shaping that environment. Chapters 5 and 6 will explore how voters often stall or accelerate partisan change through both their voting decisions and their influence on the decisions of potential candidates to seek office and their choice of a party label.

Before turning to these questions in the following chapters, this chapter explores how institutional rules play a similar role in conditioning elite decisions and southern electoral outcomes. As any visitor to a casino knows, the rules of the game can powerfully shape the outcome of the game. It is hardly accidental that far more people leave casinos with lighter wallets than when they entered. The casino controls the odds of every game and sets them so that they favor the house. Even if a lucky gambler beats the house at first, odds are that the chance of losing money rises the longer the gambler plays.

Southern history teaches the same lesson. As chapter 1 outlines, the historical dominance of the Democrats was not the result of free democratic choice. During Reconstruction, Democrats rigged the political game to favor their party. The democratization of southern politics put an end to many of these unjust rules that favored preservation of the Democratic regime. However, just because the rules were changed and made less anti-democratic does not mean that the rules of the game ceased to matter. Many of the rules, particularly those not closely associated with racial injustice, remained unchanged.

Some institutional rules, such as the intentional creation of majority-minority electoral districts, resulted from efforts to make the South more democratic by making it possible for people previously excluded from the political process to participate in government. On the other hand, primary elections, long a central process in southern elections, are so taken for granted that it is easy to overlook their importance in shaping partisan change. Finally, even small rules, such as Virginia's ban on placing party labels on the ballot, quietly influenced outcomes despite their obscurity. After a brief review of the history of institutions in shaping southern politics, this chapter turns to an analysis of the institutional rules and processes that mold the evolution of southern politics today.

The History of Institutions in Southern Politics

As outlined in chapter 1, disfranchisement laws were a key pillar of the institutional structure that maintained the undemocratic Democrats in power. Literacy tests and understanding clauses were just two of the many devices used to prevent most blacks and many poor whites from exercising their right to vote. However, disfranchisement was only one component of the complex array of devices used to perpetuate the American version of apartheid in the South. Federal action in the form of the Voting Rights Act of 1965 finally ended disfranchisement, but other institutional structures created in the context of Jim Crow continue to this day, often with quite different effects. Before examining how the institutions discussed in this chapter helped propel partisan change forward in recent decades, particularly the 1990s, this section explores how these same institutions historically helped maintain the overwhelming dominance of the then white supremacist and elite-oriented Democratic Party.

Racial Redistricting in the Nineteenth Century

While racial redistricting now assures that African Americans gain representation, it usually minimized Republican and black representation during the late nineteenth century. During Reconstruction, race was closely tied to partisanship with southern blacks giving near unanimous support to the Republicans as the party of Lincoln and freedom. Most native white southerners viewed the Democratic Party as their regional champion, though a surprisingly large minority of populists and stalwart unionists supported alternatives.[1] The Republicans, as the party that

---

[1] Kousser 1974, 27–29.

prosecuted the Civil War that forced the southern states to remain in the Union and devastated the region, nevertheless remained anathema to most southern whites.

The black share of the region's population was higher during Reconstruction than it is today. According to the 1870 U.S. Census, blacks formed a majority of the population of Louisiana, Mississippi, and South Carolina, and more than 45 percent of the population in Alabama, Florida, and Georgia. African Americans further composed 42 percent of Virginia's population and 37 percent of North Carolina's population. Under remotely fair districting plans, Republicans would have been poised to win many of the region's seats due to their solid support in the black community, especially if former Confederates were disfranchised as required by various Reconstruction statutes.

White supremacist Democrats passed redistricting plans that packed blacks into overwhelmingly black districts in order to minimize African-American representation. Packing blacks into one district reduced the black share of the population in the remaining districts and made them more difficult for the Republicans to win. In other words, by ceding one district to black Republicans, white Democrats could tighten their grip on the remaining seats. Alabama, Mississippi, North Carolina, South Carolina, and Virginia gerrymandered congressional districts in this manner in order to minimize black and Republican influence during the second half of the nineteenth century.[2]

Ironically, in the aftermath of the Civil Rights Movement and the passage of the Voting Rights Act, white supremacists resisted the creation of majority-minority districts because they feared that they would advance black representation. The black share of the population of each southern state declined significantly between 1870 and 1970. Racist mapmakers realized that they did not need to concede even one district to blacks in order to preserve white control of the remainder, so they worked to dismantle black districts rather than create them. In *Black Votes Count*, Frank Parker describes how gerrymanders minimized the election of black officials in Mississippi, the state where blacks form a greater share of the population than anywhere else in the nation.[3] Court challenges culminating in *Allen v. State Board of Elections* in 1969 and *Thornburg v. Gingles* in 1986 ultimately thwarted these anti-black gerrymanders and resulted in the election of greater numbers of black officials. However, as we will see below, the creation of majority-black districts ultimately had negative consequences for the Democrats.

---

[2] J. Morgan Kousser, "The Voting Rights Act and the Two Reconstructions" in *Controversies in Minority Voting*, ed. Bernard Grofman and Chandler Davidson (Washington: Brookings Institution, 1992); Lublin 1997, 19–21.

[3] Parker 1990, 41–51, 102–47, 151–66.

The Establishment of Primary and Runoff Elections

Primary elections were established to resolve conflicts within the dominant Democratic Party. During Reconstruction, widespread disfranchisement had not yet occurred and strong opposition parties often challenged the Democrats. Democrats perceived that primaries would help legitimate the Democratic nominee and make it difficult for the loser of a nomination to defect to the opposition. Eliminating splits naturally aided Democratic efforts to defeat Republican and Populist opponents. Casting the Democratic primary as the white primary bolstered the Democratic candidate and facilitated negative attacks on their opponents as dependent on black, northern, and Unionist support. Unlike during the twentieth century, the white primary was not so much a product of exclusion as the nearly unanimous choice by most blacks to participate in Republican politics.[4]

Even after disfranchisement eliminated any real threat to white supremacy, white elites viewed the primary as vital to avoiding splits within the Democratic Party. They feared that any serious opposition would result in the inevitable enfranchisement of blacks and efforts to appeal to them by competing groups of white politicians. Efforts to establish primary elections were also sometimes intertwined with progressive efforts to fight party bosses and corruption.[5] Primaries continued to legitimate the selection of the Democratic nominee and tamped down any effort to build a genuine non-Democratic opposition. To the extent that the South experienced real political contests, they occurred in the Democratic primary.[6] Scholars argue that the confining of competition to the Democratic Party prevented the emergence of sustained factional competition around issues in most states and favored the ongoing control of southern politics by the minority of whites who formed the traditional southern elite.[7]

By the early 1930s, all southern states except Tennessee established runoffs between the top two primary finishers if no candidate received a

[4] Kousser 1974, 72–82.

[5] Cortez A. M. Ewing, *Primary Elections in the South* (Norman: University of Oklahoma Press, 1953), 4–6; Albert D. Kirwan, *Revolt of the Rednecks: Mississippi Politics: 1876–1925* (Lexington: University of Kentucky Press, 1951), 122–35; Kousser 1974, 72–82.

[6] Key 1949, 407–9; John L. Moore, Jon P. Preimesberger, and David R. Tarr, eds., *Congressional Quarterly's Guide to U.S. Elections*, 4th ed. (Washington: CQ Press, 2001), 1–129.

[7] Key 1949, 142–50; Kousser 1974, 72–82. Louisiana formed a notable exception to this pattern: the Long faction promoted a corrupt form of populism and the anti-Longs preached reform and financial rectitude. See Key 1949, 164–79. See Jack M. Bloom, *Class, Race, and the Civil Rights Movement* (Bloomington: Indiana University Press, 1987), for more on the use of race to maintain upper-class economic and political dominance in the pre–Civil Rights Movement South.

majority in the primary.[8] Runoffs helped assure that the Democratic nominee would be perceived as the choice of a majority of white voters. In states with highly factional Democratic parties, a real possibility existed of a candidate winning the primary with far less than majority support. Without a runoff, this candidate would take the nomination even if more voters preferred the second-place candidate over the primary winner if given a chance to choose between the two of them. Since the presence of a runoff assured that no one would win the Democratic nomination without majority support, they helped further assure the acceptance of the Democratic nominee by white voters. Losing candidates could no longer bolt the party claiming that the nominee represented only a narrow faction within the broader Democratic Party.

RACIAL REDISTRICTING

Racial redistricting is the intentional drawing of majority-minority districts in order to assure the election of candidates preferred by the minority community, called "candidates of choice" in racial redistricting jargon. Racial redistricting is a product of the Voting Rights Act as interpreted by the courts. Section 5 of the Act, requires "covered jurisdictions" to submit their redistricting plans for "preclearance" to the U.S. Attorney General.[9] If the attorney general believes that a plan reduces minority strength relative to the current plan, he can block it from going into effect. Alabama, Georgia, Louisiana, Mississippi, South Carolina, Virginia, and portions of North Carolina were designated as covered jurisdictions under the original 1965 version of the Act. Extensions of the Act expanded the number of covered jurisdictions to include other areas, including places outside the South. Even if the attorney general preclears the plan, plaintiffs who believe vote dilution has occurred can sue under Section 2 of the Act.

In 1986, the Supreme Court outlined a three-pronged test for vote dilution in *Thornburg v. Gingles*. The Court decided in *Gingles* that Section 2 of the Voting Rights Act requires courts to order the drawing of majority-minority districts if: (1) the minority group is "sufficiently large and geographically compact to constitute a majority in a single member district," (2) politically cohesive, and (3) usually unable to elect its preferred candidate due to racial bloc voting. The first condition essentially

[8] Charles Bullock III and Loch K. Johnson, *Runoff Elections in the United States* (Chapel Hill: University of North Carolina Press, 1992), 1–4. Tennessee established runoffs in the unlikely event of a tie between the top two primary candidates.

[9] Covered jurisdictions may also seek preclearance from the U.S. District Court of the District of Columbia. However, they have rarely pursued this option.

states that there must be a remedy for a court to act. If one cannot draw a district in which minorities can elect their preferred candidate, then courts cannot solve the problem of minorities consistently being out-voted by the majority without changing the electoral system. More recent Supreme Court decisions, beginning with *Shaw v. Reno* in 1993, have had the effect of giving much greater weight to the compactness requirement.

The second *Gingles* requirement simply means that members of the minority group must consistently vote as a bloc. If a minority group is usually divided between parties and candidates, then it makes little sense to draw majority-minority districts to advance minority interests because members of the group clearly do not agree on how to advance their interests. Due to high levels of support by African Americans for the Democrats in general elections and strong support for black candidates in Democratic primaries, proving political cohesion has not usually been difficult for plaintiffs in vote-dilution cases. One should note that political cohesion is not the same as unanimity. Even when a group, such as African Americans, is relatively cohesive in its voting behavior, individuals often do not act in concert with the group. Many individual African Americans may vote Republican, even if the vast majority of black voters consistently cast their ballots for the Democrats.

The final *Gingles* prong is really the most critical. Plaintiffs must prove that racial bloc voting is sufficiently strong that the minority consistently cannot elect its preferred candidate. In other words, one must show that the white majority is sufficiently cohesive to regularly outvote the black minority. Simply proving that most whites prefer one candidate and most blacks another is not sufficient to prove racial bloc voting under the *Gingles* test. Even if most whites vote against a black-preferred candidate, the black-preferred candidate may still win election due to a coalition of strong black support combined with a minority of white voters. If the black-preferred candidate can win, there is no need for a court to intervene.

In the context of the South, racial redistricting has usually meant drawing black majority districts in order to promote the election of black-preferred candidates. All but two of the new majority-black congressional districts drawn during the 1990s round of redistricting were drawn in the South.[10] Alabama, Louisiana, South Carolina, Texas, and Virginia each created one new black-majority congressional district. Georgia and North Carolina created two new districts apiece, and Florida drew three. The 1975 extension of the Voting Rights Act expanded

---

[10] Maryland and Pennsylvania each drew one new majority-black district during the 1990s redistricting round.

the application of the act to language minorities, including Latinos. In Florida and Texas, racial redistricting increasingly means drawing districts for an expanding Latino population. Mapmakers drew new Latino-majority congressional districts in both states prior to the 1992 elections for the U.S. House.

Racial redistricting did not just affect congressional elections. As we shall see, new majority-black districts were created in every southern state legislature during the 1990s. Although it is not discussed in more detail here, plaintiffs successfully brought challenges to numerous at-large systems for electing county and municipal councils. Under at-large systems of election, there are no districts and all members of the community can vote for all members of the council. Where whites outnumbered blacks at the polls, they were often able to outvote blacks in elections for all of the seats on the county or town council. Lawsuits forcing a switch from an at-large to a district system for elections made it possible to create districts in which African Americans could elect their preferred candidate to the county or town council.[11]

Criticisms and Defenses of Racial Redistricting

Racial redistricting has been under intense criticism since the 1990s redistricting round greatly expanded the number of intentionally drawn majority-minority districts. In the series of decisions limiting racial redistricting beginning with *Shaw v. Reno*, the Supreme Court claimed that making race the "predominant factor" in redistricting violates the Equal Protection Clause of the Constitution. Justice Sandra Day O'Connor fears that separating blacks and whites into separate electoral districts wrongly stereotypes individuals as holding a particular set of beliefs due to their race. She further fears that racial redistricting will "balkanize" the nation and "bears an uncomfortable resemblance to political apartheid."[12] The Court's decision in *Shaw* was the logical extension of its earlier rulings limiting the scope of affirmative action. More broadly, they express a belief that it is inappropriate for government to use race to distinguish between its citizens and as a rationale for treating them differently.

Race, however, continues to play a major role in determining outcomes in American elections. Blacks and whites very often *do* vote differently—sufficiently so that blacks can find it quite difficult to win election from majority-white districts. Moreover, some of the intentionally drawn districts with odd shapes are arguably among the most integrated in the

[11] Parker 1990; Davidson and Grofman 1994.
[12] *Shaw v. Reno.*

country. The much derided Twelfth District of North Carolina was 57 percent black, and only 53 percent black among the voting-age population. Racial redistricting had hardly resulted in racially segregated districts. Even if the black majority outvotes the white minority, this is no different from the position faced by blacks, and other political minorities, in numerous other congressional and state legislative districts.

One might support racial redistricting to aid minorities even if one opposes affirmative action more generally. In more conventional judicial disputes involving affirmative action, race is perceived to interfere with the potentially nonracial conception of merit or another nonracial means of distinguishing between citizens. However, unlike in school admissions, the awarding of a job, or assignment of a government contract, merit is not at issue in redistricting cases. Voters select one candidate over another for a variety of reasons, but qualifications for the job are not ordinarily the primary consideration. In contrast to ordinary hiring decisions, voters are legally free to discriminate on the basis of race in casting their ballots.

From another perspective, racial redistricting merely addresses the discrimination inherent in the single-member district electoral system. Dispersed minorities of any type find it hard to elect members against the will of the majority under this type of system. This problem is not unique to the United States. The Liberal Democrats of Britain and the Progressive-Conservatives of Canada regularly win more than 15 percent of the vote for the House of Commons in their respective nations, but neither comes close to winning 15 percent of the seats.[13] Racial redistricting can be viewed as an attempt to make sure that a previously excluded minority has a voice in governance without abandoning the existing electoral system. It thus makes American legislative institutions more representative and helps legitimate them to a greater extent in the eyes of the minority.

Several scholars have attacked racial redistricting as unnecessary to assure the election of racial minorities. Carol Swain and Abigail Thernstrom rely primarily on anecdotal evidence to prove their case.[14] They

---

[13] In the 2001 United Kingdom general election, the Liberal Democrats received 18.3% of the total vote but only 7.9% of the seats. In 1997 the Liberal Democrats similarly received only 7.0% of the seats for 16.8% of the vote; see Robert Waller and Byron Criddle, *The Almanac of British Politics*, 7th ed. (London: Routledge, 2002). In the 2000 Canadian parliamentary election, the Progressive-Conservatives won 12.2% of the vote but only 4.0% of the seats. In 1997 the Progressive-Conservatives captured 6.6% of the seats with 18.8% of the vote; see "Thirty-seventh General Election 2000: Official Voting Results: Synopsis" and "Thirty-sixth General Election 1997: Official Voting Results Synopsis," *Elections Canada On-Line* at http://www.elections.ca.

[14] Charles Cameron, David Epstein, and Sharyn O'Halloran, "Do Majority-Minority

point to specific examples of the election of African Americans from majority-white jurisdictions as proving that minorities do not need racial redistricting. In 2002, African-American Georgia Attorney General Thurbert Baker and Commissioner of Labor Mike Thurmond won reelection even as the incumbent white governor and senator went down to defeat; the voting-age population of the Peach State is only 27 percent black. African-American Harvey Gantt won several terms as mayor of 30 percent black Charlotte, North Carolina. In 1992, African-American Ralph Campbell Jr. won election to the office of state auditor and became North Carolina's first black statewide official. Campbell was reelected in 1996 and 2000. Perhaps most impressively, African-American L. Douglas Wilder won election as the first black lieutenant governor of Virginia in 1985 and then the first black governor in 1989. Similarly, Cuban-American Bob Martinez was elected governor of Florida in 1990. However, these examples may be exceptions to a general pattern, rather than definitive proof that barriers to minority representation have fallen. Most scholars who have systematically examined election data have concluded that African Americans and Latinos usually find it difficult to win election outside of majority-minority districts.[15]

Recently, Grofman, Handley and Lublin have argued that Republican gains among whites may surprisingly aid the election of blacks from majority-white districts under certain circumstances. The defection of whites to the Republican Party may leave African Americans in control of the Democratic primary and able to nominate a black candidate even if they do not form a majority of the overall population. If sufficient numbers of whites remain Democrats and are willing to vote for a black Democrat, a minority candidate can then win the general election with a biracial coalition of blacks and liberal whites. However, if too many whites have abandoned the Democrats for the Republicans, the black Democratic nominee will likely lose the general election to a Republican

---

Districts Maximize Substantive Representation?" *American Political Science Review* 90: 4 (December 1996): 794–812; Carol M. Swain, *Black Faces, Black Interests: The Representation of African Americans in Congress* (Cambridge, MA: Harvard University Press, 1995); Abigail Thernstrom, *Whose Votes Count? Affirmative Action and Minority Voting Rights* (Cambridge, MA: Harvard University Press, 1987); Stephan Thernstrom and Abigail Thernstrom, *America in Black and White: One Nation, Indivisible* (New York: Simon and Schuster, 1997), 286–312. Of these authors, only Cameron, Epstein, and O'Halloran undertook a systematic statistical analysis of the election of African Americans. None of these authors discusses Latino representation at any length.

[15] Davidson and Grofman 1994; Bernard Grofman and Lisa Handley, "Minority Population and Black and Hispanic Congressional Success in the 1970s and 1980s," *American Politics Quarterly* 17 (October 1989): 436–45; David Lublin, "The Election of African Americans and Latinos to the U.S. House of Representatives, 1972–1994," *American Politics Quarterly* 25 (1997a): 269–86; Lublin 1997, 39–52; Parker 1990, 136–43.

candidate. In short, for a black candidate to win election, African Americans need to compose a majority of the Democratic primary electorate, and loyal Democrats need to form a majority in the general election.[16]

Racial Redistricting Stimulates Partisan Change

Finally, some criticize racial redistricting as paradoxically assuring the election of greater numbers of racial minorities but undermining the representation of minority interests. How does this seemingly contradictory outcome occur? The concentration of black Democrats into majority-black districts reduces the number of Democrats in adjoining districts, rendering them more vulnerable to Republican takeover. The election of a new black Democrat may come at the cost of losing one white Democrat. As white Democrats are far more supportive of African-American interests than Republicans, racial redistricting may reduce overall support for black interests in the legislature.

A hypothetical example helps to clarify further this perplexing outcome. Imagine two 35 percent black congressional districts of equal population adjoin one another. Suppose that mapmakers redraw the lines dividing the two districts so that one district is 55 percent black. The other district must lose black voters and become only 15 percent black. African-American candidates almost always win in 55 percent black congressional districts,[17] so the election of a black representative is virtually assured in one district. The other congressional district, however, has become far more likely to elect a Republican. While Republicans almost never win in 35 percent black districts, they often win in 15 percent black districts. Indeed, the whiter the district, the greater the Republican candidate's chance of success.[18]

CASE STUDY: RACIAL REDISTRICTING IN GEORGIA

Unfortunately for Democrats, racial redistricting has not harmed their party only in hypothetical examples. The redrawing of Georgia's congressional districts illustrates this well (see figure 4.1). Due to its burgeoning population, particularly in the Atlanta suburbs, Georgia gained one new congressional seat in the 1990 redistricting round.[19] The Justice

---

[16] Bernard Grofman, Lisa Handley, and David Lublin, "Drawing Effective Minority Districts: A Conceptual Framework and Some Empirical Evidence," *North Carolina Law Review* 79 (2001): 1383–1430.

[17] Grofman and Handley 1989; Lublin 1997, 45–48; Lublin 1997a.

[18] Cameron, Epstein, and O'Halloran 1996, 805; Lublin 1997, 99; Lublin and Voss 2000, 797–801.

[19] Georgia's population grew even faster from 1990 to 2000; it gained two new seats in the 2000 reapportionment.

Old 1980s Plan			
District	1990 Percent Black	1990 Winner Name	1990 Percent for Winner
1	33	Thomas	71
2	36	Hatcher	73
3	34	Ray	63
4	13	Jones	52
5	65	Lewis	76
6	15	Gingrich	50
7	6	Darden	60
8	35	Rowland	69
9	5	Jenkins	56
10	25	Barnard	58

Racial Redistricting Plan					
District	1992-4 Percent Black	1992 Winner Name	1992 Percent for Winner	1994 Winner Name	1994 Percent for Winner
1	23	Kingston	58	Kingston	77
2	57	Bishop	64	Bishop	66
3	18	Collins*	55	Collins	66
4	12	Linder	51	Linder	58
5	62	Lewis	72	Lewis	69
6	6	Gingrich	58	Gingrich	64
7	13	Darden	57	Barr*	52
8	21	Rowland	56	Chambliss	63
9	4	Deal	59	Deal**	58
10	18	Johnson	54	Norwood*	65
11	64	McKinney	73	McKinney	66

Post-Miller v. Johnson		
1996 Percent Black	1996 Winner Name	1996 Percent for Winner
31	Kingston	68
39	Bishop	54
25	Collins	61
37	McKinney	58
62	Lewis	100
6	Gingrich	58
13	Barr	58
31	Chambliss	53
4	Deal	66
38	Norwood	52
12	Linder	64

Figure 4.1. Georgia congressional districts, 1990–96.
Note: *Italics* denotes a white Republican; **bold** indicates a black Democrat; non-italic, non-bold text is for white Democrats. * indicates that the representatives defeated a Democratic incumbent; ** indicates that the representative switched to the GOP after the election. Georgia gained one new congressional seat in the 1990 reapportionment. Georgia conducted its normal post-Census redistricting prior to the 1992 elections, but *Miller v. Johnson* resulted in a federal court re-drawing congressional district boundaries prior to the 1996 elections. The scope of the changes resulted in incumbent Republicans Linder and McKinney choosing to run in differently numbered seats than in previous elections. These new boundaries were used through the 2000 general election.
Sources: *Almanac of American Politics*, various editions; Georgia Reapportionment Services.

Department utilized its powers under Section 5 of the Voting Rights Act to force the state to draw three black majority districts, two more than had existed prior to redistricting.[20] All three majority-black districts sent African-American Democrats to the House. Civil rights hero John Lewis won reelection from the Atlanta-based Fifth District. Sanford Bishop de-

[20] Georgia drew two black districts in its original plan but the Justice Department blocked the plan from going into effect utilizing its powers under Section 5 of the Voting Rights Act. Georgia then adopted a new plan with three black majority districts. See Robert A. Holmes, "Reapportionment Strategies in the 1990s: The Case of Georgia," in *Race and Redistricting in the 1990s*, ed. Bernard Grofman (New York: Agathon Press, 1998), 201–28.

feated white incumbent Charles Hatcher in the Democratic runoff and then won the general election from southwest Georgia's Second District. Cynthia McKinney, the only woman in the state's delegation, won election from the Eleventh District, nicknamed the "Sherman's March District" because it swept from Savannah along the coast to Atlanta.

Creating two new black majority districts required reducing the black share of the population in other districts because districts must have nearly equal populations.[21] The black share of the population dropped precipitously in several districts and the Democratic Party suffered accordingly in the 1992 elections. Incumbent Democrat Richard Ray was defeated for reelection by Republican Mac Collins after redistricting reduced the black share of the Third District's population from 34 to 18 percent. Jack Kingston similarly won the open First District; the black population had dropped from 33 to 23 percent prior to the election. Finally, John Linder very narrowly won the open Fourth District with 51 percent of the vote after the black population declined by slightly more than 1 percent.

Attributing this third Democratic loss to racial redistricting is arguably more dubious than the defeats in the first two districts as the black population declined by such a small amount. However, the black population did decline by more than the Republican margin of victory. Democrats, who controlled the redistricting process, also might have been able to help to do more to shore up their party in the district if they had not been constrained by the necessity of creating new black districts. Even the report by the NAACP Legal Defense Fund, which strongly argues that racial redistricting did not harm the Democrats, agrees that racial redistricting cost the Democrats three seats in Georgia in 1992.[22]

MITIGATING THE NEGATIVE IMPACT OF RACIAL REDISTRICTING ON DEMOCRATS

Although racial redistricting losses hurt the Democrats around the South in elections for legislative bodies selected by district, Democrats mitigated the damage due to racial redistricting through partisan gerry-

---

[21] *Baker v. Carr* 369 US 186 (1962); *Karcher v. Daggett* 462 US 725 (1983); *Reynolds v. Sims* 377 US 533 (1964).

[22] NAACP Legal Defense and Educational Fund, "The Effect of Section 2 of the Voting Rights Act on the 1994 Congressional Elections," November 30, 1994. See David Lublin and D. Stephen Voss, "The Partisan Impact of Voting Rights Law: A Reply to Pamela S. Karlan," *Stanford Law Review* 50 (February 1998): 765–78; and D. Stephen Voss and David Lublin, "Black Incumbents, White Districts: An Appraisal of the 1996 Congressional Elections," *American Politics Research* 29 (March 2001): 141–82, for why dismantling two of the three black majority districts prior to the 1996 elections did not aid Democrats or result in the defeat of any black incumbents.

mandering in some states. In Louisiana, North Carolina, Texas, and Virginia, Democrats adopted congressional district plans designed to create new African-American and Latino majority districts without reducing the total number of Democrats elected to the U.S. House. Essential to all of these gerrymanders was the packing of Republicans into very safe GOP districts. Just as creating majority-minority districts harms the Democrats, packing Republicans undermines the GOP by inefficiently concentrating their voters in only a few districts. Crafty Democrats also made sure that most new majority-minority districts did not contain many more minority group members than needed to assure the election of a minority. Democrats attempted to waste few minority Democratic voters even as they drew districts likely to elect minority-preferred candidates.

Pursuing both partisan and racial goals in tandem with the other usual concerns of the state legislators who drew redistricting plans forced the construction of noncompact districts with highly unusual boundaries. Virtually all of the plans split more counties than previous plans. North Carolina adopted a congressional plan that contained several "double crossovers," in which two separate districts effectively leap over one another, yet maintain contiguity, by meeting at a single point.

Unfortunately for the Democrats, their plans went somewhat awry. The North Carolina congressional gerrymander fell apart in 1994 when Republicans won four more seats to give them an 8-4 majority in the state's delegation. All of the plans had been constructed assuming that the Democrats would roughly maintain their share of the vote. Racial redistricting magnified the impact of any swing against the Democrats. Minority voters, especially African Americans, are not only more pro-Democratic than whites, they are also more loyal Democrats than white Democrats. Racial redistricting placed the voters most likely to stick with the Democrats even when the party fares poorly at the polls, as in 1994, in safe Democratic districts. On the other hand, many districts occupied by white Democrats held a greater share of white voters than previous plans. These white voters were much more likely to defect from the Democrats than black voters to the benefit of Republican candidates.

The Supreme Court also threw a wrench in Democratic plans by attacking the unusually shaped, noncompact new majority-minority districts as "racial gerrymanders." Beginning with *Shaw v. Reno*, the nation's highest court forced states to either draw more compact majority-minority districts that violated fewer jurisdictional boundaries or reduce the number of majority-minority districts. By the end of the 1990s, the judiciary had struck down all of the pro-Democratic congressional plans as racial gerrymanders.

Some may view this attack on racial gerrymanders as an anti-black or anti-Democratic plot by a Supreme Court dominated by conservative

Republicans. However, the Court's attack on racial redistricting may benefit Democrats over the long term as the dismantling of majority-minority districts spreads pro-Democratic minority voters more evenly across states. The problem for the Democrats in the late 1990s was that the damage caused by racial redistricting to the Democrats has already been done and Republican incumbents are now safely ensconced in citadels previously held by Democrats.

In Georgia, Republican incumbents Jack Kingston, Saxby Chambliss, and Charles Norwood all managed to win reelection in 1996 even though their districts were reconfigured to include significantly more African-American voters (see figure 4.1). Kingston won comfortably with 68 percent of the vote though the black share of the First District's population rose from 23 to 31 percent. Chambliss and Norwood won narrower victories that suggest that the incumbency advantage may have played a key role in their reelection. In the Eighth District, Chambliss won with only 53 percent of the vote after the black share of the population climbed from 21 to 31 percent. Norwood eked out a victory with 52 percent of the vote after the black population in the Tenth District skyrocketed from 18 to 38 percent.

Of course, Democrats did not control the line drawing or attempt to protect members of their party in every southern state with new majority-minority districts. Democrats felt the negative impact of racial redistricting on their party's candidates most quickly in states that did not attempt to insulate Democrats against the loss of pro-Democratic minority voters. Although Democrats controlled the redistricting process in Georgia, they were so busy attacking the district of hate-figure Newt Gingrich in a nearly successful effort to assure his defeat that they neglected to protect the districts of several rural Democrats.[23] Instead, as figure 4.1 shows, Democratic mapmakers extended several rural Democratic districts into the Republican suburbs of Atlanta with disastrous consequences for the Democratic incumbents.

ESTIMATED SEATS LOST BY DEMOCRATS IN CONGRESS
AND STATE LEGISLATURES

Table 4.1 shows the estimated number of seats lost by the Democrats due to racial redistricting at the congressional and state legislative levels. At the congressional level, racial redistricting cost the Democrats approximately ten seats in four states (Alabama, Florida, Georgia, and North Carolina). On the other hand, racial redistricting actually gained the Democrats one seat in Virginia, where Democrats adopted a plan highly favorable to their party.[24] As explained above, Democrats might

---

[23] Gingrich nearly lost the Republican primary in 1992.

[24] On the other hand, by drawing George Allen out of his district, the Democrats

have suffered even greater losses except for the adoption of pro-Democratic congressional maps. Newt Gingrich's Republican majority after the 1994 elections might have been nearly one-third smaller if new black-majority districts had not been created.

The Supreme Court has aided the Democrats, though not necessarily black and Latino Democrats, by striking down many majority-minority districts as racial gerrymanders. Prior to 2000, several states crafted minimum change plans in response to judicial demands to reduce the number of minority districts, preserving the Republican advantage gained through racial redistricting.[25] The loss of Democratic control of a number of state houses and weaker Democratic majorities in others made it more difficult for Democrats in a number of states to protect their party against the negative impact of racial redistricting on the congressional Democratic Party during the 2000 redistricting round.

Redistricting losses for the state House are also presented in table 4.1. They are further subdivided into losses due to the independent effect of racial redistricting and losses due to the interaction between racial redistricting and a swing in votes against the Democrats. Losses attributed to the independent effect of racial redistricting are losses that occurred solely because the district boundaries were changed. Even if the Democrats received as many votes as in the past, they would have lost these seats because of changes in the aggregation of votes into seats. Interaction losses are caused by the interaction between changes in district lines with any swing in votes against the Democrats. Note that these are not simply losses due to a drop in the Democratic share of votes; these losses are cataloged separately under vote-swing losses. Instead, interaction losses are losses that would not have occurred unless the Democrats lost votes *and* the district boundaries changed.

Some might classify interaction losses as the unanticipated effect of redistricting, as a major hemorrhage in the Democratic vote was not expected. Others might claim that they should be included as losses due to the swing in votes against the Democrats because they would not have happened but for the decline in Democratic votes.[26] I believe that they are fairly counted as redistricting losses because the vote swing would have occurred whether or not states created new black-minority districts. However, the seats would not have been lost if new black districts had not been established and blacks were spread more evenly across districts.

Racial redistricting accounts for a substantial number of state House seats lost by Democrats between 1990 and 1994. Specifically, the inde-

---

strongly encouraged him to run for governor of Virginia. After completing his term in 1999, he successfully challenged incumbent Democratic Senator Charles Robb in 2000.

[25] Lublin and Voss 1998, 772–77.

[26] Lisa Handley's insights on this topic are much appreciated.

TABLE 4.1
Democratic Seats Lost Due to Racial Redistricting, 1990–1994

	AL	FL	GA	LA	MS	NC	SC	TN	TX	VA	Total
U.S. House											
Redistricting Losses	2	2	3	0	0	3	0	0	0	-1	9
Number of Seats in 1994	7	23	11	7	5	12	6	9	30	11	121
Number of New Black Districts	1	3	2	1	0	2	1	0	1	1	12
Democratic Gerrymander				x		x			x	x	4
State House											
Redistricting Losses	2.7	9.1	9.9	2.2	2.8	2.5	8.3	1.8	3.4	2.3	45.0
Independent Effect	1.8	7.2	6.3	2.5	2.6	2.5	6.0	1.0	1.2	2.6	33.7
Interaction with Vote Swing	.9	1.9	3.6	-.3	.2	.0	2.3	.8	2.2	-.3	11.3
Vote Swing Losses	3.3	1.9	20.1	-4.2	5.2	25.5	8.7	-3.8	-.4	3.7	60.0
Net Democratic Losses	6	11	30	-2	8	28	17	-2	3	6	105
Number of Seats	105	120	180	105	122	120	124	99	150	100	1225
Number of New Black Districts	7	4	9	7	4	7	7	1	2	3	51

Note: A negative sign indicates a negative Democratic loss; in other words, the Democrats gained seats. Calculating the total number of congressional seats lost by Democrats is tricky because the number of seats in the delegation changed in six of the states due to reapportionment, so they are not reported here. Arkansas is excluded because data on its former 1990 state legislative plan was not available and it did not create any black-majority congressional districts.

Congressional losses were estimated by exploring whether the downward shift in the black composition of a district exceeds the Republican margin of victory. The effect of the incumbency advantage that would have been held by Democrats in 1994 is also considered for districts lost by Democrats due to racial redistricting in 1992.

In order to calculate state legislative losses, logit models were first constructed of the relationship between the racial composition of a district and the party of the state representative for all states and pre- and post-redistricting election years. We decomposed changes in the number of Democrats across elections into three categories: a redistricting effect, a vote-swing effect, and an interaction (of redistricting and vote-swing) effect.

The redistricting effect is the change in the number of seats Democrats would have won under new districts, assuming that voter preferences remained unchanged. Calculating the redistricting effect required plugging the 1990s district racial compositions into the logit models developed for the last pre-redistricting election and summing the changes in the probability of Democratic victories across all seats. The vote-swing effect is the change in the number of seats held by Democrats assuming the same Republican swing as occurred from the pre- to the post-redistricting election, but that district lines had remained unchanged. Calculating the vote-swing effect required plugging the 1980s district racial compositions into the logit models developed from the post-redistricting election. The interaction effect reconciles the redistricting and vote-swing effects with the actual change in the number of seats held by Democrats.

Sources: David Lublin, The Paradox of Representation (Princeton, 1997); and David Lublin and D. Stephen Voss, "Racial Redistricting and Realignment in Southern State Legislatures," *American Journal of Political Science* 44:4 (October 2000): 792–810; David Lublin and D. Stephen Voss, "Boll-Weevil Blues: Polarized Congressional Delegations into the 21st Century," *American Review of Politics* 21 (fall and winter 2000): 427–50.

pendent effect of redistricting alone accounts for 34 of 105 Democratic losses, or 32 percent of all state House seats lost by Democrats. Including losses due to the interaction between the vote swing and redistricting in the total of redistricting losses raises the total number of Democratic state House losses explainable by redistricting to 45, or 43 percent. Forty-five seats is equivalent to 3.7 percent of the seats in the ten southern states included in the analysis—not a bad gain for the Republicans at the state House level from racial redistricting.

The number of state House seats lost due to racial redistricting varied quite a bit from state to state. Losses in Florida, Georgia, and South Carolina appear particularly high with redistricting costing the Democrats approximately 7.6, 5.5, and 6.7 percent, respectively, of the seats in the state House. Even more important, Democrats lost control of several chambers as a result of racial redistricting. South Carolina Democrats might have controlled the state House throughout the 1990s if racial redistricting had not forced them to cede control of the chamber to the GOP in 1992. Similarly, North Carolina Democrats would probably have regained control of the state House in 1996, instead of 1998. After several special elections, the Virginia state House was evenly split in 1998. Democrats would have maintained sole control until after the 1999 elections but for the negative effect of racial redistricting on their party.[27]

One should emphasize that racial redistricting nevertheless remained a decidedly secondary problem for the Democrats compared to the more critical problem of white voters shifting to the GOP. Democrats continued to lose seats in many southern states during the 1990s and most of these further losses should not be attributed to racial redistricting. Racial redistricting might benefit the party if Republicans become so dominant among whites that Democrats can only carry majority-minority districts. However, there is little sign of the Democratic debacle extending remotely this far except in a few isolated sections of the region, such as the Mississippi Delta. Rather than continuing to make seemingly inexorable gains, the GOP has suffered reversals in recent elections in some states. North Carolina Democrats retook the state House in 1998 and maintained their hold on the chamber in 2000.[28] Democrats already held over two-thirds of state House seats going into the 1999 Mississippi state legislative elections, but the GOP still managed to lose seats in the 1999 elections despite the potential for gains.

---

[27] Lublin and Voss 2000, 801–3.

[28] In 2002, Republicans won 61 of the 120 seats in the North Carolina House. However, one Republican switched to the Democrats and the two parties shared control of the evenly split House.

IMPACT ON ELITE INCENTIVES AND OPPORTUNITIES

The real long-term damage of racial redistricting to Democrats may not be so much the seats immediately lost as the restructuring of incentives and opportunities for white political elites. As detailed in chapters 5 and 6, elites respond to political context. Racial redistricting systematically alters the political context for multiple levels of government in a manner unfavorable to Democrats. Moreover, efforts to create majority-minority districts extend beyond congressional and state legislative seats to county boards of supervisors and school boards as well as other elections held by district. Across all of these contests, racial redistricting increased the number of majority-minority and heavily white districts at the expense of districts with a white majority but a substantial minority presence. Like plants that flourish in certain types of sunlight and soil, white Democrats fare best in these districts. Racial redistricting makes it less likely for white Democratic candidates to win and provides a strong incentive for white elites to run as Republicans.

Analyzing data from southern state legislative elections supports these conclusions. Table 4.2 shows the chance of a Democrat winning election by percent black of a district for state legislative elections held during the mid to late 1990s. The probability of a Democratic victory consistently declines as the percentage of blacks falls. In a separate study, Charles Cameron, David Epstein, and Sharyn O'Halloran show that probability of a victory by a white Democrat in congressional contests also declines rapidly as the black share of the population falls below 30 percent. Seats less than 20 percent black were especially likely to elect Republicans.

TABLE 4.2
Percent Chance of a Democratic Victory in the State House by Percent Black

% Black	AL	AR	FL	GA	LA	MS	NC	SC	TN	TX	VA
10	40	75	37	31	48	39	20	0	77	18	34
20	74	84	66	56	72	49	63	35	80	65	50
30	96	91	85	78	87	72	94	45	76	92	70
40	98	95	93	90	94	89	99	97	96	98	85
50	98	98	97	96	97	96	100	100	100	100	93

Note: A variety of a logit models relating the racial composition of districts to the party of state representatives were tested for each state. The model that empirically best fit the data for each state was used to estimate the probability of Democratic victory for districts of various black percentages. Estimates presented here are based on analysis of elections held in 1998 in all states except Louisiana, Mississippi, and Virginia. The Louisiana and Mississippi elections were held in 1995; the Virginia elections were held in 1997.

Source: David Lublin and D. Stephen Voss, "Racial Redistricting and Realignment in Southern State Legislatures," American Journal of Political Science 44:4 (October 2000): 792–810.

White Democratic success also slips as the black population rises above 50 percent because African-American Democrats become increasingly likely to win the seat.[29]

Racial redistricting greatly reduced the number of seats in the 20–50 percent range during the 1990 redistricting round. Many of these districts had their black populations increased in order to turn them into black majority districts or reduced so that the black populations could be included in the construction of other black majority districts. Table 4.3 shows the impact of racial redistricting on the distribution of districts by racial composition. All seats were placed in one of six categories of percent black: less than 10 percent, 10–20 percent, 20–30 percent, 30–40 percent, 40–50 percent, and greater than 50 percent. Each cell in the table shows the change in the percentage of all seats that fall into that category of percent black under the districting plan used in the 1994 or 1995 elections as compared to the plan used for the 1990 elections. For example, the "7" in the Alabama less than 10 percent black category means that the share of Alabama state House seats less than 10 percent black in 1994 increased by 7 percent over 1990.

The percentage of black-majority districts and districts less than 20 percent black increased in all districting plans for the state House. In all states except Louisiana and Mississippi, the number of districts less than 10 percent black increased the most. As table 4.2 reveals, these districts

TABLE 4.3
Impact of Redistricting on the Distribution of Seats by Racial Composition

	State House											Congress
% Black	AL	FL	GA	LA	MS	NC	SC	TN	TX	VA	All South	All South
<10	7	12	6	2	−1	8	7	4	8	6	6	13
10–20	−2	−4	6	6	12	−3	−2	−3	−5	−2	0	−1
20–30	−1	−7	−2	−1	0	−2	2	−1	−3	0	−1	−8
30–40	−8	−3	−8	−9	−8	−10	−6	−1	0	−3	−6	−14
40–50	−3	−1	−7	−5	−7	1	−7	0	−1	−4	−3	−1
50+	7	3	5	7	3	6	6	1	1	3	4	10

Note: Each number in the table shows the change in the percentage of all seats that fall into that category of percent black under the districting plan used in the 1994 or 1995 elections as compared to the plan used for the 1990 elections. For example, the "7" in the Alabama less than 10% black category means that the share of districts less than 10% black in 1994 in Alabama increased by 7% over 1990. Arkansas is excluded because data on the racial composition of districts under the 1990 plan was unobtainable.

Source: David Lublin and D. Stephen Voss, "Racial Redistricting and Realignment in Southern State Legislatures," *American Journal of Political Science* 44:4 (October 2000): 792–810.

[29] Cameron, Epstein, and O'Halloran 1996, 805.

are exactly the ones most likely to elect Republicans. The impact of racial redistricting was particularly injurious to white Democrats in congressional elections. In 1992, 10 percent of all southern districts were new black-majority districts; the share of seats less than 10 percent black grew by 13 points.

When the extremes grow, the center must suffer. Racial redistricting institutionalized a change in the incentive structure for white politicians by greatly increasing the number of districts likely to be won by a Republican or a black Democrat at the expense of districts favorable to white Democrats. White politicians who remained Democrats faced more limited opportunities due to racial redistricting. While becoming black was clearly not an option for white politicians, they could choose to become Republicans. For many of the moderate to conservative politicians who traditionally dominated southern politics, racial redistricting provided a real incentive to seek office as a Republican instead of a Democrat. The appeal of the GOP for aspiring politicians has only grown as Republicans have won more offices and taken control of more legislative bodies. Racial redistricting directly helped Republicans win more seats. Over the long term, it further aids Republicans by providing an incentive for a greater share of political elites who used to seek office as Democrats to make their home in the GOP.

PRIMARY ELECTIONS

In the South, primary elections are a legacy of the pre–Voting Rights Act South that has gradually spurred Republican gains. As explained earlier in this chapter, primaries were established as a means of promoting unity within the Democratic Party during Reconstruction. After disfranchisement, primaries were maintained in order to discourage the establishment of a strong opposition party that might wish to expand the franchise in order to improve their party's chances. Electoral institutions, like the primary, are not easily swept away even in turbulent times like the Civil Rights Movement. Once the primary was open to blacks through litigation in *Smith v. Allwright*, the goal of civil rights reformers shifted from changing or abolishing primaries to assuring open access to them.

Almost all southern states continue to hold primary elections for party nominations. If no candidate wins a majority in the primary, a runoff for the nomination is held between the top two finishers in the primary. Louisiana, North Carolina, and Virginia are exceptions to this general rule. In North Carolina, primary winners can avoid a runoff if they win at least 40 percent of the vote. Virginia often uses party conventions to select nominees. Tennessee only uses runoffs in the rare case of a tie between candidates.[30] The Louisiana case is an unusual one that will be discussed toward the end of this section. As this section will show, the enfranchisement of black voters combined with the Democratic primary to spur southern white conservatives to choose to make their political home in the GOP instead of with the Democrats, historically the party of the white South. They helped turn the southern GOP from a moderate to liberal party into an ardently conservative haven that is now the natural political home of most middle- and upper class whites.

Enfranchisement, the Democratic Primary, and Partisan Change

During the pre–Voting Rights Act period of large-scale disfranchisement, the Democratic primary was largely representative of the highly unrepresentative shrunken white electorate. Since Democratic nominees almost invariably won the general election, usually without opposition, meaningful political participation was confined to the Democratic primary. Voters of all ideological stripes registered as Democrats and participated in the primary as the only game in town. Strong efforts by southern Democrats to identify their party as the southern regional champion, as opposed to the Republicans who had prosecuted the "War of Northern Aggression," helped prevent the electorate from dividing along ideological lines. Democrats further enforced racial unity by playing the race card; they claimed that groups that split away from the party would pave the way for black enfranchisement and the end of segregation.

The end of disfranchisement immediately modified Democratic primary dynamics. First, participation by African Americans in Democratic primaries injected a new liberal element into the party. Highly supportive of racial liberalism and a strong federal government, African-American political beliefs were antithetical to the values of traditional conservative Democrats. Combined with white moderates and liberals, black voters potentially formed a powerful bloc. In the aftermath of black enfranchisement, conservative white politicians attempted to stigmatize, often with success, any moderate white candidate who appealed to black voters as a liberal integrationist. Conservative candidates nevertheless often lost to strong moderate candidates as defending the old, undemocratic system became an obviously lost cause. Moreover, as the altered racial situation gained acceptance, candidates promoting overt racism and segregation gradually faded away as they failed to win votes and were regularly beaten by moderates.

The demise of the old system also caused large groups of new white voters to enter into the political system. Disfranchisement had greatly

---

[30] Bullock and Johnson 1992, 1–4.

shrunk the white electorate, usually to the satisfaction of traditional elites desiring to maintain their dominance over the region's politics. While whites who strongly desired to participate faced lower barriers than blacks, they often had few choices once they made it to the polls. The region's anemic politics hardly encouraged political participation. The enfranchisement of black voters also made it easier for whites to register. Fear of black political domination galvanized efforts to add white voters to the registration rolls.

Most white voters registered and participated as Democrats. After all, the Democratic Party remained extremely dominant with the Republicans experiencing little success in the region. Richard Nixon swept the South during his successful 1972 bid for reelection as president, but native son Jimmy Carter, a Democrat, carried all Southern states but Virginia during his 1976 challenge to incumbent Gerald Ford, a Republican. Republican success below the presidential level was even harder to find. Democrats continued to dominate the congressional delegations of the region and formed overwhelming majorities in all state legislatures.

However, the basis for maintaining the old system no longer existed. The Democratic Party no longer championed the South or racial segregation. Instead, many white southerners grew to view the national Democratic Party as too liberal on both racial and economic questions. As an increasingly racially liberal party in which blacks formed a key component, Democrats could not realistically expect to rely on their old tactic of vilifying people who joined the Republicans as segregationists. Democrats did benefit from historic ties between the party and southern voters, but young whites who did not grow up during the segregationist pre–Voting Rights Act South felt these ties much less strongly. The growing number of immigrants to the South from outside the region were also more willing to consider voting Republican. The end of the segregationist regime promoted investment and economic growth that raised both black and white incomes. Conservative Republican appeals to reduce taxes and cut government spending found a receptive response in the region's burgeoning white middle class.[31] In short, the raison d'être of the region's political system no longer existed and new groups of voters were rising to change and challenge the Democratic Party as its largest remaining edifice.

South Carolina Senator Strom Thurmond was among the first traditional white Democrats to abandon the Democratic Party. Thurmond, then governor, had run for the presidency as a States Rights Democrat in

[31] Black and Black 1987; Edward G. Carmines and James A. Stimson, "Issue Evolution, Population Replacement, and Normal Partisan Change," *American Political Science Review* 75:1 (March 1981): 107–18; Carmines and Stimson 1989.

1948. While he did not support the party's nominee at that time, it is important to remember than he still ran as a Democrat, albeit as an alternative one. Indeed, Thurmond and his supporters viewed themselves as more authentic Democrats who remained true to their region and their party's principles. The goal of Thurmond's campaign was not to found a new party but to remind national Democrats of the importance of southern support to the party in order to force the party to return to its traditional unwillingness to challenge southern whites on racial questions. After the election, Thurmond served in the Senate as a Democrat.

Thurmond did not abandon his links to the party until 1964. Although many cite Barry Goldwater's transformation of the Republicans into a racially conservative party as Thurmond's inspiration, his fear of losing the Democratic primary for reelection to the Senate also factored into his decision to switch parties.[32] Blacks, who undoubtedly detested Thurmond's strong segregationist stance, composed approximately 30 percent of South Carolina's population. A moderate white candidate who could appeal to both black and moderate white voters could present a real challenge to Thurmond. The candidate would need to appeal to only a minority of whites to carry the primary, so Thurmond's strong appeal among whites might not be an insurmountable barrier to winning a seat in the Senate. In order to avoid finding out just how vulnerable he was, Thurmond became one of the first conservative Democrats to jump to the GOP.

Thurmond was not the only white conservative who observed that the GOP might be a more hospitable home for people of his political persuasion. Although slow to begin, the Democratic Party's growing hostility to conservatism created a cycle that encouraged white conservatives to leave the party. As conservatives left the Democratic Party, blacks and liberals composed a larger share of the Democratic primary electorate. As a result, it grew harder for conservatives to win Democratic primaries, which further encouraged increasingly marginalized conservatives to leave the party. Of course, the Democratic primary continued to become more liberal and less a reflection of the overall southern electorate as more conservatives gravitated toward the Republican Party, so the cycle continued until liberals dominated the Democratic Party. At the same time, the Republicans, historically a haven for blacks and moderate whites, became dominated by conservatives.

[32] Bass and Thompson 1988, 201; Black and Black 1992, 141–49, 152–53; Kari A. Frederickson, *Dixiecrat Revolt and the End of the Solid South, 1932–1968* (Chapel Hill: University of North Carolina Press, 2001), 130–86; Cole Blease Graham Jr. and William V. Moore, *South Carolina Government and Politics* (Lincoln: University of Nebraska Press, 1990), 82–99.

Analyzing data on the racial and ideological composition of people who identify themselves as Democrats, the people most likely to participate in Democratic primaries, supports these conclusions.[33] Table 4.4 shows that white conservatives composed only one-third of all Democratic identifiers by 1972, about the same share as blacks and white liberals together. The crumbling of disfranchisement clearly expanded the liberal base within the Democratic Party, giving them parity with white conservatives. White conservatives, however, could still control the party in coalition with white moderates in the early 1970s. During this period, white moderates and conservatives still formed over 60 percent of all southerners who viewed themselves as Democrats.

The position of white conservatives within the Democratic Party eroded rapidly as the exodus of white conservatives began while blacks and white liberals remained loyal Democrats. By the mid-1980s, African Americans outnumbered white conservatives within the party that historically had been a bastion of southern white conservatism. At the same time, African Americans in coalition with white liberals started to consistently outnumber the competing coalition of white moderates and conservatives. This loss of control naturally only encouraged white conservatives and (to a lesser extent) white moderates to leave the party.[34] White liberals and African Americans formed roughly one-half of the region's Democrats by the end of the 1980s. In coalition with the rapidly growing Hispanic population, they outnumbered white conservatives and moderates by a margin of 2–1. By 2000, the cycle was virtually complete as nearly all white conservatives had left the Democrats and the share of white moderates remaining Democrats had stabilized.

Examining actual primary statistics from South Carolina further confirms these trends. In many ways, the Palmetto State is the ideal state to examine primary evolution. Partisan change has progressed relatively quickly; Republicans gained control of both houses of the legislature by 2001. South Carolina has open primaries so the choice of primary participation lies with the voter at each election. Open primaries make it easier for voters to switch their party of primary participation as they do not need to go the trouble of changing their party registration in advance of the primary. Finally, South Carolina's excellent statewide voter registration database makes it possible to know the level of participation in party primaries by race without having to resort to statistical estimation.

---

[33] All data discussed here are from the National Election Study Cumulative Data File 1948–98. The measure of partisanship is a collapsed one, so Democrats include strong Democrats, weak Democrats, and independents who lean toward the Democratic Party. Figures for whites and blacks are solely for non-Hispanic members of these groups.

[34] Sundquist 1983, 374–75.

TABLE 4.4
Southern Democratic Party Identifiers by Race and Ideology

	Group Share of Democratic Identifiers						Potential Coalitions		
	White Conservatives	White Moderates	White Liberals	Black	Hispanic	Other	Blacks and White Liberals	Blacks and White Liberals and Hispanics	White Conservatives and Moderates
1972	32	31	14	22		0	37	37	63
1974	27	35	16	20		2	36	36	62
1976	33	27	14	22		4	36	36	60
1978	23	31	23	14	1	8	37	38	54
1980	24	30	19	24	3	1	43	46	54
1982	27	27	27	16	2	0	43	45	55
1984	17	24	20	24	10	5	44	54	41
1986	18	27	16	32	6	1	48	54	45
1988	19	21	13	29	11	6	43	54	40
1990	17	17	18	35	10	3	52	63	34
1992	16	21	22	29	7	5	51	58	37
1994	13	19	22	26	11	8	48	59	33
1996	14	20	27	26	10	3	53	63	34
1998	8	23	23	27	16	3	50	66	31

Note: Each number in the six columns under "Group Share of Democratic Identifiers" indicates the percentage that members of that group composed of all southerners surveyed who stated that they identified with the Democratic Party in response to a standard party identification question. For example, the "32" for white conservatives in 1972 indicates that white conservatives made up 32 percent of all Democratic identifiers in 1972. The three columns on the right, collectively labeled "Potential Coalitions," merely show various aggregations of the groups in the six columns on the left. For example, the numbers presented in the "White Conservatives and Moderates" column equal the sum of the "White Conservatives" and "White Moderates" column. Any cases in which the numbers in "Potential Coalitions" columns are exactly equal to the sum of the appropriate columns on the left are due to rounding.

Source: National Election Study Cumulative Data File 1948–98.

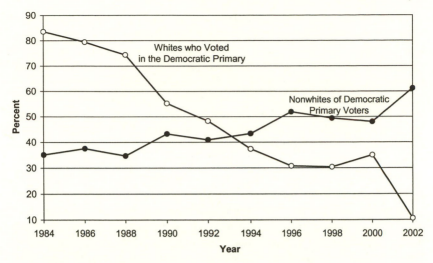

Figure 4.2. South Carolina Democratic primary participation.
Note: The black circles indicate the percentage of the Democratic primary electorate composed by nonwhites; African Americans make up the overwhelming
share of all nonwhite voters. The white circles indicate the percentage of all
whites who voted in the Democratic primary of all whites who voted in either the
Democratic or Republican primaries. These data are not based on a survey but on
data collected by South Carolina on the race and turnout of every registered
voter.
Source: South Carolina State Election Commission.

Figure 4.2 shows that the share of whites participating in Democratic
primaries in South Carolina dropped dramatically between 1980 and
2002. Over 80 percent of whites who voted in primaries chose to participate in Democratic primaries as late as 1984; however, the Democratic
share plunged to around one-third by the end of the 1990s. As a result of
white flight to GOP primaries, the nonwhite share of the Democratic
primary electorate leapt from approximately one-third to one-half. Almost all nonwhites in South Carolina are African American so black control over Democratic nominations has greatly increased.

In 2002, heated contests on the Republican side combined with a very
quiet year on the Democratic side resulted in the share of whites participating in the Democratic primary diving to a new low of 11 percent.
Republicans primaries for offices of governor, lieutenant governor, secretary of state, and attorney general were all so tightly contested that runoffs had to be held. Democrats held one statewide primary in 2002 for
the not-so-exalted office of commissioner of agriculture. As a result of
whites flocking to the Republican primary, blacks formed 61 percent of
the Democratic primary voters in 2002.

While Democrats may have taken comfort that the unattractiveness of their primary was only temporary and due to the absence of any marquee races in 2002, the presence of so many close contests between so many prominent Republicans on the GOP primary ballot is yet another indication of the increased vitality of the Republicans. The Republican gubernatorial primary alone attracted the incumbent lieutenant governor, attorney general, secretary of state, and a congressman. Unlike in the past, South Carolina Republicans no longer have any trouble finding top-tier candidates to run for office.

The 1988 Democratic presidential primaries dramatically illustrated the changed nature of the southern Democratic Party. Prior to 1988, southern Democratic elites grew highly concerned that the strong liberalism of national Democrats rendered Democratic presidential nominees, like 1984 presidential nominee Walter Mondale, unelectable in the South. They organized the nation's first regional presidential primary, called Super Tuesday, to promote a more conservative party nominee. Organizers of Super Tuesday believed that if southern states held their primaries on the same day that Democratic presidential candidates would be forced to pay greater attention to the South. As a result, a more conservative Democrat, who would not alienate southern voters in the general election, would win the nomination.

It did not work that way. The southern Democrats who organized Super Tuesday apparently did not realize that their party resembled the national Democratic Party more than the old southern Democratic Party. Prominent conservative southern Democrats, like Georgia Senator Sam Nunn, chose not to seek their party's nomination, rightly suspecting that they could not win. Indeed, the results proved that liberals dominated Democratic primaries in the South as well as the North. African-American Jesse Jackson, the most liberal candidate in the race, carried Alabama, Georgia, Louisiana, Mississippi, and Virginia. Massachusetts Governor Michael Dukakis, a liberal technocrat who opposed the death penalty, won Florida and Texas. The presence of several liberal candidates and the absence of any other moderates or conservatives had been expected to benefit Tennessee Senator Al Gore's campaign. Perceived as relatively conservative compared to the other major candidates, Gore had a moderate to liberal voting record in the Senate. However, he carried only three states: his home state of Tennessee as well as neighboring Arkansas and North Carolina.[35]

The 1992 Democratic primary campaign further emphasized the liberal nature of the southern Democratic primary electorate even though

[35] Black and Black 1992, 260–71; *Presidential Elections, 1789–1996* (Washington, DC: Congressional Quarterly, 1997), 204–7.

"New Democrat" Bill Clinton won thumping majorities in almost every state in the region. Clinton fought off a tough challenge from former Massachusetts Senator Paul Tsongas in the Florida primary by making a traditional Democratic left-wing appeal. Clinton accused Tsongas of wanting to cut Social Security, a social welfare program dear to the hearts of Florida's large retiree population. Clinton's comfort in campaigning among blacks and ties to southern black leaders, hardly a tactic of traditional white conservatives, greatly aided his efforts as he won strong support from African Americans. Clinton also picked up votes as a regional and native son candidate who worked hard to attract more traditional southerners by emphasizing his respect for religious values and his own affiliation with the Baptist Church. Despite these bows to the center, Clinton's core appeal did not rest on a call to return to old-style Democratic conservatism. Instead, he called for a major expansion of social welfare spending in the form of national health insurance. His championship of health care reform and gay rights after his election quickly lost Clinton any conservative support he might have gained during the 1992 campaign.

Louisiana

Governor Edwin Edwards established Louisiana's unique electoral system in 1975 because he was tired of having to win three elections (the Democratic primary, the Democratic runoff, and the general election) in order to serve as governor of the Pelican State. The new law created an arguably simpler system, but one with less predictable effects on Republican growth than the traditional primary system. Under the new law, all candidates regardless of party run together in a single primary. If a candidate wins a majority in the primary, the candidate is elected. If no candidate receives over 50 percent of the vote, a runoff is held between the top two finishers of the primary, even if they are of the same political party. Fellow partisans often end up competing against each other under this system.

The selection of candidates who choose to run in the first primary often greatly influences the outcome of the general election.[36] The outcomes of recent statewide contests suggest that Republicans can benefit if a viable Republican candidate can survive the first primary and if the

[36] David Canon's *Race, Redistricting, and Representation* and his article coauthored with Matthew M. Schousen and Patrick J. Sellers provided inspiration for this argument; see Canon 1999 and Canon, Schousen, and Sellers 1996. Even as I acknowledge my intellectual debt, I should note that they cannot be held responsible for any faults in my extension of their argument about the importance of the supply of candidates on determining outcomes in majority-minority districts.

surviving Democrat is unacceptable to most white voters. In 1995, this is exactly what happened. Conservative Republican Mike Foster, a descendent of one of the major proponents of Louisiana's disfranchisement laws, received 26.1 percent in the first primary. Black Democrat Cleo Fields also survived to the runoff with 19.0 percent of the vote. Fields was a young rising star in Louisiana politics who had left Congress after severely disadvantageous alterations to his congressional district as the result of a successful racial gerrymandering lawsuit. Being black unfortunately remains a strong liability among many white voters in Louisiana, and Fields lost to Foster in an extremely racially polarized runoff election. Polls indicate that Fields received only 16 percent of the white vote while Foster gained only 4 percent of the black vote.[37]

The choice of candidates in the first primary helped assure Foster this easy ride in the runoff. The outcome might have been quite different if Fields had not sought the governorship. White Democrat Mary Landrieu, the incumbent state treasurer and daughter of former New Orleans Mayor Moon Landrieu, narrowly failed to win the second spot in the runoff with 18.4 percent of the vote. If Fields had not run, Landrieu probably would have faced Foster in a runoff. While it is not certain she would have won the runoff, she would have had an excellent chance as she had assiduously courted white moderate voters and would likely have received the support of most black voters as the only Democratic candidate. Similarly, under the traditional primary system, she likely would have defeated Fields in a racially polarized Democratic primary and then faced Foster in the general election. The selection of candidates along with Louisiana's unique electoral system played a critical role in Foster's elevation to the governor's office.

The comeback bid of former Republican Governor Buddy Roemer, originally elected as a Democrat in 1987, similarly aided Foster. While Foster might have received the lion's share of Roemer's 17.8 percent of the vote if he had not run, it would have been insufficient to give Foster a victory in the primary. However, Landrieu likely would have received enough support from Roemer voters to surpass Fields's vote tally. Few of Roemer's conservative supporters could have been expected to choose Fields if he was not in the race. Just as Fields squeezed Landrieu's vote from the left, Roemer pressed from the right and she failed to make the runoff. One should not feel too badly for Landrieu; she won election to the U.S. Senate in a squeaker just one year later.

On balance, however, it is not at all clear that Louisiana's system has usually helped the GOP. The traditional primary system guarantees Re-

[37] Michael Barone and Richard E. Cohen, *Almanac of American Politics 2002* (Washington, DC: National Journal, 2001), 662–63.

publicans a spot on the ballot in the general election. Under Louisiana's system, it is possible (and common) for a Democrat to simply win the election by winning a majority in the primary. Historically, the Republican base was so small that there was no guarantee a Republican could gain the second spot even in a crowded primary. As Republicans gain electoral muscle, this may change and the system may aid further Republican growth. The Republican base may increasingly assure the Republicans of a runoff spot, but the system may prevent Democrats from nominating their strongest candidate as white moderate candidates lose votes to black and conservative candidates.

Of course, even if the Republican base guarantees the Republican a spot in the runoff, they may sometimes also nominate unelectable candidates. The campaigns of Republican State Legislator David Duke, best known for his role in the Ku Klux Klan and affection for the Nazi Party, may have prevented Republicans from taking a U.S. Senate seat in 1990 and keeping the governor's office in 1991. Incumbent Democratic Senator J. Bennett Johnston cruised past Duke in the primary with a tepid 54 percent of the vote in 1990. While Duke certainly had charisma, one wonders if a Republican without his history might have unseated Johnston. Similarly, Duke's presence in the 1991 primary prevented incumbent Republican Governor Buddy Roemer from winning a spot in the gubernatorial runoff; Duke received 32 percent to Roemer's 27 percent.[38] Duke's nomination was a windfall for the other winner of a runoff spot: former Democratic Governor Edwin Edwards. Having survived several corruption indictments, Edwards was a decidedly flawed candidate. However, white elites viewed the potential election of Duke as disastrous for the state's image and, along with black voters, opposed his election. As one bumper sticker supporting Edwards put it: "Vote for the Crook, It's Important." Presumably Roemer would have had a better shot at unifying the anti-Edwards vote than Duke. Nevertheless, few Republican candidates carry Duke's unique baggage so the Louisiana electoral system may hurt Democrats more than Republicans.

Despite Republican success, including Foster's election in 1995 and reelection in 1999, Louisiana remains one of the strongest Democratic states in the region. Perhaps because of its strong populist tradition, Louisiana is more receptive than other southern states to Democratic appeals on economic issues and more supportive of Democratic presidential candidates. No Republican has won election to the U.S. Senate from Louisiana since Reconstruction. However, in 2000 Louisiana gave unusually strong support to George W. Bush's presidential bid. His residence

---

[38] A third Republican candidate, former U.S. Representative Clyde Holloway, received 5 percent of the vote and arguably also played a role in denying Roemer a runoff spot.

in a neighboring state combined with his unwavering support of the oil industry probably aided his bid for Louisiana votes.

THE INITIATIVE PROCESS AND TERM LIMITS

Two institutions, the initiative process and term limits, came together to aid Republican prospects in state legislative elections in the early 1990s. Voters in three southern states joined the national movement in favor of term limits for elected officials by utilizing the initiative process to adopt term limits for state legislative officials. In 1992, Arkansas voters passed the strictest term limits yet adopted in the South. In Arkansas, individuals may serve a lifetime maximum of eight years in each house of the state legislature. Florida voters passed an initiative requiring legislators to relinquish their seats after serving eight consecutive years in one office. Unlike in Arkansas, legislators may seek election to the same job again at some future date. Louisiana passed an even weaker form of term limits in a 1995 initiative. Louisiana legislators may serve a maximum of twelve years in one office before being forced to give up their seat.[39] As in Florida, former Louisiana legislators can fight to win their old jobs back after sitting out an election.

The presence of the initiative process was vital to the passage of term limits. Like most people, legislators generally loathe the idea of losing their jobs. Most legislators worked hard to win election and do not want to leave until they are ready to retire or run for higher office. Candidates may publicly support term limits and even vote for them in the legislature, but this support is given with the knowledge that the chances of term limits actually passing are quite low. Congressional Republicans, for example, made a promise to vote on term limits a cornerstone of the 1994 Contract with America, a united platform signed by most Republican candidates in that year. With a few notable exceptions, few Republicans showed much interest in actually passing term limits once they took control of the U.S. House in the November elections. Several congressional candidates of both parties reneged on campaign promises to serve only a limited number of terms after the issue faded.

Term limits have already forced legislators to seek other employment in Arkansas and Florida, though no Louisiana legislators will be shoved out until 2007. In 1998, Arkansas became the first southern state in which term limits took effect. Fully one-half of the 100 members of the Arkansas House could not seek reelection in 1998. In 2000, term limits

[39] The Louisiana law requires legislators not to seek reelection if they have served twelve consecutive years or more than 2.5 four-year terms. The latter provision affects only legislators not elected during the regularly scheduled general elections held every four years.

required an additional 24 members of the Arkansas House to leave office. Seven of the 17 Arkansas senators whose terms expired in 2000 similarly could not seek reelection; the Arkansas Senate has a total membership of 35. The Florida House lost 51 of its 120 members to term limits in 2000. Term limits also forced out 11 of the 18 Florida senators whose terms ended in 2000; the Florida Senate complete membership equals 40.

Republicans benefited most from the open seats resulting from term limits in elections for the Arkansas House. Democrats held so many seats in Arkansas that open seats could only benefit the Republicans as the vast majority of incumbents were Democrats. The reduction in the number of Democratic incumbents presented an array of new opportunities for the GOP. The number of Republicans sitting in the Arkansas House rose from 14 to 24 in 1998—an impressive gain for just one election. The Florida GOP also made impressive gains in the 2000 election. The presidential election in the Sunshine State was essentially a tie and Republicans already formed majorities in both houses of the state legislature. Yet Republicans increased their share of seats by 3 percent in the House and 5 percent in the Senate.

Parties that already occupy a share of seats reflective of their strength in the electorate are also unlikely to gain much from the rise in open seats due to term limits. The high share of seats already held by the Republicans in 2000 probably explains why the GOP's gains in Florida in 2000 were smaller than in Arkansas in 1998. The Arkansas GOP holds so few seats that open seats present the party with few risks and many opportunities.

Term limits only go so far in aiding a party. If a party lacks a base of support and candidates to run for open seats, term limits will not help much. The Arkansas GOP actually lost seats in the Arkansas Senate in 2000 despite a wealth of open seats. The state GOP had probably benefited in past elections from the uncovering of corruption at high levels of the Arkansas Democratic Party. The Whitewater scandal plagued former Arkansas Governor Bill Clinton and First Lady Hillary Rodham Clinton during much of the Clinton administration. President Clinton's successor as governor was also forced to resign from office because of another scandal. Republicans won control of the governorship of Arkansas and a U.S. Senate seat in the wake of these Democratic problems. Arkansas Democrats nevertheless remain formidable and the GOP continues to struggle to build their party.

No Party Labels on the Ballot: The Case of Virginia

Except for the offices of president and vice president, Virginia did not place the party of the candidates on the ballot prior to the 2001 elections.

Partisanship cannot serve as a cue to voters in the election booth unless they are aware of the party of the candidates before they vote. Historically, the absence of a party cue mattered little because few voted in Virginia and the Democratic machine of Senator Harry Byrd dominated Virginia politics. Virtually all blacks and most whites did not participate in elections due to the great success of disfranchisement laws. Between 1925 and 1945, only 12 percent of adults, on average, voted in Democratic primaries. The level of white nonvoting was high even compared to other southern states.[40] The size of the electorate exploded after the elimination of the poll tax and passage of the Voting Rights Act. The Byrd machine died as a result during the 1960s, and party competition expanded greatly. Liberal Republican Linwood Holton won the first post–poll tax gubernatorial election in 1969. In statewide contests, the key election shifted from the Democratic primary to the general election.

In areas with competition from both major parties, voters often find partisanship a highly useful voting cue. Particularly for low-level offices, voters often have little or no information about the candidates and may vote purely on the basis of their partisanship. Most voters have little inclination to use their valuable time to investigate candidates for minor office. Partisanship serves as a valuable timesaving shortcut to determine which candidate probably shares a voter's views most closely. Even if one puts in the effort to gather the available information about candidates for low-level offices, it usually is not terribly enlightening. Candidates tend to take lots of stands that offend no one and avoid taking positions that alienate sizable blocs of voters. Not so mysteriously, candidates for sheriff oppose crime while candidates for the board of education vow to improve schools. Has anyone ever seen a successful candidate for sheriff campaign on a platform of being less aggressive in combating crime? Or a winning candidate for the board of education who distributed brochures explaining why children and schools really do not matter much?

In most states, party labels help sort through the confusion and the candidates. By not placing party labels on the ballot, Virginia eliminated this opportunity for voters and uniquely changed the role of parties in elections. Moreover, the absence of party labels on the ballot may alter the calculations of candidates on whether it is better to affiliate with a party or to run as an independent. The party brand label loses a lot of its value when voters have far less exposure to it. Just like companies put their logos on products so that people can immediately identify them, candidates like having their party label next to their name on the ballot if they think it will benefit them. People interested in opening a burger

[40] Key 1949, 20; Thomas R. Morris and Neil Bradley, "Virginia," in Davidson and Grofman 1994, 271–76.

joint would be much less interested in opening a McDonald's if they could not put the golden arches out front. Even if they have never been to a particular McDonald's, the presence of golden arches alerts customers to what they will find inside. Just as customers are drawn to (or repelled by) a new McDonald's based on past experience, voters may choose their party's candidates based on past positive experiences with candidates of that party.[41]

For a candidate, being listed as the candidate of a party on the ballot may be the primary value in associating with the party brands of Democratic and Republican. If no one knows about the label, the value of joining the party declines markedly. Running as an independent avoids the necessity of exhausting resources in a party primary or convention. Evading a party nomination battle also eliminates one chance of losing the election. However, independent candidates may also forfeit the support of party organizations and their supporters. The teachers union, for example, often provides volunteers to the candidacies of sympathetic Democrats. Similarly, independent candidates may find it more difficult to raise money for their campaigns. Political parties do not support independents and many donors like to support candidates of only one party. Additionally, party candidates can use targeted mail to alert fellow partisans of their party label.

The absence of party labels on the ballot probably has two major effects. First, one should see greater numbers of independent officeholders in elections for offices where party networks of support are not very useful. If party labels maintain sufficient value to candidates in terms of attracting support from elites who can provide campaign resources, particularly money, or in winning voter support through campaign activities, most officeholders will identify with one of the two major parties. Second, the absence of party identification on the ballot will tend to spur Republican growth in an era of heavy Democratic partisanship. The historic dominance of the Democrats in partisanship should serve as less of a drag on Republican growth in a political arena where many voters remain unaware of a candidate's party.

Examining data from Virginia elections confirms both of the above hypotheses. Unlike in other southern states, a sizable share of Virginia's local officials are independents. Between 1981 and 1999, independents won 44 percent of the local elections for the city and county offices (clerk, commonwealth attorney, revenue commissioner, sheriff, and treasurer) included in the study. Independents won a greater share of offices than either Democrats or Republicans; Democrats won 41 percent and

[41] Morris P. Fiorina, *Retrospective Voting in American National Elections* (New Haven: Yale University Press, 1981).

Republicans captured 15 percent of offices over the same period. The share of offices won by independents increased slightly toward the end of the period. In the 1997–99 election cycle, independents won 48 percent of offices as compared to a reduced 31 percent for the Democrats and a more encouraging 21 percent for the Republicans. Successful independent candidacies were quite rare in other southern states with independents winning less than 4 percent of contests in all other states.

Interestingly, state legislative and federal officeholders are almost always partisans even in Virginia. Throughout the 1990s, no independent won election to the U.S. Senate, Congress, or the Virginia Senate as an independent.[42] One independent, who usually voted with the Republicans, won election to the Virginia House of Delegates throughout the 1990s.[43] Strong incentives other than party labels likely explain why few seek or win election to the General Assembly as independents. The partisan balance between the two parties in both houses was close throughout the 1990s, particularly toward the end of the decade as Republicans gained strength and pushed to win control of the Assembly. Both parties funneled a great deal of money to their candidates, especially in competitive races, as control of the Assembly was at stake. Unavailable to independent candidates, this money permitted state legislative candidates to advertise themselves through the mail, and sometimes on television. Party candidates could also use party mailing lists to make targeted mailings to stimulate support and turnout. Party candidates could appeal to fellow partisans for support as partisans—an option unavailable to independents who could not make a partisan appeal.

Local candidates were unlikely to benefit from most of the resources that gave state legislative candidates a strong incentive to join a political party. State party organizations have far less interest in local contests, which do not offer the chance to control the state government. In the late 1990s, federal parties targeted state legislative contests in states with closely divided state legislatures in order to maximize their party's influence on the redistricting process at the beginning of the new decade. But

[42] U.S. Representative Virgil Goode switched his party affiliation from Democratic to Independent after the 1998 congressional elections. The Republicans had unified control of Virginia's state legislature and governor's office during the redistricting cycle following the 2000 elections, so it is thought that his switch away from the Democrats may have encouraged the Republicans to treat him more kindly when Virginia adopted new district maps.

[43] Independent Delegate Lacey E. Putney was sufficiently popular among House Republicans that they elected him acting speaker in 2002 after Speaker Wilkins was forced to resign due to scandal. At the time of his election, Delegate Putney, aged seventy-three, had served longer in the House of Delegates than anyone else in its history. Tyler Whitley, "Putney Will Be Acting Speaker of the House," *Richmond Times-Dispatch*, June 14, 2000, A19.

they paid virtually no attention to local contests, often for relatively unimportant offices. Aside from party organizations, local candidates find it more difficult to appeal to a statewide—let alone national—donor base of partisans. Running as an independent may often allow local candidates to bypass a party primary without any real cost to their chances of winning the general election.

Virginia changed its law regarding party labels on the ballot once Republicans won unified control of state government in 1999. The strong historical Democratic advantage in party identification has evaporated. Republicans now believe that they have replaced the Democrats as the natural standing choice of Virginia voters. As a result, Republicans hope that party labels will help extend their advantage in federal contests down to other contests, particularly state legislative and local elections.

Conclusion

The institutions of the South were neither merely background nor incidental to Republican growth in the South. Even after the dismantling of the old white supremacist political system, many institutions established to support that system, like the primary, continued to exist and shape southern politics. However, changes in other aspects of the political system often greatly altered the operation of these old institutions in important ways.

One consistent theme of this chapter is that many institutions work to stimulate partisan change and reinforce trends created by issues or changing voter preferences. The entry of large numbers of liberals into the Democratic Party changed the political makeup of the Democratic primary, spurring some conservatives to abandon the party. As conservatives left the party, the primary only became more liberal, encouraging even more conservatives to choose to join the GOP. New white conservatives entering the electorate increasingly perceived the Republicans as their natural home instead of the Democrats, where the strength of liberals and minorities has only grown over time.

Conservative white elites are likely even more sensitive than voters to changes in the ideology of Democratic primary voters. As the Democratic primary electorate became more liberal, it became more and more difficult for conservatives, especially non-incumbents, to win Democratic primaries. Aspiring conservative politicians increasingly considered joining the GOP, an overwhelmingly conservative party, instead of the dominant Democrats. This gradual shift by conservative elites was essential to Republican growth as it is impossible to contest or to win elections without candidates. The growing dominance of minorities and white liberals in the Democratic primary made possible the increased contestation of offices, especially open seats, by the Republicans that was described in the previous chapter.

Racial redistricting similarly spurred Republican growth in the 1990s. It aided Republicans directly by concentrating the most loyal Democratic voters into majority-minority districts. Packing loyal Democrats into these districts made it easier for Republicans to win surrounding districts. Racial redistricting altered incentives for elites even more abruptly than the gradual shift in the ideology of Democratic primary voters as the creation of new black districts was highly concentrated in the early 1990s. By lifting opportunities for minority Democrats and white Republicans at the expense of white Democrats, racial redistricting encouraged ambitious white politicians to pursue their political future with the Republicans rather than the Democrats. The enhanced opportunities for the GOP further spurred more experienced Republican candidates to run for election where they might previously have been deterred by the Democratic nature of the district. Stronger candidates help fulfill the prophecies of Republican gains by running stronger and more successful campaigns. The impact of racial redistricting was directly felt in virtually all offices elected by district from county commissioner to state legislator to the U.S. House. By augmenting the pool of Republican officials, it aided the GOP even in elections for non-districted offices. Racial redistricting played an important role in the greatly increased rates of Republican contestation and victory outlined in chapters 1 and 2.

Term limits, made possible in some states through the availability of the initiative process, increased the number of open seats and the number of good political opportunities open to Republican candidates. The number of Republicans elected to the Arkansas legislature jumped after many incumbents were forced to leave the legislature due to term limits. As Republicans make gains, term limits increasingly may work against them as they force experienced, incumbent Republicans to retire. On the other hand, Virginia Republicans hope that the addition of party labels to the ballot will now help them make further gains as so many residents of the Old Dominion now identify with the GOP. Ironically, the absence of these labels may have aided the GOP in the past by undercutting the availability of party as a cue in the voting booth when Democrats dominated Virginia politics.

While institutions can greatly condition electoral outcome, they are hardly the sole influence on either elite decisions or the voting behavior of ordinary citizens. This chapter explains how institutions promoted partisan change; the next chapter begins the exploration of how the voting behavior and beliefs of people influenced Republican southern gains. More specifically, it explains how racial context influenced the pace of these gains. Ironically, even though both institutions and racial context tend to change slowly, both of these relatively fixed aspects of the southern political scene can actually promote political change. Institutions like primaries and racial redistricting aided Republican efforts to advance in the South. Racial context makes its influence felt most strongly by conditioning where Republicans are most likely to flourish. The next chapter details why blacks give such strong support to the Democrats and how this reliable support conditions political outcomes. It also explores how racial context can influence both white elites and white voting behavior. Regardless of the importance of racial issues, explored in more detail in chapter 6, racial context can have a huge impact on the success of Republican candidates.

CHAPTER FIVE

The Impact of Racial Context

RACE HAS LONG BEEN declared central to southern politics by many observers. Racial issues were certainly central to political debates during the 1960s and the two major parties became newly polarized over race during this period. The 1964 election with racial conservative Barry Goldwater carrying the standard for the Republicans and racial liberal Lyndon Johnson seeking a full term as a Democrat crystalized their party's positions. Proponents of racial theories of partisan change contend that racial conservatism attracted racially conservative white voters to the Republicans and accounts for the GOP's gradual ascendance over the past several decades. Considering the historical power of racial issues and their particular salience during the upheavals of the 1960s makes it seem foolish to challenge this viewpoint.

Nevertheless, I believe that the role of race in southern politics has often been misunderstood even if it has played a critical part in shaping the politics of the region. In contrast to past work that has emphasized the centrality of racial issues, I argue that the role of race in southern politics has varied over time and for different groups of southerners and has not been the only issue to spur partisan change. Race played a critical role in shattering the institutions that maintained Democratic dominance in the South.

Racial issues continue to spur most black southerners to identify and vote Democratic. The racial conservatism of the Republicans has rendered the GOP unacceptable to the vast majority of African Americans. However, for most whites, racial issues are less critical.[1] While racial issues may remain of great importance for a subset of whites, other factors, including economic and social questions, compete for the attention of most whites in the political arena. Indeed, the very success of the Civil Rights Movement in transforming the South has changed the nature of racial issues. The destruction of the old system actually allowed healthy partisan conflict over nonracial issues. The decline of white supremacy

[1] Abromowitz 1994; Harold W. Stanley, "The 1984 Presidential Election in the South: Race and Realignment," in *The 1984 Presidential Election in the South: Patterns of Southern Party Politics*, ed. Robert P. Steed, Lawrence W. Moreland, and Tod A. Baker (New York: Praeger, 1986); Stanley 1988, 67–73; Raymond Wolfinger and Michael Hagen, "Republican Prospects: Southern Comfort," *Public Opinion* 8 (October/November 1985): 12.

and the rise of blacks as a key Democratic constituency meant that Democrats could no longer attack Republicans as a threat to white racial unity and the racial status quo. The racial status quo had been destroyed and the Democrats began to court the previously much excoriated and feared black voter.

That racial issues should play a smaller role for the dominant majority than a minority with a long history of political oppression is unsurprising. However, just as it would be mistaken to assume that race has retained the same centrality for whites as in the past, it would be misguided to assume that southern politics has moved beyond race. The near unanimous support given to Democrats by black voters means that racial context plays an extremely important role in constraining partisan change. After explaining in more detail why African Americans continue to back the Democrats so solidly, this chapter then explores how the presence of black voters inhibits the Republicans from both recruiting candidates and winning elections. Like the institutions examined in the previous chapter, racial context has a very strong impact on the patterns of elite behavior and electoral outcomes observed in chapters 2 and 3.

The latter part of this chapter will explore whether racial context continues to influence the voting behavior of white southerners. Historically, whites who lived in areas with many black voters most feared the end of white supremacy because racial equality, especially racial political equality, would likely threaten their political and economic dominance. I find that there is little evidence that whites may react to the presence of blacks by supporting the more racially conservative party at a greater rate than other whites.

This chapter only really begins the discussion of the impact of race on partisan change. It focuses primarily on racial context: explaining why African Americans vote Democratic and the impact of these voting patterns both on white voting behavior and overall electoral outcomes. The next chapter broadens the discussion of race by moving beyond racial context to explore the relative impact of racial and other issues on partisan change in the South over the past several decades.

RACE REMAINS CENTRAL TO BLACK PARTISANSHIP

The level of support for the Democratic Party approaches unanimity to a greater extent among African Americans than virtually any other racial, ethnic, or religious group in America.[2] The consistency and depth of this

---

[2] Tate 1994, 67–68, 72, 128–35, 148–50, 181–98. Puerto Ricans who live on the mainland also provide very high levels of support for the Democrats, though the low levels of

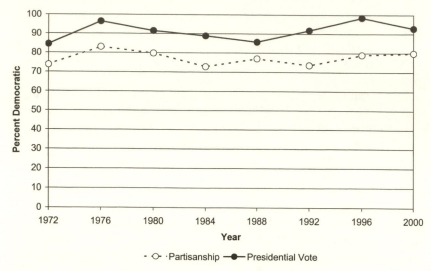

Figure 5.1. Percent of Blacks who vote and identify Democratic.
Note: Percent Democratic partisanship is the percentage identifying as Democrats of the total number who identify as either Democratic, Republican, or Independent.
Source: NES Cumulative Data File 1948–98; NES 2000 Post-Election Study.

support has been well documented by surveys and studies over the years. Figure 5.1 presents the percentage of southern blacks who voted Democratic for president and who identify themselves as Democrats according to the National Election Study. Over 90 percent of southern blacks regularly cast their ballots for Democratic presidential candidates and the percentage of southern blacks identifying as Democrats has never dipped below 70 percent since 1972.[3] African Americans are unusually loyal Democrats compared to white Democrats; black Democrats are far less likely to defect from the party in the polling booth by voting for Republican candidates.

These numbers perplexingly contradict media reports implying greater

voter turnout, even by America's low standards, among eligible Puerto Ricans somewhat mitigate the reliability of voting as a measure of Puerto Rican public opinion; Rodolfo O. de la Garza, Louis DeSipio, F. Chris Garcia, John Garcia, and Angelo Falcon, *Latino Voices: Mexican, Puerto Rican and Cuban Perspectives on American Politics* (San Francisco: Westview Press, 1992); Lublin 1997, 60.

[3] The sample size of southern blacks in the NES for the presidential vote question is rather small with the number of cases ranging from 47 to 98 depending on the year (mean: 68). However, these conclusions on southern black voting behavior are confirmed by other surveys. The sample size for the partisanship question is somewhat larger with the number of cases ranging from 66 to 182 (mean: 123).

willingness on the part of African Americans to consider voting Republican. Moreover, more black Republicans have risen to prominence lately. Secretary of State Colin Powell, perennially mentioned as a candidate for the Republican presidential and vice-presidential nominations, usually leads the list. Condoleezza Rice advised George W. Bush on foreign policy during the 2000 campaign and now serves as national security advisor. Two black Republicans, Gary Franks of Connecticut and J. C. Watts of Oklahoma, have won election to Congress in recent years, though Franks was defeated for reelection in 1996 and Watts retired from the House after the 2000 elections. Anita Hill may have accused Clarence Thomas of sexual harassment during Thomas's confirmation hearings, but Hill largely shared the conservative view of Justice Thomas. Finally, though hardly exhaustively, Californian Ward Connerly led the fight to end affirmative action. Interestingly, none of these African-American Republicans currently lives in the South.[4]

The clash between media reports and polling results may partly indicate misperceptions or efforts to highlight minorities who do not fit political stereotypes about African Americans on the part of the media. Black Republicans like Colin Powell and Clarence Thomas reflect that there is invariably a diversity of opinion within every group. Even when the political preferences within the group are overwhelmingly in one direction, various individuals may deviate from the usual preference by members of the group. Exit polls may show that a huge majority of blacks vote Democratic, but they also show that a persistent, albeit small, minority of blacks vote Republican. Nevertheless, when studying African-American voting behavior, it is important not to get carried away by the impression left by prominent black Republicans. Black Republicans remain highly unusual within the overall group. The few elected black Republicans never win election thanks to African-American support. A majority of black voters opposed the elections of Representatives Franks and Watts. Both owed their election to the willingness of white voters to support their candidacies.

The History of Black Partisanship

African Americans have not always been such ardent supporters of the Democrats. In the aftermath of the Civil War, African Americans voted in large numbers and voted heavily for the Republicans.[5] Blacks of that era identified the Republicans as the party of Lincoln and gave staunch

---

[4] There are very few black Republicans elected in the South. For example, there was exactly one black Republican, Charleston County Councilman Tom Scott, elected to any office throughout South Carolina in the 1998–2000 period.

[5] Kousser 1974, 14–29.

support to the party indissolubly linked with the great achievements of the Emancipation Proclamation and the post–Civil War amendments to the Constitution. African Americans contrarily perceived the Democrats as aligned with their former enslavers and efforts to return to oppression through Jim Crow–type laws. Prominent advocates for black rights, like Representative Thaddeus Stevens and Senator Charles Sumner, were invariably Republicans while opponents of black political equality, particularly vocal ones, were usually Democrats.

The shift of African Americans from loyal Republicans to staunch Democrats was a decades-long process. The fraying of ties to the Republicans, largely due to lack of interest in black civil rights on the part of national Republicans, was the first step. Republicans continued to fight an increasingly rearguard action to support black rights until close to the end of the nineteenth century but gave scant attention to black concerns after 1896. Political interest explains the disjuncture in Republican advocacy between the two periods. Prior to the national shift toward the Republicans during the 1896 election, the GOP needed to appeal for black votes in order to have a shot at winning the usually tight presidential elections. Republicans similarly required black votes in order to carry a few southern congressional districts, and they needed to win at least a small minority of southern districts to control the U.S. House. After William Jennings Bryan's 1896 campaign for "free silver" alienated many northerners, the movement toward the GOP allowed the Republicans to win comfortably both the presidency and majority control of Congress without black support. Republicans then sidelined the highly controversial issue of black rights that alienated northern whites who sympathized with southern white supremacists.[6] The Dunning school of historians at Columbia University leant scholarly support to this decision through their skewed work arguing that Reconstruction was an abject failure and that blacks could not hope to responsibly govern or to exercise the right to vote.[7] More broadly, many northern whites, eager to move past the Civil War, had long tired of the problems of southern blacks, including denial of the right to vote.

Blacks began to shift their votes to the Democrats during the presidency of Franklin Roosevelt. While blacks actually cast a smaller share of their votes for Roosevelt in 1932 than they had for Democrat Al Smith in 1928, Roosevelt's New Deal economic policies attracted blacks, as well as whites, to the Democratic banner. Many New Deal agencies and programs discriminated against blacks. Social Security did not cover domestic servants or agricultural laborers, the two largest classes of employ-

---

[6] Valelly 1995.
[7] Du Bois 1935), 717–19; Foner 1988, xix–xxi.

ment for southern blacks. The receipt of any benefits from the federal government, however, was a new experience for a black population accustomed to not-so-benign neglect. The severity of the Great Depression made government aid particularly welcome to a community as discrimination made even good economic times a challenge for most black families. Roosevelt's "Black Cabinet," led by Mary McLeod Bethune, gave African Americans a voice within the administration. First Lady Eleanor Roosevelt was particularly solicitous of black concerns, most famously resigning her membership in the Daughters of the American Revolution after African-American Marian Anderson was denied permission to perform a concert at DAR–owned Constitution Hall.[8]

Support for the New Deal lifted black support for the Democrats to approximately one-half of the black vote. Most southern blacks could not express support for or against the Roosevelt administration due to their continued disfranchisement. There was nevertheless evidence of changing perceptions of the Democrats among southern blacks, though the total absence of any effort by the Roosevelt administration to advance black civil rights tempered black support for the Democrats. The administration even declined to endorse federal anti-lynching legislation, the central federal legislative goal of the NAACP at the time. Roosevelt relied on the support of southern senators to pass New Deal legislation and did not want to lose their support for his economic agenda over civil rights legislation. The failure of the Democrats to support the most basic civil rights legislation, such as the anti-lynching bill, combined with the prominence of white supremacist southern Democrats discouraged many blacks from breaking long-held ties to the Republicans. Republicans continued to win around one-half of the black vote in presidential elections though Republican efforts to advance a black agenda were as dead as Thaddeus Stevens long before the 1940s.[9]

Both major parties competed actively, if discreetly, for African-American votes from 1948 through the presidential election of 1960. Just as political necessity drove the Republicans to abandon their previous active support for southern black rights after 1896, political competition encouraged the parties to battle for black votes.[10] During the Great Migration, thousands of blacks left the South for northern cities in hope of a securing a brighter economic future. Northern black ghettos were deeply

---

[8] Weiss 1983, 257–66.

[9] Ibid., 98–119.

[10] Paul Frymer, *Uneasy Alliances: Race and Party Competition in America* (Princeton: Princeton University Press, 1999); Frymer argues that competition for black votes is critical to success in advancing a pro-black agenda. According to Frymer, African Americans fare poorly when they overwhelmingly support one party and the parties do not compete for their votes.

overcrowded, but they provided a great degree of insulation from white control impossible in the largely rural South. Blacks established cultural and civic institutions independent of white supervision. World War II accelerated black migration to the North as demand for labor in factories geared for the war effort attracted blacks from an economically under-developed South. Blacks may have been an often despised minority in the North as in the South, but they could vote and their almost equal division between the two parties made them a tempting target for strategists of both parties trying to win the electoral votes of closely divided key northern states.[11]

The share of blacks voting Democratic increased sharply in 1948 due to President Truman's leadership. Truman integrated the armed forces, and the Democratic Convention that nominated him for reelection in 1948 adopted a pro–civil rights plank in its platform for the first time in the history of the party. Deep South Democrats reinforced the break with the past by bolting the Democratic Convention and nominating South Carolina Democrat Strom Thurmond for the presidency on the State Rights Democratic ticket. "States rights" had long been none-too-subtle code language for allowing southern states to maintain white supremacy without interference from the national federal government.[12] One should nevertheless stress that Republicans continued to support black rights, arguably even more strongly, than the Democrats. Note that Thurmond and other defenders of the white supremacist status quo did not join the Republicans as they remained anathema. Instead, they organized a breakaway version of the *Democratic* Party. During the mid-twentieth century, African-American support for the Democrats was not nearly as unanimous or solid as it is today. The GOP continued to receive around one-quarter to one-half of the black vote.[13]

African Americans started voting overwhelmingly Democratic after the relative positions of the two major parties shifted drastically during the 1964 presidential election campaign. Incumbent President Lyndon Johnson established the Democratic Party as the party of racial liberalism by shepherding the Civil Rights Act of 1964 into law over the fevered opposition of southern Democrats. He continued these efforts by gaining passage of the Voting Rights Act of 1965, the other monumental civil rights legislation passed during the period. In contrast, the Republicans nominated racially conservative Arizona Senator Barry Goldwater for the presi-

[11] Carmines and Stimson 1989, 31–44; Frymer 1999, 93–100; Weiss 1983, 180–208.

[12] South Carolinian John Calhoun explicitly expounded his theory of states rights as a mechanism for preserving slavery. While states rights is not inherently a racist theory of governance, it has historically been linked to race in the context of the American South.

[13] Black and Black 1992, 141–49; Carmines and Stimson 1989, 27–37; Frederickson 2001, 118–86; Weiss 1983, 287.

dency. Goldwater claimed to oppose segregation, but he nevertheless voted against the Civil Rights Act of 1964 as an unconstitutional extension of federal power. He closed his presidential campaign in Columbia, South Carolina, at an all-star lineup of southern segregationists. The contrast between the two parties on an issue of crucial concern to black Americans led to near unanimous support for Johnson among blacks. Voting for Goldwater made about as much sense to blacks as voting to be the turkey on Thanksgiving.[14] On the other hand, Goldwater won the electoral votes of the Deep South.

Although they lost the 1964 presidential election in a landslide, the Republicans have continued to maintain their stance as the conservative party on both racial and economic issues. Richard Nixon, who campaigned as a racial liberal in 1960, changed tactics in 1968 when he shifted gears to court the South as part of his "southern strategy." Republicans like Nixon did not advocate white supremacy in the manner of old-fashioned Democrats. Clever Republicans realized that they could win the votes of white racists simply by being more racially conservative than the racially liberal Democratic Party.

The growing complexity of racial issues compared to the clear moral high ground held by the Civil Rights Movement has made these tactics both simpler and more broadly acceptable. Racially liberal policies like busing and affirmative action attract opposition outside the South and from many who oppose discrimination, laud the Civil Rights Movement, and wish no return to the evils of segregation. The consistency of Republican opposition to these and other civil rights policies nevertheless makes it difficult for the GOP to successfully appeal to blacks.

Maintaining Black Support for the Democrats Today

For most blacks, economic issues reinforce the relative appeal of the Democrats on racial issues. African Americans have made major economic strides since the Civil Rights Movement, which enabled blacks to enter the American economy on a more equal basis than in the harshly discriminatory past. Nevertheless, African Americans benefit to a greater extent from federal policies, usually advocated by Democrats and opposed by Republicans, designed to help the poor and working class. Moreover, federal intervention to aid groups in need of assistance remains much more broadly acceptable among blacks than whites. This difference should hardly surprise when one considers that blacks closely identify many great economic and racial advances with the national gov-

[14] Black and Black 1987, 269–71; Black and Black 1992, 149–58; Carmines and Stimson 1989, 44–47.

ernment. The New Deal and the Great Society liberal economic pro-grams were developed and financially supported by the federal gov-ernment. Even more obviously, the Thirteenth Amendment abolishing slavery, the Civil Rights Act of 1964, and the Voting Rights Act of 1965 were adopted due to strong federal support over the deep opposition of southern states.

Republicans, especially President Ronald Reagan, worked to link racial and economic images in the mind of voters. During his 1980 campaign, Reagan successfully associated anti-poverty programs with "welfare queens," implicitly minority women, who supposedly live high-on-the-hog at the expense of hardworking taxpayers. The 1988 Bush campaign indelibly linked crime with the image of Willie Horton, a rapist and murderer. The goal of this strategy was to attract the white majority, especially working- and middle-class whites in northern cities increas-ingly suspicious of policies targeted to aid the poor, rather than the mid-dle class.[15] However, this approach inevitably engendered and maintained an enduring hostility toward Republicans among the great majority of African Americans.

The 1998 senatorial campaign by South Carolina Representative Bob Inglis vividly demonstrates the difficulty that both blacks and Republi-cans have in overcoming this mutual suspicion and hostility. In virtually every respect, Inglis is a poster child for right-wing conservative Repub-licanism. A firm religious conservative who opposed government spend-ing to the extreme of voting against highway spending for his own con-gressional district, Inglis defeated an incumbent Democrat in 1992 to win his congressional seat centered on Greenville and Spartanburg in the "buckle" of the Bible Belt.[16] Inglis refreshingly dissociated his firm eco-nomic and religious conservatism from race. He campaigned repeatedly among blacks, including visits to all-black university campuses. Perhaps most impressively, unlike when Newt Gingrich campaigned among blacks in the District of Columbia, Inglis did not trim his sails and at-tempted to sell the same conservative message to blacks and whites. In-glis argued that Republicans needed to distance themselves from the ra-cial components of the southern strategy and to win black support through shared conservative values, particularly on religious issues.

Inglis paid a lot and gained little as the result of his efforts. In the Republican primary, Inglis's effort to attract African-American votes

[15] Edsall and Edsall 1992, 172–214; Theda Skocpol, *The Missing Middle: Working Families and the Future of American Social Policy* (New York: Norton, 2000); Tali Mendelberg, *The Race Card: Campaign Strategy, Implicit Messages, and the Norm for Equality* (Princeton: Princeton University Press, 2001), 134–68.

[16] Michael Barone and Grant Ujifusa, *The Almanac of American Politics 1994* (Washington, DC: National Journal, 1993), 1155–57.

earned him a challenge from the right despite his pristine record of consistent support for virtually every conservative cause. His challenger aired television commercials attacking Inglis for departing from southern traditions and values by disavowing the southern strategy. While most white Republicans, including all recent presidential nominees, would undoubtedly welcome greater black support for their party, these commercials likely reemphasized for black voters that the Republican Party contains many active members hostile to their interests. Inglis won almost no black votes in the general election, which he lost to incumbent Democrat Ernest "Fritz" Hollings.

The regular recurrence of racially tinged controversies undercuts efforts by Republican leaders like Inglis or Gingrich to reach out to black voters. Republican Senate Leader Trent Lott and Georgia Representative Bob Barr met with members of the racist Council of Conservative Citizens, heir to the notorious White Citizens Councils, and incredibly claimed that they did not know of the group's racist record. Despite negative press surrounding these meetings, Trent Lott continued to serve as the minority leader of the Senate. However, Trent Lott's expectations of leading the Republicans as majority leader after their victories in the 2002 elections were dashed after the storm of controversy unleashed by his public praise of Strom Thurmond's 1948 presidential campaign at Thurmond's one hundredth birthday party. These comments, combined with a recapitulation in the press of past indiscreet comments on racial issues, were enough for Lott to lose the support of many conservatives— and the White House. Lott stepped aside, though his position was taken by another southerner, Tennessee Senator Bill Frist.

Recent battles over the Confederate flag have likely further tarnished the image of the GOP among many blacks. The Confederate flag, actually the Confederate battle flag, remains part of the state flag of Mississippi. Until recently, it was also part of the Georgia flag. South Carolina began flying the battle flag just below those of the nation and the state on the state Capitol building at the height of the Civil Rights Movement. As part of an effort to diffuse the issue in the wake of a boycott organized by the NAACP, the South Carolina legislature voted in 2000 to transfer the flag from the dome to a monument on the grounds of the statehouse.

The debate over the flag and other monuments to the Confederacy is more complex than is often presented.[17] Many whites genuinely view the Confederate flag as simply an expression of southern pride and are not particularly aware of its racial connotations. They may not care much about African-American concerns, but their support for the flag stems

[17] Sanford Levinson, *Written in Stone: Public Monuments in Changing Societies* (Durham: Duke University Press, 1998).

from regional pride and a desire to remember their "heritage" rather than racial conflict. On the other hand, some whites want to maintain the Confederate flag as an expression of white political power. As a southern college freshman explained privately to me when articulating his support for the Confederate flag: "It's our way of telling them who's on top." Regrettably, he did not need to clarify the references to "our" and "them" to make his racism understood. Many blacks unsurprisingly find the Confederate flag a deeply offensive symbol of a dead regime dedicated to their continued enslavement. White racist backing of the flag only confirms black suspicions that the flag is really a symbol of their second-tier status in southern society.

The Confederate flag is not inherently a Democratic or Republican issue. It is easy to find white Democrats who support maintaining the prominence of Confederate emblems. Some Republicans wish to retire the Confederate flag in order to promote racial reconciliation or out of fear that racial conflict will discourage business investment. The effort to keep the flag nevertheless remains far more closely identified with the Republicans than the Democrats. The most strident advocates of keeping the Confederate flag are usually Republicans. Former South Carolina Republican Governor David Beasley promised to keep the flag flying during his 1994 election campaign. When he broke this promise, he attracted little new support but was vilified by many Republicans. House Republicans quickly organized a majority dedicated to quashing any effort to remove the flag promoted by Beasley. The South Carolina Republican Party even held a referendum, which passed, on keeping the flag flying over the statehouse as part of their effort to attract new voters to their primary.

In contrast, black Democrats have usually led the fight to remove the flag from public symbols and buildings. Many white Democrats tend to stay silent on the issue because there is little political gain in promoting the issue. They fear shattering their biracial support base by taking a strong stand either for or against the Confederate flag. The most prominent non-black advocates, however, for removing the flag from public prominence have been white Democrats. Joe Riley and Bob Coble, the white Democratic mayors of Charleston and Columbia, respectively, repeatedly called for the flag's removal from the dome of the South Carolina statehouse. Former Georgia Governor (now U.S. Senator) Zell Miller unsuccessfully fought to change the design of the Georgia flag during his first term as governor. Roy Barnes, Miller's successor as governor, persuaded the legislature to reduce the size of the Confederate flag on the Georgia flag from about two-thirds of the flag to the size of a small badge. However, white backlash against the change probably played a significant role in the loss of support for Barnes among white rural Georgians that cost him reelection. Governor Sonny Perdue, the first Republican governor of Georgia since Reconstruction, campaigned for a referendum on the flag question during his successful 2002 bid to unseat Barnes.[18] Since the election, Perdue has greatly angered supporters of the Confederate battle flag through his success in convincing the legislature to adopt yet another design that completely eliminates the battle flag from the Georgia flag.

The stances of many prominent members of the GOP on the flag and similar racial issues make it highly difficult for even conservative African Americans to consider joining or voting for the Republicans. The net effect is to make blacks feel completely unwelcome within the GOP. Many within the party seem more interested in appealing to white flag supporters than to attending to black sensibilities. During the flag controversies of the late 1990s, for example, the College Republicans at the University of South Carolina sold t-shirts with the Confederate flag prominently displayed to raise money for their organization. It is hard to imagine any black student buying one of these shirts or even going up to the table to seek information about the party. Interestingly, race appears to play a much smaller role in nonpartisan student elections. African Americans have been elected student body president at the University of South Carolina even though whites compose more than 80 percent of the student body.

More recent efforts by Republicans to diffuse racial issues and gain black support have backfired and only increased the ardor of most blacks for the Democrats. Following the lead of his brother, Texas Governor George W. Bush, Jeb Bush moderated his stances on racial issues and made concerted efforts to reach out to the black community during his successful second run for governor of Florida in 1998. Racial divisions within the Democratic Party aided his goal of gaining additional black support while in office. White Democrats in the Florida House deposed African-American Willie Logan as their leader, making black Democrats unusually receptive to approaches from Republicans.

Once in office, Bush attempted to diffuse the controversy over affirmative action in university admissions through a proposal to guarantee the admission of the top tier of students from all Florida high schools to the

---

[18] Jonathan Tilove, "Lott affair may signal watershed; Politics of race in America may never be same," New Orleans *Times-Picayune*, December 18, 2002, 6; Tom Baxter, "Election 2002: Playing field illuminated in debates," *Atlanta Journal-Constitution*, October 28, 2002, A4; Michael A. Fletcher, "A Ban on Hate, or Heritage? Ga. School Divided over Confederate-Themed Shirts," *Washington Post*, December 30, 2002, A1; Linda Feldmann, "Lott fallout: GOP forced to tiptoe on race," *Christian Science Monitor*, December 20, 2002, 1; David Von Drehle and David Balz, "For GOP, South's Past Rises in Tangle of Pride, Shame," *Washington Post*, December 15, 2002, A26.

University of Florida. At least on the surface, this proposal appeared to have the potential to please both opponents and supporters of affirmative action. By admitting only top students, the proposal pleased opponents of affirmative action who believe that only academic achievement, not race, should play a role in university admissions. At the same time, the continuing segregation of Florida high schools assured that many blacks would probably gain admission regardless of the quality of their schools or test scores. Opponents of affirmative action would likely find it difficult to object to the admission of top black students, even if they had lower test scores, because they had performed the best in their schools. It was hardly their fault if their local schools were of poor quality or they could not afford to move to localities with a stronger school system.

Regardless of its merits, the proposal alienated Florida blacks who resented the abolition of affirmative action and feared that it would result in their exclusion from public higher education in Florida. Instead of rallying blacks to the Republicans, it promoted a backlash against the Republicans in the African-American community and a higher black turnout for the Democrats. The backlash against was so severe that it nearly prevented the elevation of George W. Bush to the presidency. Between 1996 and 2000, black turnout in Florida rose sharply. Without this increased black mobilization, Al Gore would never have come close to carrying Florida and within a hair of winning the presidency in 2000.

RACIAL THREAT, ELECTORAL OUTCOMES, AND WHITE VOTING BEHAVIOR

Racial issues understandably remain a key concern of the South's black minority. As a visible minority with a long history of battling oppression, African Americans are unsurprisingly sensitive to partisan stances on racial issues. The long-term identification of the Republicans with racial conservatism and the Democrats with racial liberalism has resulted in nearly unanimous black support for the Democrats. The impact of strong black support for the Democrats on partisan change in the South is nevertheless cloudy. One might expect the Democrats to show greater strength as the black population rises due to solid Democratic preferences among African Americans. Democrats require a smaller share of the white vote to win a majority in areas where blacks form a larger share of the population. Obtaining less of something is usually easier than obtaining more of something, so one could reasonably suspect that it is easier for the Democrats to win a small share of white votes than a large one. The natural result would be that the presence of black voters should make it easier for the Democrats to win southern elections.

However, southern politics may not operate in such a straightforward manner. If white support for the Democrats is affected by racial context, then the relationship between the share of blacks in the population and the probability of a Democratic victory may change. Whites who live near blacks might be more tolerant and racially liberal than whites who live in less racially diverse communities. As a result, whites in communities with many black residents may support the Democrats at higher rates than whites who live elsewhere. In this case, there would be synergy between the presence of blacks and the response of whites to this presence that gives the Democrats an extra boost as the black population rises. As the African-American share of the electorate increases, Democrats would gain not just from the receipt of more black votes but from greater support in the white community as well.

However, racial context may influence white voting behavior in the opposite manner. One of the oldest hypotheses in southern politics is the threat hypothesis, also known as the white backlash, Black Belt, and group threat hypothesis.[19] Although fiercely debated by scholars, the idea itself is very simple. As the share of African Americans in the population rises, the black threat to white political dominance becomes more acute. Whites accordingly provide higher levels of support to racially conservative candidates as the percentage of African Americans in the population increases. Instead of expanding black political power, African-American population gains ironically promote a white backlash that reduces black political influence. Democratic success may actually decline as the share of the black population rises due to this white backlash against the presence of blacks. Most scholars accept that the racial threat hypothesis helps explain white voting behavior in the pre–Voting Rights Act South, but it may not still explain it today.

Even if the racial threat hypothesis continues to correctly describe white voting behavior, one would expect a decline in the severity of white backlash because the percentage of African Americans has declined. Unlike during Reconstruction, whites now form a clear majority in all states in the South. Blacks composed more than 46 percent of the population of six southern states in 1870 and might have formed a voting majority if ex-Confederates had been vigorously excluded from the franchise. Today,

---

[19] Hubert M. Blalock Jr., *Toward a Theory of Minority Group Relations* (New York: Wiley, 1967); Key 1949, 513–17; Michael W. Giles, "Percent Black and Racial Hostility: An Old Assumption Reexamined," *Social Science Quarterly* 58 (1977): 412–17; Giles and Buckner 1993; Giles and Hertz 1994; Herring 1990; Voss 1996; James W. Glaser, "Back to the Black Belt: Racial Environment and White Racial Attitudes in the South," *Journal of Politics* 56 (1994): 21–41; Matthews and Prothro 1963; Fossett and Kiecolt 1989; Huckfeldt and Kohfeld 1989.

blacks form under 37 percent of the total population in every southern state and an even smaller share of the voting-age population.

Educational disparities often serve to further reduce the percentage of blacks who actually cast ballots at the polls because citizens with more education participate at a higher rate in elections.[20] Moreover, felon disfranchisement has permanently disfranchised a sizable share of the black male population in many southern states. Over 30 percent of black men in Alabama and Florida currently cannot vote due to felony convictions; 24 percent of black males in Virginia and 20 percent in Texas are similarly barred from the ballot box.[21] Of course, felon disfranchisement may be viewed as simply an extension of white hostility to black political participation. Historically, whites allotted particularly severe penalties to crimes perceived as common among blacks.[22] Today, drug-related crimes committed more commonly by blacks carry higher penalties, including a record as a felon, than equivalent drug-related crimes common among whites. In any case, the result is the same. Whites have little real reason to fear that black political power can ultimately undermine their control of state politics.

Even if one examines units below the state level, one would expect a great decline in white backlash. Counties are clearly the most important political unit below the state level. Each county has its own local government and elects a number of officials. Historically, the county courthouse was the center of southern political life. Prior to the Supreme Court's decisions in *Baker v. Carr* and *Reynolds v. Sims*, each county usually elected at least one member of the state legislature, and many counties had their own state senator.

The number of counties with black majorities has declined markedly as the percentage of blacks in each state has fallen. Lightly populated rural counties that contain only a small percentage of each state's white population account for most of the remaining southern counties with black majorities. An increasing share of the white population of the South lives in heavily white suburban counties and neighborhoods, like Cobb and Gwinnett Counties outside Atlanta. In 1990, less than 2 percent of the non-Hispanic white population lived in counties with a black majority. Only 11 percent of the non-Hispanic white population inhabited a county

---

[20] Raymond E. Wolfinger and Steven J. Rosenstone, *Who Votes?* (New Haven: Yale University Press, 1980), 17–26. But Nagler argues that there is little relation between education and turnout; see Jonathan Nagler, "The Effect of Registration Laws and Education on U.S. Voter Turnout," *American Political Science Review* 85 (December 1991): 1394–1405.

[21] Sentencing Project/Human Rights Watch Report, "Losing the Vote: The Impact of Felony Disenfranchisement Laws in the United States," http://www.hrw.org/reports98/vote.

[22] Franklin 1961, 48–49; Du Bois 1935, 171–78.

where blacks composed more than one-third of the population. The overwhelming majority of non-Hispanic southern whites live in counties where they outnumber blacks by more than 2 to 1 in total population and blacks pose no threat to white political control.

Segregation is even stronger at the neighborhood level with many counties and towns divided into black and white sections. For example, blacks form the vast majority of the population in the southern portion of De Kalb County, Georgia, but few African Americans live in the northern portion. The potential for backlash still exists in counties and neighborhoods where blacks form a sizable minority. However, white reaction should not be nearly as energetic as in the past if only because the black population is so much smaller and blacks rarely form a voting majority.

Scholars continue to debate whether there is a relationship between racial context and white support for conservative policies.[23] There are several means to test the current validity of the racial threat hypothesis using election results. First, if racial threat remains a powerful force, the probability of a Democrat winning election should decline as the black population rises until blacks form a voting majority. Contrary to the past, Democrats are now clearly identified as the party of racial liberalism, or at least racial moderation, throughout the South. If the racial threat hypothesis retains significant strength, the probability of a Democratic victory should fall as the percentage of blacks rises due to white backlash against the presence of the black minority manifesting itself in the form of heightened white support for the racially conservative Republicans. Even if African Americans lend the Democratic candidates unified support, a powerful white backlash should outweigh or at least offset the effect of increases in the black share of the electorate on the outcome of the election.

Second, even after controlling for their political party, elected officials should support more conservative policies as the black share of the population rises. Until African Americans compose a majority of the electorate and thus can elect officials without white support, officials will need to cater to the majority-white population. Greater black populations should promote greater perceptions of racial threat by whites. If white backlash is a major factor in elections, elected officials should become more conservative as the black population rises as part of their effort to maintain sufficient white support to ward off a racially conservative challenger at the polls. On the contrary, if white backlash is weak or nonexis-

[23] Giles 1977; Lublin 1997; Giles and Buckner 1993; Giles and Hertz 1994; Herring 1990; Voss 1996; Glaser 1994; Matthews and Prothro 1963; Nadeau and Stanley 1993; Fossett and Kiecolt 1989; Huckfeldt and Kohfeld 1989.

tent, officials should become more liberal as the black population grows. Any backlash by whites against the presence of blacks would not be enough to override black votes and the resulting political influence.

Finally, several states have held referenda on issues with clear racial implications. According to the racial threat hypothesis, whites living in precincts and counties with sizable black populations should oppose the liberal position on these questions to a greater extent. The advantage of studying these referenda is that they are explicitly racial. Nonracial issues do not cloud the racial implications of the outcome as they may regular elections for public officials. Of course, if nonracial issues obscure the racial meaning of electoral contests, this suggests that race does not dominate southern elections.

Recent studies utilizing a variety of these methods to test the threat hypothesis uncover little evidence of white backlash. Congressional and state legislative districts always become more likely to elect Democrats as the black population increases. In many southern states, it has actually become easier for Democrats to win elections in state legislative districts with a sizable black minority even as Democratic success in heavily white districts has declined.[24] Studies of congressional elections reveal that both southern Republicans and southern Democrats consistently become more liberal as the share of blacks in their districts rises. Republicans usually win election from heavily white districts because of the linkage between the percentage of blacks in a district and the election of Democrats, so this finding has greater implications for Democrats than Republicans.[25]

If officials consistently become more liberal as the black population rises, the effect of white backlash cannot be very strong. It would nevertheless be mistaken to claim that *no* backlash against blacks occurs on the basis of these findings. Some whites may still respond to the perceived racial threat posed by a sizable black minority by supporting racially conservative candidates at a higher rate than whites in areas with few blacks. The conservative impact of the white backlash, however, is smaller than the liberal impact of the presence of black voters. As a result, the probability of a Democrat winning election or a representative taking liberal positions on issues rises with the share of the black population despite white backlash. This nonetheless indicates a far lower level of backlash than existed prior to the passage of the Voting Rights Act of

---

[24] Cameron, Epstein, and O'Halloran 1996, 794–812; Lisa Handley, Bernard Grofman, and Wayne Arden, "Electing Minority-Preferred Candidates to Legislative Office: The Relationship between Minority Percentages in Districts and the Election of Minority-Preferred Candidates" in Grofman 1998, 28–38; Lublin and Voss 2000, 797–801.

[25] Lublin 1997, 82–91, 99–101.

1965. Any amount of backlash that does not prevent greater responsiveness to African Americans as their share of the population increases would not be terribly significant and much would be weaker than claimed by proponents of the racial threat hypothesis.[26]

Analyses conducted by D. Stephen Voss of a South Carolina referendum on a highly-charged racial issue provide no indication of white backlash at the county or precinct level. In South Carolina, white voters who lived in heavily black counties did not oppose repeal of the provision of the South Carolina Constitution that banned miscegenation (interracial sex) at a higher rate than whites in other counties. State laws banning interracial sex or marriage have been inoperable for several decades because they violate various provisions of the U.S. Constitution as interpreted by the Supreme Court. The referendum still gave voters a chance to express their opinion on an explicitly racial issue in the privacy of a voting booth.[27]

The next section explores the relationship between racial context and electoral outcomes and assesses the validity of the racial threat hypothesis using aggregate election results from local, state legislative, and presidential elections. It further makes use of survey data on the party identification of white southerners linked with aggregate data on the racial composition of each respondent's home county to examine the white backlash theory. The use of both survey and aggregate data in this and the following chapter help assure greater accuracy of the results presented here. The use of two different types of data helps assure that the results are not simply artifacts of the data collection or methods used to analyze them. Moreover, while there is excellent survey data on partisanship and voting behavior in federal elections, only aggregate election data is available for local and state legislative contests. The use of both survey and aggregate data makes the certainty of the conclusions greater because one can test them across several different levels of southern government.

National Elections

Figures 5.2, 5.3, and 5.4, respectively, show southern counties divided into quartiles (four groups) based on the percentage of the total vote

---

[26] Lublin and Voss 2000, 797–801.

[27] D. Stephen Voss and Penny Miller, "Following a False Trail: The Hunt for White Backlash in Kentucky's 1996 Desegregation Vote," *State Politics and Policy Quarterly* 1 (March 2001): 63–82. Voss estimated the percentage of whites voting for and against repeal of these constitutional provisions utilizing EI, Gary King's ecological inference program. Gary King, *A Solution to the Ecological Inference Problem: Reconstructing Individual Behavior from Aggregate Data* (Princeton: Princeton University Press, 1997).

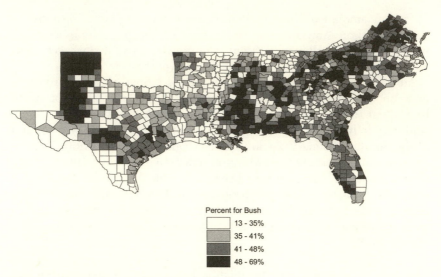

Percent for Bush

☐ 13 - 35%

▨ 35 - 41%

▨ 41 - 48%

■ 48 - 69%

Figure 5.2. Total support for Bush in 1992.
Note: One-quarter of all counties, including the equivalent units of parishes in Louisiana and independent cities in Virginia, are shaded the same. Counties in the highest quartile of support for Bush, as measured by the percentage of votes for Bush, are shaded black with lower quartiles in progressively lighter shades. The break points between quartiles are different for figures 5.2, 5.3, and 5.4.
Source: Richard M. Scammon, *America Votes 20: A Handbook of Contemporary Election Statistics* (Congressional Quarterly, 1992).

received by the Republican presidential candidate in 1992, 1996, and 2000. The darker the level of shading, the greater the support for the Republican candidate. Comparing any of these maps with figure 5.5, which shows the African-American share of the county population, reveals that Republicans consistently fared poorly in counties where blacks form a high share of the population. In 2000, no majority-black counties were in the top quartile and only one county was in the second quartile of counties supporting Republican George W. Bush. The vast majority of black-majority counties were in the bottom quartile.

Somewhat ironically, the rural Black Belt areas of the South, such as the Mississippi Delta, are white in figures 5.2, 5.3, and 5.4 because of their low levels of support for Republican candidates. Counties dominated by central cities with large black populations, like Fulton (Atlanta) in Georgia, Orleans (New Orleans) in Louisiana, Durham (Durham) in North Carolina, and Richland (Columbia) in South Carolina, also gave relatively low levels of support to Republican candidates. These urban counties consistently accounted for a much larger share of the Democratic vote than their area on the map indicates.

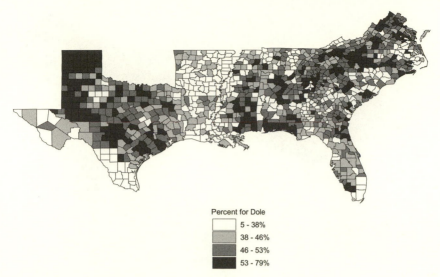

Figure 5.3. Total support for Dole in 1996.
Note: One-quarter of all counties, including the equivalent units of parishes in Louisiana and independent cities in Virginia, are shaded the same. Counties in the highest quartile of support for Dole, as measured by the percentage of votes for Dole, are shaded black with lower quartiles in progressively lighter shades. The break points between quartiles are different for figures 5.2, 5.3, and 5.4.
Source: Richard M. Scammon and Alice V. McGillivray, *America Votes 21: A Handbook of Contemporary Election Statistics* (Congressional Quarterly, 1995).

The share of blacks in a county does not come close to predicting the outcomes of presidential elections perfectly. Although blacks around the South voted overwhelmingly for Democratic presidential candidates in 1992, 1996, and 2000, white support for the Democrats varied considerably. If the share of blacks in the electorate correlated perfectly with opposition to Republican candidates, the correlation between the percent black in the voting-age population and the percent for the Republican candidate would be close to −1. If there was no relationship between the share of blacks and presidential election outcomes, the correlation would equal 0. The correlation between the percent voting-age black and support for incumbent President George Bush in 1992 was only −.23. The similar correlations with the share of votes for Bob Dole in 1996 and George W. Bush in 2000 were −.42 and −.53, respectively.[28]

[28] The growing strength of the correlation between the racial composition of the population and vote for the Republican presidential candidate reflects that total support for the GOP candidate grew over time. Since blacks consistently voted Democratic, this increased

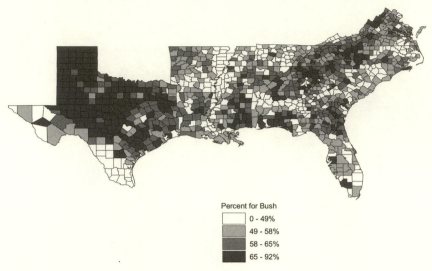

Percent for Bush
☐ 0 - 49%
▨ 49 - 58%
▦ 58 - 65%
■ 65 - 92%

Figure 5.4. Total support for Bush in 2000.
Note: One-quarter of all counties, including the equivalent units of parishes in Louisiana and independent cities in Virginia, are shaded the same. Counties in the highest quartile of support for Bush, as measured by the percentage of votes for Bush, are shaded black with lower quartiles in progressively lighter shades. The break points between quartiles are different for figures 5.2, 5.3, and 5.4.
Source: Richard M. Scammon, Alice V. McGillivray, and Rhodes Cook, *America Votes 22: A Handbook of Contemporary Election Statistics* (Congressional Quarterly, 1998).

Due to solid opposition to the Republicans among blacks but highly variable levels of support among whites, the racial context places a ceiling on Republican support rather than predicting electoral outcomes perfectly. As the black share of the population rises, the maximum possible proportion of the vote received by the GOP declines. Examining presidential election results from 1992, 1996, and 2000 reveals that the Republican share of the vote almost never exceeds the non-black share of the voting-age population. In all three elections, Republicans received a higher share of the vote than the non-black proportion of the voting-age population in 1 percent or fewer of counties.[29]

A high white population does not guarantee Republican success, though it at least makes it possible because Republicans fare so poorly

---

Republican support occurred almost exclusively among whites. The rise in white support for the GOP thus strengthened the relationship between race and Republican support.
[29] The number of counties where the Republican share of the vote exceeded the non-black share of the voting-age population was 3 in 1992, 1 in 1996, and 12 in 2000.

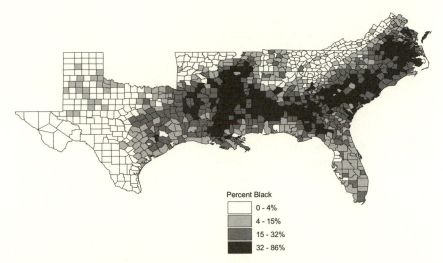

Figure 5.5. Percent black in 1990.
Note: One-quarter of all counties, including the equivalent units of parishes in Louisiana and independent cities in Virginia, are shaded the same. Counties in the highest quartile of African-American population, as measured by the percentage of people identifying themselves as Black or Negro in the 1990 U.S. Census, are shaded black. Lower quartiles are shaded in progressively lighter shades.
Source: U.S. Bureau of the Census, *United States Census 1990*.

among blacks. Racial context does not perfectly explain electoral outcomes, but it constrains severely the ability of Republicans to increase their share of the vote. Since African Americans provide few votes for Republican candidates at any level of government, this constraint exists in nonpresidential elections as well.

County and State Legislative Elections

The strong relationship between the share of blacks and Republican success extends down to the bottom rung on the office ladder. Republicans find it tough to win any office in areas where blacks form more than one-third of the population. Across the South, GOP candidates have a less than one-in-five chance of winning election to the state legislature from a 30 percent black district. The probability of a Republican victory drops to a mere 6 percent in districts where African Americans compose 40 percent of the population (see table 4.2 and the discussion in chapter 4 for more details). Similarly, no member of the GOP served as sheriff, the county office most likely to be held by Republicans, in a majority-black county during the 1990s in any of the five southern states for which data is available. The GOP won only 8 percent of all elections for sheriff in counties between one-third and one-half black as compared to 20 percent of all elections for sheriff held in counties less than one-third black.

More systematic analyses of aggregate data confirm this relationship between the presence of black voters and continued Democratic success. Figures 5.6 and 5.7 show the relationship between the percentage of African Americans in a county or state legislative district, respectively, and the probability that a Republican wins the election for county or state legislative office after controlling for other factors, such as the relative wealth of the constituency's population or its location in a rural or urban area. A few words of caution: these models show the chance of a GOP victory assuming that the Republicans have managed to find a candidate, so they overestimate the overall probability of success by the GOP. Relatedly, these figures only reveal part of the impact of race as they do not show the influence of the racial composition of a constituency on the probability of the GOP successfully recruiting a candidate. (The complete statistical models appear in tables 1 and 2 of the appendix; the figures assume that the election occurred in the late 1990s.)[30]

Both figures make clear the strong relationship between race and GOP success. The likelihood that the Republicans win a contest for either county office or the state legislature declines substantially as the share of African Americans in the population increases. Controlling for other factors, figure 5.6 shows that Republicans triumph in just over one-half (51 percent) of contests for county office in urban counties with no black residents. In rural counties with no African-American residents, the GOP carries somewhat fewer, 42 percent, of elections for county office. However, the GOP wins only around one-quarter of elections held in 40 percent black urban (27 percent) and rural (22 percent) counties.

The impact of race on state legislative contests is even greater. In state legislative districts with no African-American residents, Republicans win close to three-quarters (74 percent) of elections held in suburban districts, and nearly two-thirds (64 percent) of contests held in rural or urban districts, after controlling for other factors.[31] The chance of Re-

[30] Biprobit models were constructed for local and state legislative elections. The presence of a Republican candidate (1 = GOP candidate, 0 = no GOP candidate) served as the first dependent variable. Republican victory (1 = GOP winner, 0 = non–GOP winner) served as the second dependent variable. See tables 1 and 2 of the appendix for the models.

[31] For state legislative elections, districts were coded as urban, suburban, and rural following the coding of William Lilley III, Lawrence J. DeFranco, and Mark F. Bernstein, *The Almanac of State Legislatures: Changing Patterns, 1990–1997* (Washington, DC: Congressional Quarterly, 1998). For county elections, urban and rural were defined as in the 1990 U.S. Census: "The Census Bureau defines 'urban' for the 1990 census as comprising all territory, population, and housing units in urbanized areas and in places of 2,500 or more

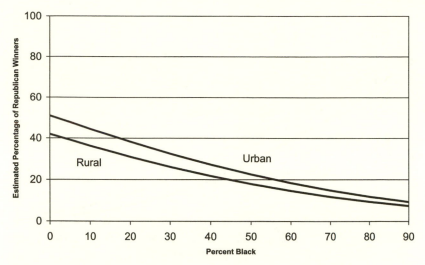

Figure 5.6. Republican victories in county elections by percent black.
Note: The estimated percentage of county races with Republican winners is based on the bivariate probit model for open county elections presented in table 1 of the appendix. This graph presents the estimated change of a Republican victory assuming that the Republicans have managed to recruit a candidate. See figure 5.8 for a graph showing the relationship between percent black and Republican candidate recruitment in county races. In producing these estimates, Median Household Income ($1000) = 22.69, Proportion Hispanic = 0, and Proportion Native to the South = .89. The year was assumed to be 1999; all dummy variables were set equal to 0. Proportion Rural was set equal to 1 for rural county projections and 0 for urban county projections.

publican success plunges as the black share of the population rises with Republicans estimated to win only slightly more than one-third (37 percent) of elections held in 30 percent black suburban districts. Republicans emerge victorious in just over one-quarter (27 percent) of contests in 30 percent black rural or urban districts. It is important to remember that these graphs actually understate differences in the total probability of Republican success between districts with low and high African-American populations because the results presented here assume the presence

persons outside urbanized areas. More specifically, 'urban' consists of territory, persons, and housing units in: 1. Places of 2,500 or more persons incorporated as cities, villages, boroughs (except in Alaska and New York), and towns (except in the six New England States, New York, and Wisconsin), but excluding the rural portions of 'extended cities.' 2. Census designated places of 2,500 or more persons. 3. Other territory, incorporated or unincorporated, included in urbanized areas. Territory, population, and housing units not classified as urban constitute 'rural.'" See the U.S. Census web site at http://www.census.gov/population/censusdata/urdef.txt for more information.

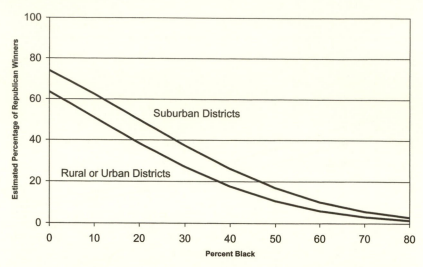

Figure 5.7. Republican victories in state legislative elections by percent black.
Note: The estimated percentage of state legislative races with Republican winners is based on the bivariate probit model for open state legislative elections presented in table 2 of the appendix. This graph presents the estimated change of a Republican victory assuming that the Republicans have managed to recruit a candidate. See figure 5.9 for a graph showing the relationship between income and Republican candidate recruitment in state legislative races. In producing these estimates, Median Household Income ($1000) = 34.22, the median value for open seats in the data set, and Proportion Hispanic = 0. Suburban District was set equal to 1 for suburban district projections and 0 for rural and urban district projections.

of a Republican candidate. As the analysis below will show, race is also closely related to whether or not the GOP manages to recruit a candidate in both local and state legislative races.

The overwhelming support by African Americans for Democrats renders the strong, consistent relationship between the presence of African Americans and Democratic victories unsurprising. However, these results are perhaps more striking in light of history. Counties with a majority of black residents, but few black voters, trenchantly resisted racial equality during the Civil Rights Movement and gave overwhelming support to Barry Goldwater because of his opposition to the Civil Rights Act of 1964. The power of black ballots now assures that these same counties provide crucial support to the Democrats, the party of racial liberalism. As in national elections, black votes overpower any white backlash against the presence of blacks. Even if whites living in areas with sizable black populations feel politically threatened, they do not turn to the Republicans at nearly sufficient rates to overcome African-American support for Democratic county or state legislative candidates. Racial context nevertheless plays a crucial role in shaping the geography of Republican gains, though in a different fashion than predicted by the proponents of the white backlash theory. While the presence of black voters constrains Republican growth, their absence accelerates it.

County and State Legislative Elites

Strong black support for the Democrats further tempers movement toward the Republicans indirectly by influencing the behavior of potential white candidates. As chapter 3 explains, high-quality candidates act highly strategically in their pursuit of public office. In majority-white areas where blacks form a sizable minority, white elites often choose to remain Democrats because Democratic nominees in these areas can win election by combining solid black support with a minority of the white vote.

Republican candidates have to unite the white vote in order to win, often a difficult task in a region where white voters are far more politically divided than black voters. As the black share of the electorate grows, Republican candidates must gain ever higher shares of the white vote to achieve victory. Even if most whites vote Republican, achieving sufficient levels of white support to offset solid black support for the Democrats is often an insurmountable task in a region where many whites continue to vote Democratic. Potential white candidates who seek office as Republicans in areas with sizable black minorities give their opponent the opportunity to form a biracial coalition between most blacks and a minority of whites. Only in areas with relatively few black residents or with high racial polarization is pursuing the Republican nomination preferable for the strategic candidate who places holding office above party. Canny white candidates pay close attention to racial context; Republicans find it much easier to recruit in heavily white areas as a result.

African-American opposition is not a minor problem that southern Republicans can easily ignore. In many counties of the South, the racial context renders running as a Democrat the savvy choice. As figures 5.2 and 5.3 indicate, Republican presidential nominees George Bush in 1992 and Bob Dole in 1996 failed to carry a majority of southern counties. Even George W. Bush, the strongest Republican nominee in over a decade, failed to win a majority in over one-quarter of southern counties (see figure 5.4).[32] And remember that Republican presidential candidates

---

[32] Chapter 4 contains more discussion of the relationship between racial composition of districts and elite party choice as well as the negative impact of racial redistricting on the Democrats.

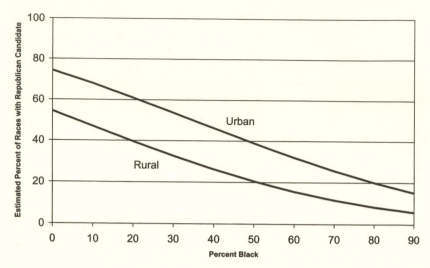

Figure 5.8. Percentage of county races with Republican candidates by percent black.

Note: The estimated percentage of county races with Republican candidates is based on the bivariate probit model for open county elections held between 1979 and 1999 presented in the full model in table 1 of the appendix. In producing these estimates, Proportion for Republican Presidential Candidate = .46; Median Household Income ($1000) = 22.69; Proportion Hispanic = .02; and Proportion Native to the South = .89. The year was assumed to be 1999; all dummy variables were set equal to 0. Proportion Rural was set equal to 1 for rural county projections and 0 for urban county projections.

fare better than other GOP candidates in the region. The presence of African Americans as a strong pro-Democratic minority in many parts of the South is one reason that the Republicans have difficulty recruiting candidates in many parts of the region.

Analysis of elections for local and state legislative office supports the conclusion that potential candidates are highly responsive to the racial makeup of their constituency. The probability of the GOP fielding a candidate declines as the percentage of African Americans in the county or state legislative district rises. According to figure 5.8, after controlling for other factors, the probability of an urban county having a Republican candidate for county office falls from 74 to 46 percent as a district shifts from 0 to 40 percent black. Republicans are generally less likely to attract candidates in rural counties. (See the discussion of social issues and partisan change in the next chapter for an explanation of why the Republicans fare better in urban areas.) However, the ability of the GOP to recruit candidates remains sensitive to the racial composition of the county with

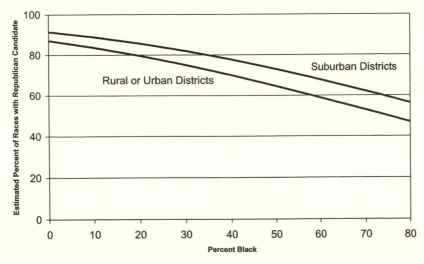

Figure 5.9. Percent state legislative races with Republican candidates by percent black.

Note: The estimated percentage of state legislative races with Republican candidates is based on the bivariate probit model for open state legislative elections presented in table 2 of the appendix. In producing these estimates, Median Household Income ($1000) = 34.22, the median value for open seats in the data set, and Proportion Hispanic = 0. Suburban District was set equal to 1 for suburban district projections and 0 for rural and urban district projections.

the probability of a Republican candidate declining from 54 to 26 percent as the black share of a county's population rises from 0 to 40 percent.

Republicans similarly run candidates at a lower rate in state legislative contests as blacks make up a greater share of the district's population (see figure 5.9), though the relationship is less strong than for county elections. The presence of black voters inhibits candidacies by Republicans even for seats not already held by Democratic incumbents. In open seats, the GOP runs candidates in approximately 90 percent of contests held in districts with no black residents. The probability of a Republican seeking election to an open state House seat declines to 77 percent in suburban districts and 70 percent in rural and urban districts as the black share of the district's population increases to 40 percent.

The presence of black voters inhibits Republican growth both directly and indirectly. Strong black support for Democratic candidates directly undermines Republican electoral chances by making it harder for GOP candidates to win a majority of votes. Elite awareness that it is usually difficult to win elections as a Republican in districts that are not heavily white further indirectly undermines Republican opportunities. Republicans find it much harder to attract candidates, let alone win elections, as the white population declines.

Submerged White Backlash?

Although any white backlash against the presence of blacks is not strong enough to overcome the impact of black ballots on election outcomes, whites may still vote more Republican as the black share of the population rises. The effect of white backlash may be submerged due to the greater weight of black votes. This negative reaction by whites to the presence of blacks is not as substantively significant as if it were usually strong enough to defeat black-preferred candidates or force officials to become more conservative, at least on racial issues. However, it may still influence white voting behavior. This section examines the link between racial context and white voting behavior in an effort to determine more exactly the extent of backlash voting among whites. Looking exclusively at white voting behavior, rather than total votes or electoral outcomes, should make it easier to identify any backlash against the presence of blacks among whites.

Figures 5.10, 5.11, and 5.12 parallel figures 5.2, 5.3, and 5.4 except that they show the estimated share of the *white* vote received by Republican presidential candidates in 1992, 1996, and 2000, instead of the actual percentage of the total vote. Since the identity of voters is secret, it is impossible to identify how white voters cast their ballots simply by examining election returns. However, it is possible to estimate the voting behavior of whites through statistical analysis of election results matched with information on the racial composition of the electorate.[33] The removal of minority voters changes the map of southern politics dramatically. Leaving aside Texas for a moment, it appears that Deep South whites tend to support Republican candidates at a higher rate than the Peripheral South whites. Most counties in Alabama, Mississippi, and South Carolina fall into the top two quartiles of support for Republicans among whites in all three elections. In contrast, Democrats maintained greater strength among whites in Arkansas, Florida, and Tennessee.

The home states of the candidates explain some of the regional varia-

[33] Estimates were derived utilizing Gary King, *EI: A Program for Ecological Inference* (found at *http://gking.harvard.edu/stats.shtml*) with estimates for each state calculated separately. The level of data aggregation and knowledge about turnout by race varied from state to state. The data sets for Louisiana and South Carolina contained turnout by race at the precinct level. The data sets for Florida, Georgia, and North Carolina contained registration by race at the precinct level. The data sets for Mississippi, Tennessee, Texas, and Virginia contained U.S. Census racial data at the precinct level. The datasets for Alabama and Arkansas contained U.S. Census racial data at the county level.

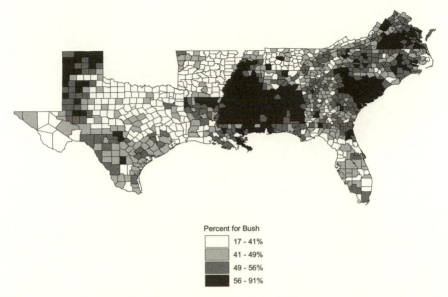

Percent for Bush

☐ 17 - 41%
▨ 41 - 49%
▨ 49 - 56%
■ 56 - 91%

Figure 5.10. Estimated white support for Bush in 1992.
Note: One-quarter of all counties, including the equivalent units of parishes in Louisiana and independent cities in Virginia, are shaded the same. Counties in the highest quartile of estimated white support for Bush, as measured by the estimated percentage of white votes for Bush, are shaded black with lower quartiles in progressively lighter shades. The break points between quartiles are different for figures 5.10, 5.11, 5.12, and 5.13.
Source: Estimates were derived utilizing Gary King, *EI: A Program for Ecological Inference* with estimates for each state calculated separately. The level of data aggregation and knowledge about turnout by race varied from state to state. The data sets for Louisiana and South Carolina contained turnout by race at the precinct level. The data sets for Florida, Georgia, and North Carolina contained registration by race at the precinct level. The data sets for Mississippi, Tennessee, Texas, and Virginia contained U.S. Census racial data at the precinct level. The data sets for Alabama and Arkansas contained U.S. Census racial data at the county level.

tions in support. Bill Clinton served as governor of Arkansas prior to winning the presidency in 1992 and 1996. His running mate, Al Gore, served as senator from Tennessee before becoming vice president in 1992 and running for president in 2000. Gore was widely pilloried for losing his and Bill Clinton's home states in 2000. Nevertheless, Tennessee whites provided very low levels of support for his opponent compared to whites in other parts of the South. Only 14 percent of Tennessee counties were not in the bottom quartile of support for Bush, an even lower

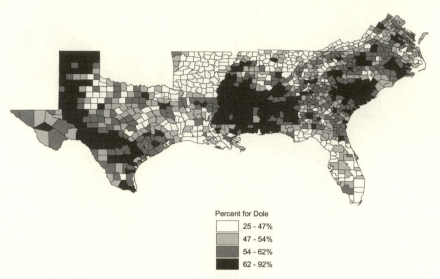

Percent for Dole

25 - 47%
47 - 54%
54 - 62%
62 - 92%

Figure 5.11. Estimated white support for Dole in 1996.
Note: One-quarter of all counties, including the equivalent units of parishes in Louisiana and independent cities in Virginia, are shaded the same. Counties in the highest quartile of estimated white support for Dole, as measured by the estimated percentage of white votes for Dole, are shaded black with lower quartiles in progressively lighter shades. The break points between quartiles are different for figures 5.10, 5.11, 5.12, and 5.13.
Source: Estimates were derived utilizing Gary King, *EI: A Program for Ecological Inference* with estimates for each state calculated separately. The level of data aggregation and knowledge about turnout by race varied from state to state. The data sets for Louisiana and South Carolina contained turnout by race at the precinct level. The data sets for Florida, Georgia, and North Carolina contained registration by race at the precinct level. The data sets for Mississippi, Tennessee, Texas, and Virginia contained U.S. Census racial data at the precinct level. The data sets for Alabama and Arkansas contained U.S. Census racial data at the county level.

share than in 1992 and 1996. Whites in Arkansas similarly voted for Gore in greater numbers than almost anywhere else in the South.

The greater success of Republicans in the Deep South might be explained by backlash against the presence of black voters. Alabama, Mississippi, and South Carolina are each at least 30 percent black. African Americans form a smaller share of the population of states in the Peripheral South. Examining white voting behavior within states also provides some evidence for a backlash against blacks. In 1992, Bush performed especially strongly among whites in the Southside section of Virginia, the most culturally southern section of the Old Dominion and the portion of

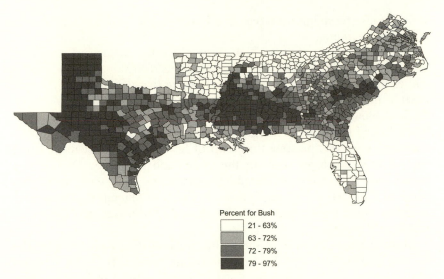

Percent for Bush
21 - 63%
63 - 72%
72 - 79%
79 - 97%

Figure 5.12. Estimated white support for Bush in 2000.
Note: One-quarter of all counties, including the equivalent units of parishes in Louisiana and independent cities in Virginia, are shaded the same. Counties in the highest quartile of estimated white support for Bush, as measured by the estimated percentage of white votes for Bush, are shaded black with lower quartiles in progressively lighter shades. The break points between quartiles are different for figures 5.10, 5.11, 5.12, and 5.13.
Source: Estimates were derived utilizing Gary King, *EI: A Program for Ecological Inference* with estimates for each state calculated separately. The level of data aggregation and knowledge about turnout by race varied from state to state. The data sets for Louisiana and South Carolina contained turnout by race at the precinct level. The data sets for Florida, Georgia, and North Carolina contained registration by race at the precinct level. The data sets for Mississippi, Tennessee, Texas, and Virginia contained U.S. Census racial data at the precinct level. The data sets for Alabama and Arkansas contained U.S. Census racial data at the county level.

the state with the highest share of blacks. Similarly, Republicans did well among whites in eastern North Carolina. The concentration of blacks generally rises as one moves from west to east in North Carolina and this same area provided support crucial to the reelection of North Carolina Senator Jesse Helms. Senator Helms was one of the most racially conservative members of the Senate and widely known for his willingness to play hardball racial politics. Helms ended his 1990 reelection campaign against Harvey Gantt, the first African American to attend Clemson University and the first black mayor of majority-white Charlotte, with the infamous "white hands" commercial. The advertisement showed a pair of white hands crumpling a job rejection letter—a job he did not get due to affirmative action.

Other areas of the South show signs of similar patterns. Republican presidential candidates consistently performed relatively strongly among whites in the counties of southwest Tennessee that contain a higher proportion of blacks than any other area of the state. In 2000, George W. Bush demonstrated greater strength among whites in the traditional Black Belt of rural south Georgia than in whiter north Georgia. In South Carolina, once one passes a thin strip of heavily white settlement along the Atlantic, the black share of the population usually declines as one moves away from the coast. Republican candidates consistently racked up some of their largest margins in South Carolina among whites in rural counties where blacks form a greater share of the population than elsewhere in the state.

More evidence in favor of the white backlash theory comes from the relative decline in support for Republicans in Appalachia. These counties remained pro-Union during the Civil War and retained their Republican sympathies long after the end of the conflict. Traditionally, Appalachia formed the backbone of Republican support in the heavily Democratic pre–Civil Rights Movement South. However, the chance of counties in Appalachia appearing in the top quartile of white support for the Republican presidential candidate declined somewhat over the course of the 1990s. In 2000, whites living in the Appalachian mountain and foothill regions of Virginia, Tennessee, North Carolina, Georgia, and Alabama were less likely to support George W. Bush than whites living in other portions of their states.[34]

However, the relative decline in Appalachia's support for the Republicans may reflect factors other than white backlash. The strong opposition of today's Republicans to most social welfare spending may have alienated some traditional Republicans in Appalachia—a relatively economically depressed region of the nation and the South. Moreover, much historical support for the Democrats outside of Appalachia was based in the desire to maintain the white racial dominance. The rise in support for the Republicans in the non-Appalachian South could well reflect that racial issues no longer top the agenda for many of the region's whites.

Comparing areas of heavy support for States Rights Democrat Strom Thurmond in 1948 and Republican candidates in 1992, 1996, and 2000 provides more telling evidence that racial issues continue to play a role in southern politics (see figure 5.13). Thurmond sought the presidency in order to protest the shift by national Democrats toward support of racial

[34] Lublin and Voss 2000, 797–801, provides evidence that Appalachia also no longer represents the core bastion of white support for the Republicans in state legislative elections.

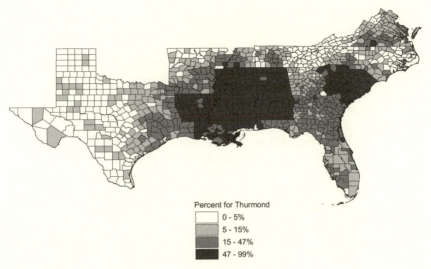

Percent for Thurmond
☐ 0 - 5%
▨ 5 - 15%
▨ 15 - 47%
■ 47 - 99%

Figure 5.13. Support for Strom Thurmond in 1948.
Note: One-quarter of all counties, including the equivalent units of parishes in Louisiana and independent cities in Virginia, are shaded the same. Counties in the highest quartile of estimated white support for Bush, as measured by the estimated percentage of white votes for Bush, are shaded black with lower quartiles in progressively lighter shades. The break points between quartiles are different for figures 5.10, 5.11, 5.12, and 5.13.
Source: Alexander Heard and Doland S. Strong, *Southern Primaries and Elections 1920–1949* (University of Alabama Press, 1950).

liberalism under the leadership of President Truman. Thurmond's goal was to force deference to the South on racial issues by depriving the Democrats of key southern support. As the 1948 election occurred prior to the passage of the Voting Rights Act of 1965, the map of total support for Thurmond largely represents a map of the level of *white* support for Thurmond. Thurmond fared best in the same states where Republicans fare best among whites today. Similar regional patterns also appeared within states in 1948 with Thurmond winning his heaviest support in regions of states with high black populations.

Despite this evidence, one should proceed with caution before giving too much weight to the role of race or accepting the white backlash theory. The probability of a Republican victory consistently declines as the black share of the population rises, so any backlash is not strong enough to counteract heavy black support for the Democrats. Whites obviously cannot outvote blacks in majority-black counties. However, whites do not usually vote sufficiently as a bloc to succeed in swamping the black vote in areas where blacks form a sizable minority. Except in areas of unusually high racial polarization, like the Mississippi Delta, a minority of whites often votes with a solid bloc of blacks to carry the county for the Democrats.

One also has to be careful to avoid confusing the effect of race with other variables. An apparent bivariate relationship between the racial composition of a county or its past support for the racist candidacy of Strom Thurmond and the current voting behavior of its white population may mask other factors that explain why whites in these particular areas tend to vote Republican. Whites may vote Republican because of economic interests or their opposition to the social liberalism of the Democrats. The strong support given by whites throughout much of western Texas, a region with few blacks, even when someone named George Bush was not the nominee suggests that other factors play a role in white voting behavior.

Figure 5.14 shows the relationship between percent black in a county and the probability that a white voter identifies as a Republican after controlling for a variety of issue beliefs (such as views on economic issues and abortion) and demographic characteristics (such as gender and income) of the voter. As a result, unlike the simpler comparison between the percentage black in a county and support for the Republican candidate, the relationship between racial context and white partisanship presented in figure 5.14 is not confounded with white beliefs on a variety of important issues or demographic characteristics. (The full model of white partisanship can be seen in table 4 of the appendix.)[35]

Contrary to the white backlash theory, a rising share of blacks is associated with greater Democratic partisanship as the black population increases. After controlling for other factors, the percentage of Republican identifiers among whites declines mildly from 53 to 48 percent as the share of blacks rises from 0 to 25 percent according to figure 5.14. Increasing the black share of the population to 50 percent further reduces the Republican share of party identifiers to 43 percent. Support for Republican congressional candidates falls even more sharply as the black share of the population increases. However, examining the relationship between racial context and the presidential vote reveals that there is no significant relationship between the percentage of blacks and support for Republican presidential candidates. (The full models of white congressio-

[35] The model of white partisanship was created using the 1980–1998 portion of the 1948–2000 NES cumulative data set. Utilizing the county codes provided in the NES data set, county racial data from the U.S. Census were linked with NES data set. This linkage made it possible to assess the impact of county racial context on white voting behavior even after controlling for a number of individual-level demographic characteristics and issue attitudes.

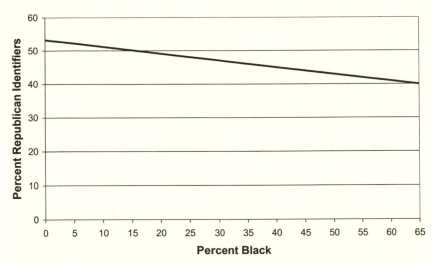

Figure 5.14. White Republicans by percent black in the county.
Note: The relationship between percent black and white party identification presented here is based on the model of white party identification presented in table 4 of the appendix. The figure shows the relationship between the racial composition of a county and white partisanship after controlling for many other factors, including issue positions on racial issues. Removing issue positions on racial issues from the model does not alter the basic relationship between percent black and white party identification.

nal and presidential voting behavior are located in table 4 of the appendix.)[36]

These results confirm previous studies indicating that white backlash generally does not aid the Republican quest to overtake the Democrats.[37] As these findings constitute a pattern rather than a firm rule, white backlash may nevertheless hurt the Democrats in some parts of the South. The overwhelming weight of these findings, however, remains clear. Support for the Democrats and the liberalism of officials consistently rises with the African-American share of the population, suggesting that any white backlash is overcome by black voting power. Looking exclusively at whites provides only weak evidence in support of the white backlash theory.

[36] The coefficient on proportion black in the model of presidential voting behavior is negative but fails to achieve statistical significance (p = .69).
[37] See, for example, Voss 1996; Voss and Miller 2001.

CONCLUSION

Since 1964, Republican conservatism on racial issues has rendered the Republican Party an unacceptable alternative for the vast majority of African Americans. Sporadic attempts by GOP nominees to attract blacks have failed to overcome black hostility. The Republicans remain more racially conservative than the Democrats and most blacks remain opposed to the Republican efforts to advance both their economic agenda and decentralization to the states. Efforts by some Republicans to alter black perceptions of the Republicans as hostile to African Americans fail, at least partly because of the presence of a vocal racially conservative minority committed to the southern strategy and symbols of southern heritage perceived as racist by many African Americans. The Republicans are now viewed by most blacks as the party of Goldwater rather than the party of Lincoln.

African-American opposition to the GOP constrains Republican success. As the black population rises, it becomes increasingly difficult for Republican candidates to attract the larger majority among whites required to outvote black Democratic ballots. If whites felt sufficiently threatened by the power of black votes, Republican candidates might actually have found it easier to achieve the racial polarization needed to win as the black population rises. However, the evidence for the white backlash theory is quite thin. The preponderance of the evidence suggests that whites actually become more likely to vote Democratic as the black population becomes a large instead of a small minority. Republicans fare best in heavily white contexts as a result and find it harder to advance in biracial contexts.

While racial context shapes the geography of Republican opportunity, it is hardly the only factor shaping the contours of Republican success. Whites are highly variable in the level of support they give the Republicans. Even if a majority of whites throughout the region supports the Republicans, the size of the white minority who votes Democratic is very often the difference between success and failure for Democratic candidates.

Through its examination on how issues shape white voting behavior, the next chapter sheds more light on why many southern whites identify and vote as Republicans but others stick with the Democratic Party. Race will continue as a focus as many suspect views on racial issues of being the primary determinant of white voting behavior. Racial conservatism can still work to the advantage of Republicans even if it does not operate primarily by spurring whites living in areas with many African Americans to vote Republican at higher rates. Whites may appreciate Republican support of racially conservative policies regardless of the racial context. However, the next chapter will show that views on economic issues actually played a more substantial role in promoting the current success of the Republicans than racial issues. Highly divisive social issues also cannot be ignored in explaining Republican growth.

CHAPTER SIX

Issues and White Partisanship

THE PREVIOUS CHAPTER explains how the shifting positions of the two major parties on racial issues promoted strong African-American support for the Democrats. Barry Goldwater's transformation of the Republicans into the party of racial conservatism in 1964 rendered the GOP unacceptable to the vast majority of African Americans. In contrast, Lyndon Johnson's embrace of racial liberalism and success in getting Congress to pass first the Civil Rights Act of 1964 and then the Voting Rights Act of 1965 proved very attractive to black voters. As chapter 5 explains, this issue cleavage between the two parties has endured, perhaps especially strongly in the South, and so has strong black support for the Democratic Party.

Strong black support for the Democrats conditions where Republicans both pursue and win public office. As the African-American share of the population rises, Republicans find it increasingly difficult to win elections and fewer of them run. As the black population declines, Republicans find the electoral territory more hospitable. However, not all largely white areas are equally congenial to Republican candidates. Some whites are more likely than others to vote Republican. This chapter explores which issues have shaped white voting behavior and promoted white movement away from the Democrats to the GOP. Examining which issues promote black support for the Republicans is relatively pointless as black support for the Republicans has been so consistently low. Moreover, most agree that African-American support for the Democrats is due primarily, though not exclusively, to differences between the parties on racial issues. As a result, this chapter focuses almost entirely on white voting behavior.

EXPLAINING WHITE PARTISAN CHANGE IN THE SOUTH

Many scholars of partisan change argue that racial issues played the central role in promoting Republican gains at the expense of the Democrats. In particular, observers point to the role of the 1964 presidential election in reshaping southern public opinion.[1] Racial issues were certainly critical to supporting and destroying the institutions that maintained the artifi-

[1] Carmines and Stimson 1989; Black and Black 1992, 2002; Phillips 1969; Sundquist 1993; Whitby and Gilliam 1991.

cial dominance of the Democrats. The racial conflicts of the 1960s ultimately resulted in the arrival of broadly based democratic institutions
and the liberty to participate in them freely in the South. However, the
evidence that race alone explains Republican gains appears thin on the
ground. The examination of racial context in the last chapter provides
little evidence in support of white backlash. This chapter's exploration of
how issues influenced partisan change will show that racial issues began
to influence partisanship only later.

The traditional New Deal divide over economic and class questions
asserted itself much earlier. New Republicans were attracted more by
economic than racial conservatism once the institutional stranglehold of
the Democratic Party over the region's institutions was removed. The
conservatism or moderation of most southern Democrats on racial issues
helped mute the appeal of Republicans on these issues despite the racial
liberalism of Democratic presidential nominees. Only when old-style
southern Democrats retired and new Democrats who depended on black
votes to win election replaced them did the two parties diverge dramatically on race. At this point, racial issues began to assert themselves and
aid the Republicans. At the same time, partisan divisions over social issues, especially abortion, began to appear. These new sources of partisan
cleavage did not result in the demise of economic issues as a major
source of division between the two parties. The relative influence of economic issues on white southern voting behavior and partisanship may
have declined due to the rise of racial and social issues. However, in
absolute terms, economic issues remain a potent source of partisan division. Republicans have increasingly benefited from all three issues due to
white support for conservative positions.

Racial Explanations

Carmines and Stimson articulate the dominant theory of partisan change
in their book, *Issue Evolution*.[2] Although they intend their theory to be a
general one, they developed it in the context of studying the impact of
race on American politics since 1945. According to Carmines and Stimson, elite efforts to garner additional popular support by changing issue
positions can precipitate major partisan change. Party elites, such as
members of Congress and presidential candidates, shift their positions on
an important issue so that the two major parties disagree on the issue.
Party movement may occur intentionally when party leaders stake out
new ground on an issue, as when Republican Barry Goldwater adopted
the mantle of racial conservatism in 1964. Change in party issue stances

[2] Carmines and Stimson 1989.

can also occur somewhat accidentally when election victories or defeats, unrelated to the rising issue, enhance the relative size of one wing of a party over another. Change often occurs gradually, as older members retire or are defeated and are replaced by new members, though it may be punctuated by critical moments of change within a party. For example, the Democratic landslide of 1958 shifted the balance within both parties on racial issues. The replacement of large numbers of northern liberal Republicans by northern liberal Democrats made the Republicans more conservative and the Democrats more liberal on racial issues than in the past.[3]

The impact on the electorate of changes in the issue positions held by party leaders and elected officials is not evenly distributed by age. Carmines and Stimson argue that shifts in the issue positions of the parties primarily alter the voting behavior of new voters. The impact of the issue on election outcomes increases over time as more and more new voters enter the electorate. Partisan change is not caused by the conversion of existing voters already aligned on the old cleavage or the mobilization of nonvoters. Generational replacement, rather than conversion or mobilization, explains the bulk of partisan change according to Carmines and Stimson's theory.[4]

Carmines and Stimson contend that race is the key issue propelling partisan change since the foundation of the New Deal alignment. The establishment of the Democrats as the party of racial liberalism and the Republicans as the party of racial conservatism took decades.[5] However, the 1964 election crystalized the new stands of the party in the mind of the electorate. Democratic President Lyndon Johnson had pushed through Congress the then-radical Civil Rights Act of 1964. His Republican opponent, Barry Goldwater, crusaded against the Act as a violation of state sovereignty. Johnson confirmed the salience of race to the new alignment by successfully pressing Congress to pass the Voting Rights Act of 1965 after his reelection.

Class or Social Issue Explanations

Others dispute that race explains the revitalization of the southern GOP, arguing that divisions over economic issues, the hallmark of the New Deal alignment, continued to shape southern partisanship long after the 1964 election. Alan Abromowitz directly attacks Carmines and Stimson's theory of racial issue evolution. He contends that economic and defense

[3] Ibid., 69–72.
[4] Edward G. Carmines and James A. Stimson, "Issue Evolution, Population Replacement, and Normal Partisan Change," *American Political Science Review* 75 (March 1981): 107–18.
[5] Carmines and Stimson 1989; Weiss 1983; Black and Black 1987, 241–45.

issues played a much greater role in spurring whites to abandon the Democratic Party during the 1980s. Contrary to this hypothesis of racial issue evolution through generational replacement, Abromowitz found that racial attitudes were unrelated to party identification among either younger or older whites even by the end of the 1980s.[6] In a more recent study, Jeffrey Stonecash forcefully argues that differences in economic class and on class issues relate more strongly to voting behavior today than in the 1960s around the nation, but especially in the South.[7] In a similar vein, Nadeau and Stanley argue that high-income native southern whites became more likely to support the Republicans by the 1970s, indicating that the class cleavage characteristic of the New Deal alignment had finally arrived in the South.[8] This finding fits claims that the South became more like the rest of the nation once the monolithic dominance of the Democrats ended.

Unlike Abromowitz or Nadeau and Stanley, Adams does not dispute Carmines and Stimson's theory of issue evolution but argues that a new issue evolution centering on the abortion question played a major role in shaping southern politics in the 1980s and 1990s.[9] Abortion has remained a sharply disputed issue since the Supreme Court's ruling legalizing abortion throughout the nation in *Roe v. Wade*. Over time, Republicans have become more identified with the pro-life position and Democrats with the pro-choice position. Southern Republicans have gained more support as pro-lifers entering the electorate identify with the GOP.

Multiple Factors?

Carmines and Stimson are not alone in highlighting the role of race in southern politics. However, their argument that race explains Republican gains in isolation from other issues stands out as unique. Other scholars argue that multiple factors have played an important role in promoting Republican growth over the past several decades. In particular, some argue that race has interacted with other issues to cause realignment.

In *Politics and Society in the South*, *The Vital South*, and *The Rise of Southern Republicans*, Earl Black and Merle Black explain the critical role of race in gradually eroding the basis of support for Democratic presidential candidates in the region. Indeed, Black and Black argue that Republican manipulation of racial issues was critical to breaking the Democratic lock on the region's electoral votes. Equally important, the Democratic Party has become more closely identified with blacks but less identified with

[6] Abromowitz 1994.
[7] Stonecash 2000.
[8] Nadeau and Stanley 1993.
[9] Adams 1997.

institutions popular among the moderate to conservative white electorate. Black and Black nevertheless also give weight to the role of other factors, such as economic and social issues, in shaping southern politics over the past several decades.[10] Black and Black were probably right to suspect that race played a critical role in shattering Democratic hyperdominance, but it was not the only factor to shape the resulting new political alignment in the South.

One should not contrast their conclusions too much with those of Carmines and Stimson. Even as they acknowledge the role of nonracial factors, ongoing and increasing racial polarization convinces Black and Black that race was probably the most important. They highlight surveys showing that majorities of almost all groups of whites, regardless of economic status or beliefs on social issues, regularly voted Republican in federal elections by the turn of the century. Only secular white women often cast narrow majorities for the Democrats. In contrast, huge majorities of African Americans usually vote Democratic. At the same time, Black and Black concede that economic and social issues play a huge role in determining the size of the Republican majority.[11]

In *Chain Reaction*, Tom Edsall and Mary Edsall argue that President Reagan's victory in not only winning the presidency but rolling back social welfare programs was due to his success in convincing whites to identify these programs with an unpopular black community. However, rather than focus solely on race, Edsall and Edsall explain that it was the *interaction* of race with economic and social issues that made the racial appeals so effective. The disagreement of many white voters with the Democratic Party on social issues, such as abortion and gay rights, made these voters more open to Republican appeals. Similarly, Reagan's appeals were more effective among middle-class whites than poor whites, who stood to lose more from the elimination of social welfare programs and the Reagan administration's effort to shift the tax burden from progressive income taxes to regressive Social Security taxes.[12] On the other hand, Huckfeldt and Kohfeld suggest that low-income whites who are open to racial appeals were more likely to support the Republicans.[13]

Perhaps the crucial insight is that different factors can motivate different individual voters. While race likely drove some white voters into the arms of the Republicans, other separate issues may have spurred other whites to take leave of the Democrats. Racial and class explanations of

[10] Black and Black 1987, 232–56; Black and Black 1992, 141–75, 219–34; Black and Black 2002.

[11] Black and Black 2002, 242–326.

[12] Edsall and Edsall 1992.

[13] Giles and Hertz 1994; Huckfeldt and Kohfeld 1989, 49–53.

partisan change are not mutually exclusive. Both can press sections of the electorate to alter their voting behavior or party identification. Economic issues may explain why most white southerners who vote Democratic earn relatively low incomes. At the same time, racial or social issues may explain why many low-income voters cast votes for the GOP. For other voters, different issues are mutually reinforcing.

The Overemphasis on Racial Issues

Contrary to much past scholarship, racial issues do not appear to do a satisfactory job of explaining partisan change in the South. This failure is all the more shocking as one might expect theories that focus on the role of race in American politics to fit more closely in the South than other regions of the country. Racial issues are felt more intensely in a region with sizable African-American populations. The Civil Rights Act of 1964 and the Voting Rights Act of 1965 both targeted the South. Most of the Voting Rights Act applied to the entire nation, but certain "covered jurisdictions" were forced to preclear any changes in voting practices with either the D.C. District Court or the U.S. Attorney General. Not accidentally, only the most white supremacist areas of the Deep South were designated as "covered jurisdictions" under the 1965 version of the Act.[14]

Nevertheless, examining the actual issue positions of white southerners suggests that racial theories of partisan change do not fit white southerners very well. Figure 6.1 shows the difference between the position of the average white Democrat and average white Republican on questions asked by the National Election Study (NES) that tap public opinion on racial, economic, and social issues. On race, the NES asked individuals to rate themselves on a seven-point scale as to whether they believed the government should make "every effort to improve the social and economic position of blacks" with seven being the most conservative position (strong opposition to government aid because blacks should make it on their own) and one being the most liberal position (strong support for government aid to blacks). Similarly, individuals were asked to rate themselves on a similar seven-point scale as to whether they believed it is the responsibility of the individual or the federal government to make sure that "every person has a job and a good standard of living." Respondents were asked to gauge their support for opposition to abortion on a similar scale.[15]

Rather than shrinking over time as the racial issue became more and

[14] Renewals of the Voting Rights Act in 1970, 1975, and 1982 expanded the definition of a "covered jurisdiction" to include many non-southern areas of the United States.

[15] In recent years, the actual question asked on race by the NES was: "Some people feel that the government in Washington should make every effort to improve the social and

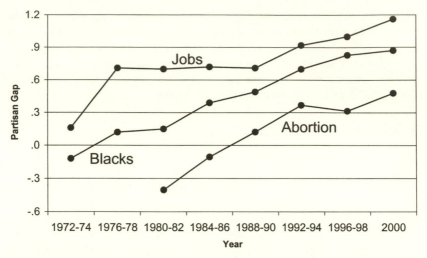

Figure 6.1. Interparty Polarization among Southern whites on three issues.
Note: The scale on the vertical axis shows the gap in views on each issue between the average white southern Democrat and the average white southern Republican. Economic and racial attitudes were measured by 7-point scales and abortion attitudes were measured by a 4-point scale with high numbers indicating greater support for the conservative position, so a positive gap indicates more conservative views are held by the average Republican compared to the average Democrat. See footnote 15 for the wording of the survey questions.
Source: NES Cumulative Data File, 1948–98: CF0303, CF0809, CF0830, CF0838. The responses to the abortion question in the NES were multiplied by −1 to give it the same direction as the questions on economic and racial issues.

---

economic position of blacks. Suppose these people are at one end of a scale, at point 1. Others feel that the government should not make any special effort to help blacks because they should help themselves. Suppose these people are at the other end, at point 7. And, of course, some other people have opinions somewhere in between, at points 2, 3, 4, 5 or 6." The actual version of the economic question was: "Some people feel that the government in Washington should see to it that every person has a job and a good standard of living. Suppose these people are at one end of a scale, at point 1. Others think the government should just let each person get ahead on his/their own. Suppose these people are at the other end, at point 7. And, of course, some other people have opinions somewhere in between, at points 2, 3, 4, 5 or 6." The abortion question has been constructed somewhat differently: "There has been some discussion about abortion during recent years. Which one of the opinions on this page best agrees with your view? You can just tell me the number of the opinion you choose. 1. Abortion should never be permitted. 2. Abortion should be permitted only if the life and health of the woman is in danger. 3. Abortion should be permitted if, due to personal reasons, the woman would have difficulty in caring for the child. 4. Abortion should never be forbidden, since one should not require a woman to have a child she doesn't want. 9. Don't Know; other." For purposes of comparing opinions on abortion to opinions on racial and economic issues, the direction of the abortion more important, partisan differences on economic issues have actually grown larger over the same period among white southerners. Even if partisan differences over racial issues have lately increased, it does not appear to be at the expense of economic issues. Among white southerners, partisan differences over economic questions consistently remained larger than partisan differences over racial issues during the last three decades. Party polarization over racial issues may have grown but so did polarization over economic issues.

---

scale has been reversed and the magnitude rescaled. The collapsed version of the traditional 7-point party identification scale used by the NES was used to determine partisanship; pure independents were excluded but leaning independents and weak partisans were collapsed with strong partisans. See NES Cumulative Data File Codebook 1948–98, variables CF0303, CF0830, CF0837, and CF9121.

Tracking the standard deviation within each party in addition to the average helps assess the extent to which many members of the party depart from the average position of party members. Presumably, the more central an issue is to party choice, the smaller the standard deviation as fewer members will depart from the central tendency. The following table shows changes in the size of the standard deviation over time for the three issues examined in the text:

	Economic		Racial		Social	
	D	R	D	R	D	R
1972–74	1.82	2.02	1.76	1.86		
1976–78	1.57	1.88	1.67	1.87		
1980–82	1.72	1.79	1.36	1.70	1.99	2.11
1984–86	1.75	1.87	1.55	1.65	2.10	2.11
1988–90	1.79	1.97	1.54	1.93	2.12	2.12
1992–94	1.68	1.79	1.52	1.74	2.10	2.16
1996–98	1.59	1.78	1.42	1.75	2.07	2.18

The parties appear somewhat more homogenous on racial issues than economic issues with the standard deviation declining for members of both parties over time since 1972–74. Over the entire period covered in the table, the standard deviation on economic issues declined around 12% for both parties. On racial issues, the standard deviation for the Democrats declined by 19%, but the standard deviation for the Republicans shrank by only 6%. The greater change among Democrats likely reflects the departure of racial conservatives for the Republicans, rendering the Democrats a more homogenous party but leaving the Republicans essentially unchanged. On social issues, the standard deviation for members of both parties has increased slightly. However, the increase was under 5% between 1980–82 and 1996–98. The size of the standard deviation on social issues was larger than the standard deviation on either economic or racial issues, suggesting that social issues may perhaps be somewhat less central than economic and racial issues to party identification. Neither the amount nor the direction of change in the standard deviation was usually consistent, so the meaning of the size and the changes in the standard deviations should be interpreted with caution.

Moreover, past scholarly reports of the decline of economic issues likely exaggerated the level of the decline or depended on any decline to continue beyond the period for which data was available. For example, Carmines and Stimson examine interparty polarization over economic issues among all partisans around the nation from 1930 through 1980 utilizing a very similar question, also with a seven-point scale, from the General Social Survey. In their national sample, partisan differences over the role of government in the economy gradually declined between 1930 and 1950 from a height of 1.4 but remained mostly stable after 1950 at around 1.1—a decline of around 20 percent.[16] Considering the severity of economic conditions in 1930 as compared to the period since 1950, the decline in party polarization on economic issues appears relatively small. And even the figure presented by Carmines and Stimson shows a slight rise in polarization on economic issues by 1980.

One should also note that Carmines and Stimson were attempting to explain partisan change in the entire nation. However, examining the nation as a whole likely helped obscure the importance of structural changes in southern politics as well as the striking rise of economic issues in the South. During the period of Democratic hyperdominance, there could hardly have been much in the way of party polarization over issues because there really was not an alternative party to the Democrats. Democratization of the South changed the political system, which in turn allowed party polarization over issues to occur. As the stranglehold of the old white supremacist Democratic elite was gradually broken and more blacks and whites went to the polls, the unnatural dominance of the Democrats began to erode. Even if the Democrats retained a commanding position, the Republicans now existed as a potential alternative. Party polarization on some issues was bound to increase as the new party—and the Republicans were effectively a new party in the South—attracted individuals disaffected from the Democrats.

This pattern was unlikely to occur outside the South, especially on economic issues that had long divided the two parties. Looking at data from the entire United States likely hid this trend, especially since southern Republicans only formed a small minority of all Republicans during

---

[16] Carmines and Stimson 1989, 146–48. The question used by Carmines and Stimson is from a Center for Political Studies survey: "The question is the familiar seven-point forced choice between 'The Government should see to it that every person has a job and a good standard of living' and 'Each person should get ahead on his own.'" The graph presented by Carmines and Stimson (1989) on page 148 (figure 6.3) gives the appearance of much greater decay in party polarization over economic issues than has actually occurred because the horizontal axis of the graph is set at 1.0 rather than at 0. On the other hand, the text and the graph on page 147 (figure 6.2), which presents the same data in a slightly different format, shows more clearly that the decay has been smaller and more subtle.

the earlier part of this period. Division over economic issues was merely a perpetuation of the status quo outside of the South rather than a new pattern reflecting fundamental structural change and the democratization of politics in the South.

As the primary existing national cleavage between the two parties centered on economic, not racial, issues, it was natural that economic conservatives joined the Republicans. Indeed, the collapse of the old order effectively freed economic conservatives to vote for the GOP. In the past, Democrats argued that voting Republican might lead to federal intervention to end white supremacy. Since this had so obviously occurred, it was no longer a convincing reason to vote Democratic.

Though racial issues were highly salient in the wake of these dramatic changes, racial issues were not a convincing reason for most southerners to vote Republican in nonpresidential elections or shift their party identification. Most southern Democrats adopted conservative or moderate stands on racial issues in the immediate aftermath of all of these radical changes to the structure of southern politics.[17] Only later as old-style politicians retired and blacks began voting in larger numbers and black support became critical in Democratic primaries did white southern Democrats become more liberal on racial issues. As a result, for most southerners, racial issues only became a reason to abandon the Democrats once the gap between the two parties became more acute in the 1980s.

The data presented in figure 6.1 confirm that racial issues emerged more slowly than economic issues. Southern white Democrats did not become substantially more liberal than their Republican counterparts on racial issues until the 1980s. At first glance, the rise of racial issues does not appear to have been at the expense of economic issues. The partisan gap over economic issues among southern whites has grown further since Carmines and Stimson published their major work on issue evolution in 1989.

Ultimately, *Issue Evolution* is probably not so much wrong as incomplete in its explanation of partisan change in the South. Though it underestimates the continuing power of economic issues, Carmines and Stimson's analysis of the growing importance of racial issues appears roughly on target. The rise of racial issues occurred more slowly than expected in the South due to the conservatism of Democratic officials on these issues, suggesting that more attention needs to be paid to regional differences in elites and institutions. However, the conservatism of southern Democrats slowly eroded and polarization over racial issues steadily increased as indicated by the *Issue Evolution* model of partisan change. This gradual rise

[17] Black and Black 2002, 148–73.

in the salience of racial issues may reflect that only new voters viewed racial issues as critical. As Carmines and Stimson argue, the importance of race rose gradually as new voters entered the electorate and old voters, who formed their partisanship prior to the partisan divide on racial issues, passed from the scene and no longer formed such a large portion of the southern white electorate.

Finally, as Adams has argued, partisan differences on abortion also rose dramatically during the 1990s in a manner consistent with the *Issue Evolution* model.[18] Amazingly, among southern whites, the average Democrat was actually *less* likely than the average Republican to support a woman's right to have an abortion in 1980 (see figure 6.1). President Reagan's outspoken pro-life position appears to have caused a strong shift in the relationship between partisanship and abortion. By the end of his second term in 1988, the partisan gap on the abortion issue had almost vanished. During the 1990s, the average Democrat took a more liberal position on the abortion issue.

Abortion may serve as a proxy for a number of moral issues on which the parties disagree. Besides abortion, national Democrats usually take more liberal positions on controversial cultural issues like gay rights and school prayer. These sorts of social issues may be unusually amenable to shaping party identification because of their very nature as moral issues. The conservative position on almost all of these issues has a firm basis in deeply held religious beliefs. Many—perhaps most—opponents of abortion do not merely believe that abortion is wrong but that it is murder. Similarly, cultural conservatives view homosexual behavior as sinful and keeping prayer out of school as an attack on religion and an attempt to promote secular beliefs. While the liberal position on these issues is not often rooted in religion, it is grounded in core beliefs surrounding the critical importance of tolerance and individual freedom.

Social issues are arguably not as amenable to easy compromise as economic ones. One can split the difference on the size of a tax cut or an increase in spending on social programs. People who believe that abortion is murder or that a woman must absolutely have control over her own body are unlikely to agree on a compromise. Indeed, taking a centrist position on social issues may merely serve to alienate both sides of the divide. Neither the Christian Coalition nor the National Organization for Women is likely to give more than tepid support to a candidate who believes in protecting a women's right to have an abortion but in constraining it greatly by limiting it to the very early part of pregnancy and requiring parental notification. Politicians who pick a side are at least guaranteed a team of supporters.

[18] Adams 1997.

Assessing the Relative Importance of Racial, Economic, and Social Issues

Figure 6.1 shows that southern white partisans increasingly disagree on economic, racial, and social questions. However, it does not prove that any of these issues relates to partisanship after controlling for the impact of other issues. It additionally does not demonstrate that party elites disagreed over these issues. If party leaders do not disagree over these questions, it makes little sense for voters to choose their party or cast votes on the basis of them.

The remainder of this chapter is devoted to assessing the relative importance of the three issues on southern white partisanship and voting behavior. The roll-call voting records of members of the U.S. House will be utilized to show that party elites increasingly disagree on each of the three issues. As in the last chapter, both aggregate data from local and state legislative elections and survey data on partisanship and federal elections will be used to assess the influence of racial, economic, and social issues on partisanship and voting behavior. Since the relationship of racial context to partisanship and voting behavior is so thoroughly examined in chapter 5, this chapter will not repeat the aggregate analysis of racial context. Aggregate data analysis indicates that economic class continues to shape both the decision of elites to seek election as Republicans and whether GOP candidates win office. Close study of local and state legislative results further indicates that social issues divided urban partisans earlier than rural ones but that social issues now influence both rural and urban elections. Analysis of survey data confirms suspicions that economic issues promoted Republican growth among white southerners in the immediate aftermath of the Civil Rights Movement. More recently, racial and social issues have joined economic questions in shaping southern white voting behavior. The rise of these new issues, however, has not reduced the importance of economic issues.

Racial Issues and Democratic Officials

Evidence suggests that Democrats rely increasingly on their African-American base and are careful not to offend it through support of racial conservatism. As Glaser points out, white Democrats tend not to shout about their support for racial liberalism in their campaigns for fear of alienating key white swing voters. They tend to quietly support racial policies favored by blacks while in office, though they may brag of it to all-black audiences.[19] Increased Democratic responsiveness to black vot-

[19] Glaser 1996, 43–79.

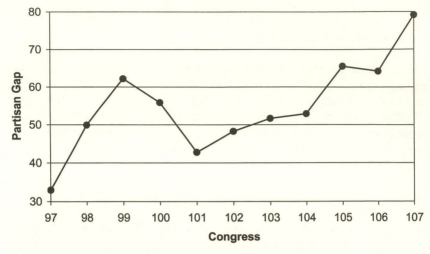

Figure 6.2. Partisan gap in LCCR scores.
Note: The partisan gap is the difference between the rating given by the Leadership Conference on Civil Rights (LCCR) to the average Democrat and the average Republican. Every Congress is numbered sequentially with a new Congress elected every two years. The 97th Congress was elected in 1980; the 102nd Congress was elected in 1990; the 107th Congress was elected in 2000.
Source: Leadership Conference on Civil Rights.

ers has expanded the gap between Democratic and Republican members of the House on racial issues. Figure 6.2 shows the difference between the average score awarded Democratic and Republican members of Congress by the Leadership Conference on Civil Rights (LCCR), an interest group that promotes racially liberal policies supported by blacks. The scores track the percentage of time that representatives voted in favor of policies supported by the LCCR and can range from 0 to 100.

The gap in LCCR scores rose from a relatively small 33 for the 97th Congress, elected in 1980, to 62 in the 99th Congress, elected in 1984. However, the party gap on race issues as measured by LCCR scores declined to 43 in the 101st Congress, elected in 1988. Over the next decade, the party gap on LCCR scores steadily increased with the gap rising to 66 in the 105th Congress, elected in 1996. Party differences over racial issues temporarily reached a plateau as the party gap on LCCR scores was roughly the same at 64 in the 106th Congress. However, the party gap shot up to a new high of 79 in the 107th Congress. Unlike prior to the Civil Rights Movement, southern Democrats now support racially liberal policies far more often than southern Republicans. And the gap between the southern wings of the two major parties has steady grown since the election of the 101st Congress in 1988.

Several factors account for this change. Racially liberal Republicans, like Arkansas Governor Winthrop Rockefeller and Virginia Governor Linwood Holton, were driven out of the party as it became more identified with the racial policies of Barry Goldwater and Ronald Reagan. Additionally, old-line white supremacist Democrats who energetically worked to block civil rights legislation have gradually retired or been defeated for reelection. Younger white Democrats do not carry the segregationist baggage of their predecessors and openly court black voters. In other cases, they shifted their positions to accommodate the new reality of black participation in both Democratic primaries and general elections. Regardless of whether the shift results from a change of heart on racial issues by white candidates or political necessity, the result has been a Democratic Party that demonstrates greater responsiveness to the core concerns of African-American voters.[20]

Pressure from their more liberal northern colleagues and changes in the rules of the House account for some of the shift in southern Democratic voting behavior on the House floor. Traditionally, seniority governed which members ascended to the powerful post of committee chair. Southern Democrats historically chaired a disproportionate number of congressional committees regardless of their ideology due to their long seniority.[21] The Democratic Caucus in the U.S. House is now dominated by northern liberals and increasingly unwilling to tolerate southern conservative members who support conservative legislation too often. Democrats decided to let their members vote on the retention of committee chairs as part of reforms to House rules designed to make it easier to pass liberal legislation and to give junior members a greater say in running the House.[22] Southerners who voted out of line with the wishes of the Caucus suddenly faced the prospect of losing the power they had accrued over the course of decades of service in the House. Accordingly, they quietly pursued a more moderate rather than conservative course.

The long careers of Mississippi Representatives Sonny Montgomery and Jamie Whitten illustrate this sort of evolution. Representative Sonny Montgomery served from 1967 through 1996 and rose through seniority to become chair of the Veterans Affairs Committee. Montgomery was arguably the House Democrat most beloved by Republicans during his tenure and rarely faced opposition for reelection. Through 1984, Mont-

[20] Lublin 1997, 68–71, 81; Whitby and Gilliam 1991. The political science literature is not unified on the question of the relationship between seniority and racialism among southern white Democrats. All agree, however, that southern Democrats as a group have become more liberal on racial issues over time.

[21] Lublin 1997, 62.

[22] Black and Black 2002, 176–81; Berard 2001; David W. Rohde, *Parties and Leaders in the Postreform House* (Chicago: University of Chicago Press, 1991), 17–25, 71–77.

gomery had never voted with his party more than one-third of the time on key votes in which a majority of Democrats voted on the opposite side of a majority of Republicans. Republicans liked Montgomery so much that he nearly lost his committee chair due to unhappiness among House Democrats. In order to keep his powerful position, Montgomery hewed a less conservative course. Starting in 1985, he consistently voted with his party more often than not. However, this tepid level of support provoked a challenge to his continuance as committee chair by a more liberal, northern Democrat. In 1992, the Democratic Caucus voted by only 127–123 to allow Montgomery to retain his position. The vote seems to have spurred Montgomery to rediscover his attachment to the Democrats. During the first two years of the Clinton administration, he supported the Democratic position over 70 percent of the time. Interestingly, during his last term when Republicans controlled the House and he no longer had to fear retribution from his party, Montgomery once again voted with the Republicans more often than not.[23]

Representative Jamie Whitten's career in the House spanned an amazing forty-eight years, from 1947 through 1994. From 1961 through 1976, Whitten regularly voted with House Republicans against a majority of his own party more than twice as often as he supported the Democrats. In 1979, Whitten became chair of the powerful House Appropriations Committee, probably the most powerful committee in the House, but only after facing down a challenge from within the Caucus by a vote of 157–88. Whitten started voting more and more with his own party in 1977 and voted with the Democrats over three-quarters of the time after 1983. Whitten's shift was likely prompted by a need to protect himself at home and in Washington. In Mississippi, Whitten increasingly needed black support to secure reelection when he faced a serious Republican challenger. In Washington, he needed to protect himself against another challenge to his committee chair from within the Democratic Caucus.[24]

The election of committee chairs is yet another example of a relatively obscure institutional rule that helped propel partisan change. By forcing committee chairs to conform to the wishes of the Democratic Caucus, the election of committee chairs spurred greater divergence between Democratic and Republican elected officials on racial issues. Chapter 4 explains how various institutions related to the electoral process but external to government operations, like racial redistricting and the primary,

---

[23] Barone and Ujifusa 1993, 719–21; J. Michael Sharp, *Directory of Congressional Voting Scores and Interest Group Ratings*, 3rd ed. (Washington, DC: Congressional Quarterly 2000), 1022.

[24] Black and Black 2002, 177–79; Sharp 2000, 1514–16; Rohde 1991, 71–72, 75–76; Michael Barone and Grant Ujifusa, *The Almanac of American Politics 1986* (Washington, DC: National Journal, 1985), 738–40.

aided the GOP. In contrast, the election of committee chairs is an internal process that shapes the actions of elected officials. By influencing the behavior of elected officials, these sorts of internal rules that shape the actions of officials during the actual process of governing can promote partisan change even if they do not directly shape electoral outcomes in the manner of external rules related to elections.

Class, Economic Issues, and Partisan Change

Since Franklin Roosevelt's New Deal, economic issues have divided Democrats and Republicans. Democrats believe that government has a major role to play in assuring the social welfare of all Americans and the prosperity of the economy. Republicans have fought the intrusion of government, especially the federal government, into these areas. Scholars have fiercely debated whether this cleavage over economic issues remains vital to American politics so many years after the Great Depression.[25]

Figure 6.1 reveals that differences between the average Democrat and average Republican over the role of government in promoting jobs and social welfare has grown substantially among white southerners over the last several decades. The takeover of the Republican Party by staunch economic conservatives under the leadership of Barry Goldwater and Ronald Reagan may have revitalized the debate over economic issues and assured their continued salience to American political debates. In the 1964 election, Goldwater clashed with incumbent President Johnson on economic as well as racial issues. Goldwater personally opposed segregation but voted against the Civil Rights Act of 1964 because he believed it went beyond the constitutional powers of the federal government. In contrast, Goldwater's ardent campaign for reducing the role of the federal government in addressing economic and social welfare problems was motivated by strong personal belief as well as his conservative ideology. Goldwater's opposition to federal programs to aid the needy clashed sharply with Johnson's advocacy of his beloved Great Society in which the power of the federal government would be harnessed to help the poor. Johnson's initiatives followed in the Democratic tradition formed under Roosevelt during the New Deal of enacting new federal programs to fight economic problems. Needless to say, Johnson's vision of an active government ready to address the economic plight of impoverished Americans did not jibe with Goldwater's vision of a small government in which individuals took the initiative to solve their own problems.

Goldwater lost the 1964 election but his ideas did not die. Former

[25] Carmines and Stimson 1989; Abromowitz 1994; Black and Black 1987; Nadeau and Stanley 1993.

California Governor Ronald Reagan campaigned on a similarly conservative agenda and, with the help of a deep economic recession and the ongoing Iranian hostage crisis, won the presidency in 1980. Reagan opposed the expansion of government programs and government spending much more strongly than his predecessors both on the stump and in office. During the first two years of his presidency, many social welfare programs treasured by Democrats, like the Comprehensive Employment and Training Act, were eliminated or severely cut back. The tax code also underwent great changes with taxes on the affluent declining but regressive Social Security taxes increasing the tax burden on taxpayers of more modest means.[26]

Despite criticisms from the right that the first President George Bush was insufficiently committed to either economic or social conservatism, a more liberal vision of Republicanism did not emerge after Reagan left office. The party became even more conservative under the leadership of fiery southern Republicans committed to reducing taxes and the role of government. Despite support for racial conservatism, this conservative economic agenda was the central unifying goal of the Republican congressional majority elected in 1994. After Georgian Newt Gingrich became the first Republican Speaker of the House in forty years, the Republicans promptly reformed welfare in a manner that requires recipients receive assistance for only a limited period. George W. Bush campaigned for a major tax cut and persuaded Congress to pass a major income tax cut in 2001. All Americans who pay income taxes received some tax reduction, though the amount of money returned to the taxpayer rose with income. On the other hand, Americans who work and pay Social Security taxes but do not earn enough to pay income taxes received no benefit from the Bush tax cut as Social Security taxes were not cut along with income taxes. Further tax cuts passed by Congress with bipartisan support and signed by President Bush in the wake of the September 11, 2001, attack on the World Trade Center and the Pentagon provided rebates on payroll taxes similar to the earlier rebates on income taxes.

Reflecting the heightened salience of economic issues, the divide between congressional Democrats and congressional Republicans elected from the region increased according to the AFL-CIO's Committee on Political Education (COPE) scores (see figure 6.3). COPE scores range from 0 to 100 and indicate the percentage of the time that a representative voted pro-labor on selected important roll-call votes. Members of Congress with low COPE scores are very pro-business in contrast to representatives with high scores, who are very pro-labor. The gap be-

[26] Edsall and Edsall 1992, 160–62, 233–35.

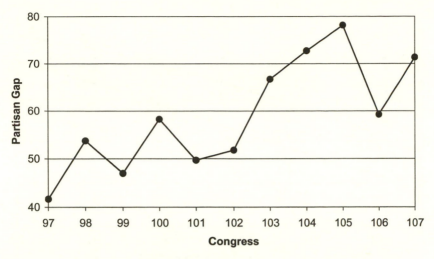

Figure 6.3. Partisan gap in COPE ratings.
Note: The partisan gap is the difference between the rating given by the AFL-CIO's Committee on Political Education (COPE) to the average Democrat and the average Republican. Every Congress is numbered sequentially with a new Congress elected every two years. The 97th Congress was elected in 1980; the 102nd Congress was elected in 1990; the 107th Congress was elected in 2000. Source: AFL-CIO's Committee on Political Education.

tween the scores received by the average southern House Democrat and southern House Republican rose from 42 in the 97th Congress, elected in 1980, to 78 in the 105th Congress, elected in 1996. The gap dropped to 59 in the 106rd Congress, elected in 1998, but rose back up to 71 in the 107th Congress, elected in 2000.

One might reasonably expect a relationship between income and support for Republican policies. Poorer Americans are more likely to benefit from programs backed by Democrats and to support their continuation. Less affluent Americans may oppose tax cuts that undercut the financing of social welfare programs but benefit them only marginally. On the other hand, the chances of benefiting from the tax cuts passed under Republican leadership rise with income. Wealthy Americans have less need to rely on a social welfare safety net for health care, unemployment insurance, or income.

INCOME AND ELITE BEHAVIOR

Chapter 5 demonstrates that elites remain highly sensitive to racial context. Republicans find it more and more difficult to recruit candidates as the black share of the population rises due to strong African-American support for the Democrats. Strategic elites become less likely to seek

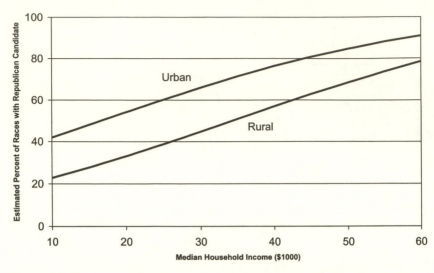

Figure 6.4. Percentage of county races with Republican candidates by income.
Note: The estimated percentage of county races with Republican candidates is based on the bivariate probit model for open county elections held between 1979 and 1999 presented in the full model in table 1 of the appendix. In producing these estimates, Percent Black = .25, Proportion Hispanic = 0, and Proportion Native to the South = .89. The year was assumed to be 1999; all dummy variables were set equal to 0. Proportion Rural was set equal to 1 for rural county projections and 0 for urban county projections.

election under the banner of a party as their chances of victory fall. Economic context similarly conditions the attractiveness of the GOP. Low-income white voters support the Democrats at a higher rate than high-income white voters, so economic context influences where candidates run as Republicans.

The economic status of a constituency's residents is tightly linked to the ability of the Republicans to attract candidates in both county and state legislative elections. Figures 6.4 and 6.5 reveal the variation in probability of a Republican candidate running, after controlling for other factors, along roughly the actual range of inflation-adjusted median household income for southern counties and state legislative districts. In urban counties, the chance of Republicans running a candidate for open county offices rises from 54 to 84 percent as the median income of a county rises from $20,000 to $50,000. The percentage of contests with Republican nominees similarly rises from 33 to 69 percent as income rises the same amount in rural counties.

The relationship between the income of a district's residents to the attraction of candidates to the Republican banner is comparatively muted

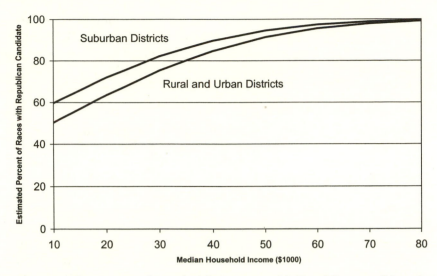

Figure 6.5. Percentage of state legislative races with Republican candidates by income.
Note: The estimated percentage of state legislative races with Republican candidates is based on the bivariate probit model for open state legislative elections presented in table 2 of the appendix. In producing these estimates, Proportion Black = .20, and Proportion Hispanic = 0. Suburban District was set equal to 1 for suburban district projections and 0 for rural and urban district projections.

in state legislative elections but still far from small. Republicans consistently run candidates for more than nine out of ten state House contests in seats with median household incomes of $50,000 or more. The GOP, however, does not run nominees in over one-third of rural or urban districts with median incomes of only $20,000. In similar suburban districts, the GOP does not manage to recruit candidates in over one-quarter of all districts.[27]

The link between income and Republican success does not stem from any relationship of income levels to race. The models used to construct

[27] These results are not an artifact of the relationship between race and income. The two figures assume that blacks compose 20% of the constituency population, slightly less than the median for the South. However, estimating the relationship between income and Republican candidacies for districts with almost no black residents reveals that the GOP does not manage to attract candidates for approximately one-fifth of suburban districts and one-quarter of urban and rural districts with median household incomes of only $20,000. This result indicates that white southerners with relatively low incomes probably prefer Democrats more often than Republicans so potential candidates are more likely to run as Democrats in constituencies with many low-income whites regardless of the racial composition of the district.

both figures 6.4 and 6.5 controlled for the racial composition of the county or state legislative district. The increased success of GOP recruitment efforts as income rises derives from the relationship of income to white voting behavior. (See tables 1 and 2 of the appendix for the complete models of southern county and state legislative elections.)

INCOME AND REPUBLICAN VICTORIES

The median income of a district's inhabitants has an enormously powerful effect on Republican chances of winning elections that is completely separate from the impact of income on GOP chances of attracting a candidate (see figures 6.6 and 6.7).[28] In county elections, the chance of a Democratic victory in open-seat contests nosedives as median income rises. Republicans win only about 25 and 32 percent of elections held in rural and urban counties, respectively, with median incomes of $20,000. In counties with median incomes of $50,000, the GOP captures around two-thirds of all elections held in rural counties and three-quarters of all elections held in urban counties. The pattern is equally strong in state House contests. The model indicates that the GOP should win a desultory 19 percent of races in rural and urban districts and a not much more impressive 27 percent of contests in suburban districts with median incomes of $20,000. However, the Republicans should carry nearly two-thirds of contests in rural and urban districts and three-quarters of elections in suburban districts once median income rises to $50,000.

Money matters. Contrary to arguments suggesting a decline in the influence of economic class on voting behavior, income has a powerful influence on local and state legislative elections in the South. Figures 6.6 and 6.7 actually underestimate the impact of income on politics as they assume that the Republicans successfully managed to recruit a candidate. But, as figures 6.4 and 6.5 show, income is also closely related to GOP candidate recruitment. The analyses of survey data presented at the end of the chapter reinforce these findings. They indicate that views on economic issues continue to play a major role in explaining both partisanship and voting behavior in federal elections.

Social Issues and Partisan Change

Beliefs about racial and economic issues that influence voting behavior have obvious potential relationships to demographic characteristics that

---

[28] In other words, the two figures presented here show the relationship between median household income and the probability of a Republican victory conditional on the presence of a Republican candidate. The relationship between income and the chances of Republicans attracting a candidate is not confounded with the separate relationship between income and the probability of a Republican victory.

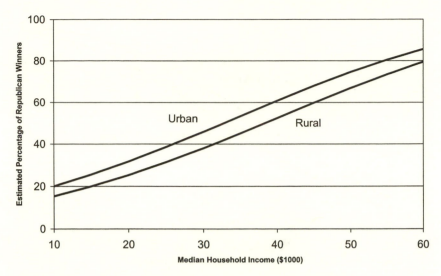

Figure 6.6. Republican victories in county elections by income.
Note: The estimated percentage of county races with Republican winners is based on the bivariate probit model for open county elections presented in table 1 of the appendix. This graph presents the estimated change of a Republican victory assuming that the Republicans have managed to recruit a candidate. See figure 6.4 for a graph showing the relationship between income and Republican candidate recruitment in county races. In producing these estimates, Percent Black = .25, Proportion Hispanic = 0, and Proportion Native to the South = .89. The year was assumed to be 1999; all dummy variables were set equal to 0. Proportion Rural was set equal to 1 for rural county projections and 0 for urban county projections.

vary across southern counties. African Americans understandably feel passionately about racial equality. As chapter 5 shows, counties with many African Americans may support the Democrats, the party of racial liberalism, at a higher rate. Similarly, the previous section demonstrates that affluent white voters identify with the Republicans, the party of lower taxes and smaller government, to a greater extent than voters with more modest incomes who might benefit from government spending.

Figure 6.1 suggests that abortion began to cleave Democrats from Republicans more recently than economic or racial questions. This makes sense as the Supreme Court issued its decision in *Roe v. Wade* forcing the national legalization of abortion in 1974—a full decade after the racially charged 1964 presidential election. Ronald Reagan was one of the first national politicians to emphasize his conservative positions on abortion and other social questions. However, incumbent President Ford, perceived as relatively moderate and not nearly as attractive to southern

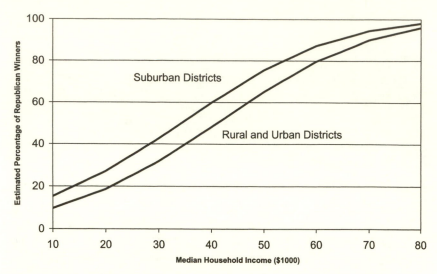

Figure 6.7. Republican victories in state legislative elections by income.
Note: The estimated percentage of state legislative races with Republican winners is based on the bivariate probit model for open state legislative elections presented in table 2 of the appendix. This graph presents the estimated change of a Republican victory assuming that the Republicans have managed to recruit a candidate. See figure 6.5 for a graph showing the relationship between income and Republican candidate recruitment in state legislative races. In producing these estimates, Proportion Black = .20, and Proportion Hispanic = 0. Suburban District was set equal to 1 for suburban district projections and 0 for rural and urban district projections.

religious conservatives, narrowly fought off Reagan's challenge for the nomination in 1976. It was unlikely that Ford, even if he were so inclined, would have had much success in attracting religious conservatives against Jimmy Carter. Carter projected a more pleasing image to southern conservatives than any Democratic nominee in the decade before or after him.

With strong support from religious conservatives, Ronald Reagan gained the Republican nomination in 1980. Indeed, organized support by religious conservatives in southern states was crucial to both his remaining a viable candidate in 1976 and ultimately winning the nomination in 1980. Religious conservatives were not just passive reactors to bids for Republican support. Increasingly, they organized in order to force Republican candidates and party organizations to adhere to their positions. "The Moral Majority," led by Reverend Jerry Falwell, was one of the most nationally prominent politically active Christian Right organizations in the early 1980s. Pat Robertson, founder of the Christian Broadcasting Network, later eclipsed Falwell and unsuccessfully sought the presidency in 1988. He nevertheless forced George Bush, the eventual nominee, to aggressively seek the support of Christian conservatives by taking a strong pro-life position and discussing his relationship with Jesus Christ in videos circulated at southern conservative Christian churches. Robertson later founded the Christian Coalition, the leading pro–social conservative lobby in Washington. Under Ralph Reed, now a leading Republican campaign strategist, the Christian Coalition achieved great prominence in the mid-1990s, taking credit for much of the Republican electoral success in 1994.

No demographic characteristic is so clearly related to beliefs about social issues and the U.S. Census does not collect public opinion data. However, social issues likely caused partisan change more quickly in urban than rural areas, especially in down-ballot contests for local and state legislative elections. Urban areas contained far greater concentrations of social liberals and socially liberal institutions than rural areas. The presence of these social liberals spurred Democratic candidates seeking office in urban areas to adopt more liberal positions on social issues than their counterparts in rural areas. At the same time, the visible presence of social liberals and their institutions outraged social conservatives into political action. However, social conservatives acted within the Republican Party, which increasingly became identified with their beliefs in the mind of voters.

In rural areas, the situation was quite different because there were few social liberals to push Democrats to adopt liberal positions on these issues. Rural Democrats would have been foolish to adopt liberal positions on social issues as they would have alienated many potential voters but gained virtually no new support. As a result, Democrats and Republicans alike adopted the dominant social conservative positions in rural areas. Rural social conservatives had no need to mobilize within the GOP to fend off challenges to their beliefs by socially liberal Democrats. The conservative consensus on social issues in rural areas suggests that rural partisans should have been slower to disagree over social issues than urban partisans who live in counties where social issues are highly divisive.

Rural partisans should nevertheless eventually have disagreed on these issues due to differences in the positions of the parties and their presidential candidates at the national level. Additionally, urban voters likely pressed statewide Democratic candidates to adopt more liberal positions than the Republicans on social issues, so rural voters gained exposure to prominent state Democratic candidates who take more liberal positions than their Republican counterparts on these issues. Rural voters may also gradually have become aware of liberal positions held by Democrats, such as state legislators, from outside their area. The social conservatism

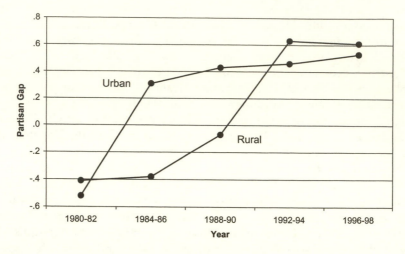

Figure 6.8. Partisan differences among Southern whites on abortion.
Note: The scale on the vertical axis shows the gap in views on abortion between the average white southern Democrat and the average white southern Republican. Abortion attitudes were measured by a 7-point scale with high numbers indicating greater support for a conservative or pro-life position, so a positive gap indicates more conservative views on abortion are held by the average Democrat compared to the average Republican.
Source: National Election Studies Cumulative Data File 1948–98: CF0838. The abortion question in the NES has a 4-point scale that was converted here into a 7-point scale in order to be comparable to the questions used to examine racial and economic issues.

of local and state legislative Democrats in rural areas delayed partisan change surrounding passionate disagreements over social issues, but it could not prevent it.

Figure 6.8 confirms that partisan differences over abortion among white southerners actually arrived later in urban areas than rural areas. The scale on the vertical axis of the graph shows the gap in views on abortion between the average white southern Democrat and the average white southern Republican. Abortion attitudes were measured by a seven-point scale with high numbers indicating greater support for a conservative or pro-life position, so a positive gap indicates more conservative views on abortion by the average Republican compared to the average Democrat. On the other hand, a negative gap reveals that the average Democrat holds more conservative views than the average Republican.

In 1980, the average white Democrat held more conservative attitudes on abortion than the average white Republican in both urban and rural areas. However, partisan positions on abortion began to quickly change in urban areas. By 1984, urban white Democrats, on average, held more liberal positions on abortion than urban white Republicans. In contrast, rural white Democrats did not become more liberal on abortion than rural white Republicans until 1992. The remainder of this section further develops the argument outlined above regarding the delayed impact of social issues on rural areas in greater detail and argues that this explains why rural areas have been slower to shift toward the Republicans than urban areas.

SOCIALLY LIBERAL PEOPLE AND INSTITUTIONS ARE CONCENTRATED IN URBAN AREAS

On an entire range of social issues, institutions that promote socially liberal positions are concentrated in urban centers but virtually nonexistent in rural counties throughout the South. Abortion is probably the most divisive social issue and Planned Parenthood is one of the most prominent pro-choice organizations. Planned Parenthood is widely known not only for its support of abortion rights but for its operation of clinics where doctors perform abortions. Planned Parenthood additionally supports anonymous HIV testing as part of its commitment to privacy and individual control over sexual matters. Planned Parenthood has clinics in various cities around the South, but none in rural areas. As in much of the rest of the nation, rural women seeking an abortion must travel to an urban center.

In a similar vein, one can find institutions that serve the gay and lesbian community in virtually every southern city, but not in rural areas. All southern cities of even medium size are home to at least one gay bar. Many southern cities have neighborhoods, such as Midtown in Atlanta, known to be home to especially high numbers of gays and lesbians. Such highly visible evidence of the presence of a vibrant gay community is absent from rural areas. In rural areas, gays and lesbians generally try to blend into the community. Even if their sexuality is widely known, they do not bring attention to it. Many rural gays and lesbians abandon rural areas for more welcoming cities.

Rural and urban differences over school prayer likely spurred earlier activism by social conservatives in urban areas. Contrary to popular perception, the Supreme Court's decision in *Engel v. Vitale* did not immediately bring an end to school prayer. Many schools, especially in rural areas, simply ignored the decision and continued with the past practice of teacher-led prayer in schools and even with religious training during school hours. Urban areas ended school prayer more often than rural areas because greater religious diversity in urban areas makes it much more difficult to adopt a universally acceptable school prayer. The smaller, tight-knit nature of rural communities further raises the price of challenging school prayer in rural areas.

Moreover, rural areas are more religiously homogenous and less likely to contain residents desiring to challenge prayer in schools. For example, while some Jewish southerners inhabit rural areas, the vast majority of the South's Jewish population lives in urban areas.[29] Cities are more likely to be home to Jewish institutions such as synagogues and Jewish Community Centers. Jews in rural parts of the South often have to travel sizable distances to pray as a group.[30] The one small synagogue in Florence, South Carolina, serves the entire Pee Dee region in the northeastern portion of the state. As a group, Jews tend to be more socially liberal than other Americans on a whole range of cultural issues, so the presence of Jews and Jewish institutions injects a socially liberal presence into urban areas. Even conservative Jews often oppose school prayer simply because they do not want their children praying to Jesus.

Jewish southerners have long been identified as one of the more liberal elements of the southern white community. Perhaps as a religious minority, Jewish Americans tend to be especially sensitive to minority rights. Large numbers of Jewish synagogues were bombed during the Civil Rights Movement due to the association of many ordinary Jews and Jewish leaders with the Movement. The bombing of the Reform Jewish Temple in Atlanta was highlighted in one scene of *Driving Miss Daisy* and described in detail in Melissa Faye Greene's *The Temple Bombing*. Not all southern Jews held liberal positions on racial issues. South Carolina House Speaker Sol Blatt, then one of the most influential politicians in his state, publicly advised his coreligionists to avoid getting involved in racial controversies in a speech during the Civil Rights Movement at a synagogue in Columbia. Of course, it may have been the racially liberal leanings of the congregation that inspired Speaker Blatt to deliver such a warning.

There is also greater diversity of Christian churches in urban areas. Just like Jews but unlike Baptists, Unitarians are far less likely to have churches in rural areas. As tolerance is a core precept of Unitarians, they tend to hold even stronger liberal positions than the Jewish population.

Institutions such as abortion clinics, gay bars, and Jewish synagogues not only suggest the presence of social liberals but probably help nurture the expansion of the number of social liberals through their presence.

---

[29] *American Jewish Yearbook 1986* (New York: American Jewish Committee, 1986), 223–30.

[30] Noah Gordon, *The Rabbi* (New York: Ballantine, 1965), nicely dramatizes the problems facing isolated Jews in the rural South when writing about a young Jewish rabbi who traveled circuit around the Ozarks.

Social liberals likely perceive southern cities as a more supportive environment than rural areas. Jews thinking of settling in the South may be more likely to choose an urban area with various Jewish institutions because they believe that it will be more difficult to raise their children as Jewish in an area with few other Jewish residents. In a similar fashion, secular Christians may find rural areas inhospitable as the church may be the only major viable social institution outside of the school. Separating oneself from the church may be quite socially isolating even if your neighbors do not find your lack of religious belief, or at least church attendance, shocking.

Additionally, urban areas are economically expanding rapidly throughout much of the South. They attract migrants from outside the region who come to take advantage of economic opportunities and bring with them a wide range of views on issues. In contrast, economic growth has not been quite as dynamic in the rural South. Due to the relatively fewer economic opportunities and the attractions available in urban areas, rural areas are less likely to attract new residents than urban areas. Consequently, few new arrivals come to challenge the dominant local social conservatism in rural areas.

GREATER SOCIAL CONSERVATIVE MOBILIZATION IN URBAN AREAS

If social issues have a strong influence on southern politics, one might expect to find greater support for the Democrats in urban areas than rural areas due to greater numbers of social liberals in urban areas. However, the opposite appears to be true. Indeed, figure 6.9 indicates that Republicans almost never win elections for sheriff in rural areas. Unlike in the North, where rural areas are often bastions of Republican support, Democrats have continued to maintain a strong position in the rural South, at least in election for local offices. As figures 5.2, 5.3, and 5.4 reveal, some of the strongest bastions of support for Republicans in presidential elections have been suburban counties surrounding majority black cities. This seemingly perplexing contradiction between the greater concentration of social liberals and their institutions in metropolitan areas and the failure of Republicans to gain a foothold in the rural South requires an explanation. How can social issues be a growing force for partisan change toward the Republicans if the most socially conservative counties in the South remain so supportive of Democrats?

One should first realize that social conservatism remains dominant in both urban and rural areas of the South. Social liberals are far more numerous and active in urban areas, but they remain outnumbered by social conservatives. As a drive around any southern city will confirm, southern metropolitan areas are dotted with churches, often of an enormous size and membership. While the rural South certainly does not lack

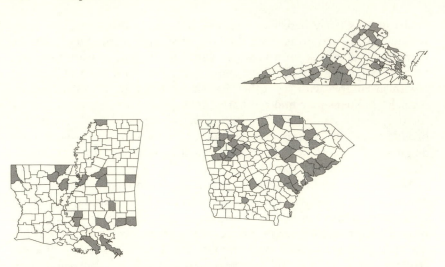

Figure 6.9. Counties with Republican sheriffs.
Note: Shaded counties are counties that elected a Republican as sheriff in the elections held between 1996 and 1999. Data were unavailable statewide during this period for states not shown.
Source: Data compiled by author.

churches, large urban churches can offer more services and play a larger part in the lives of their members than the smaller churches that dominate religious life in the rural South. The high density of population in metropolitan areas facilitates the attraction of a large membership located within a short distance of the church. The greater affluence of whites living in metropolitan areas, as compared to rural whites, means that their churches are wealthier as well, so large urban and suburban churches can offer an array of services, such as day care, meals, and classes.

Despite the thriving presence and even dominance of conservative religious institutions in metropolitan areas, social liberals are more likely to be politically active within urban areas. The larger population and greater diversity reduces the threat of social exclusion or economic punishment for taking socially liberal positions. Social conservatism remains highly dominant within urban as well as rural areas, but communities exist to support and nurture social liberalism within urban areas. The greater diversity of urban areas may make liberal views somewhat less shocking to most members of the conservative majority even if they remain unacceptable. Rural residents rightly fear that they pay a greater price for taking deviant positions on social issues. In a small community, no one wants to lose clients or business by taking a publicly unpopular position. A threat of violence may also remain in the background even though its actual appearance is now far less common than in the past.

This point was driven home to me vividly when I attended Rosh Hashanah (Jewish New Year) services in one of the few rural southern synagogues. During his sermon, the rabbi encouraged the congregation to put pro-choice bumper stickers on their cars in order to make a small difference by showing support for choice on abortion. While many of the worshipers likely shared his pro-choice views, they laughed at the bumper sticker idea when I mentioned it later. Even if they were economically successful, they had little desire to attract negative attention from their socially conservative neighbors. Studies of black politics explain that the preacher was often the only individual in rural African-American communities free to argue in favor of civil rights because he was the only individual employed by blacks. A small religious minority may similarly feel vulnerable to pressure even if they are not oppressed in the manner of the black community in the pre–Civil Rights Movement South. Just like rural black religious leaders, rural rabbis may feel freer to express their views than their congregants.

The reaction to people who choose not to conform may vividly demonstrate the price of liberal political action. Publicly demanding an end to prayer in the public school will almost certainly incur a united negative reaction in rural areas. The religious majority will likely perceive this opposition to prayer in school as opposition to prayer more generally and an attack on religion and their beliefs. Even if the vast majority stick to peaceful support for school prayer, the social ostracism can be difficult to bear, especially for children enrolled in the school. Of course, one also has to consider potential economic consequences if the family depends on local individuals or businesses for their livelihood. Supporters of school prayer may take their business elsewhere. Other social liberals in rural areas may choose to remain quiet after witnessing the price paid for going public with socially liberal views.

Active social liberals are more likely to be politically active within the Democratic Party, nationally identified as the party of social liberalism. The two parties enshrine opposite positions on abortion into their platforms every four years with the Republicans staunchly opposing abortion and the Democrats defending a woman's right to choose. Democrats are also far more supportive of gay rights and welcoming of gays within their party than the GOP. In contrast, some Republicans left the hall during the 2000 Republican Convention when openly gay Republican Representative Jim Kolbe addressed the convention on the issue of free trade. The Texas delegation formed a prayer circle to express their concern that Kolbe was allowed to speak before the Convention. Congressional Democrats are much more likely to vote in favor of legislation, such as the

Employment Non-Discrimination Act, designed to protect the rights of gays and lesbians, than Republicans. Even though southern Democrats are less supportive of gay rights than their northern colleagues, they remain much more supportive than southern Republicans.[31]

High concentrations of social liberals, often active in liberal political causes and the Democratic Party, spur southern Democratic candidates running in urban areas to take more liberal positions than Democrats seeking office in rural areas. Activists are especially likely to vote in primaries and socially conservative positions may alienate core Democratic socially liberal voters in urban areas. On the other hand, it would be political suicide for Democrats to take similar positions in rural areas. It is hard to imagine Democrats running on a platform of gun control in the Southside of Virginia or expanding gay rights in the Mississippi Delta. The position of rural Democrats on social issues is often indistinguishable from those held by rural Republicans.

The greater diversity of people and the relative liberalism of Democrats in urban areas promotes a reaction among social conservatives that simply does not occur in rural areas. Social conservatives living in rural areas find wide acceptance for their views in both political parties. They have little need to resort to political activism because of the absence of almost any challenge to social conservatism. In rural areas of the South, social conservatism is usually so pervasive and part of the fabric of rural life that it is taken for granted like the absence of traffic on rural roads. Ideas such as gun control and tolerance for open or obvious homosexuals are hardly ever voiced and would be regarded by most as startling or bizarre at best. Naturally, rural Democrats, as part of the local culture, do not express liberal social views. Smart rural politicians would not express liberal views on social issues even if they happened to hold them. As a result, socially conservative rural southerners were slower to identify the Democrats with socially liberal positions and felt less pressure to abandon the party of their forebears, the Democrats, over social issues.

Urban residents live in a quite different political environment. Indeed, this environment was crucial to incubating the conservative Christian, or religious right, movement that became a pillar of the Republican Party. Social conservatism may be dominant in the urban South, but challenges to it exist almost everywhere. The very diversity of urban life in contrast to the homogeneity of rural communities presents a challenge to social conservatism. Social conservatives may find the diversity of religious and political beliefs threatening. Urban residents are more likely to know people who hold beliefs at odds with their own. School prayer is far less

[31] David Lublin, "Explaining Support for Gay and Lesbian Rights in the 106th Congress," unpublished paper.

likely to continue in urban areas, and schools may also present other cultures and beliefs in positive terms that social conservatives may believe threaten their value system. In a similar vein, the large library systems of urban areas often carry books that social conservatives abhor. The wealth of urban library systems also often allows them to provide Internet access. Parents may fear that their kids may access not only ideas that they dislike but highly graphic pornography.

Perhaps most crucially, both political parties do not provide equal support for Christian conservatism in metropolitan areas. Democratic candidates are more likely to hold socially liberal positions. In metropolitan areas, unlike in rural areas, social liberals present a challenge to the dominant social conservatism of the South. Social conservatives react by undertaking political activism; the social liberalism of Democrats encourages most social conservatives to channel that activism in support of Republicans. Contrary to stereotype, the Christian Right is not populated by uneducated, poor, rural southerners. Middle-class suburbanites are the driving force in the conservative Christian movement.[32]

Studies confirm that Republican activists are much more likely to hold conservative views on abortion than Democratic activists.[33] The greater liberalism of Democratic activists on the abortion issue is not due to a concentration of black party activists within the Democratic Party. According to a 1991 survey, 74 and 78 percent of white and black county party activists, respectively, agreed that "By law a woman should be able to obtain an abortion as a matter of personal choice." In contrast, only 43 percent of white Republicans agreed.[34] Unfortunately, there is no data available comparing rural and urban Democratic activists.

The strong reaction to social issues helps propel partisan change away from the Democrats. Urban social conservatives, due to their relative wealth and population concentrations, are in a much better position to organize politically than their rural counterparts. Large churches facilitate the dissemination of information about candidates, such as the Christian Coalition voter guides distributed at conservative churches in advance of the election. Political movements require money, and social conservatives living in metropolitan areas are more likely to have it than the relatively poorer residents of rural counties.

In sum, the presence of social liberals in urban areas pressed the Dem-

[32] Clyde Wilcox, *Onward Christian Soldier? The Religious Right in American Politics* (Boulder, CO: Westview, 1996), 48.

[33] Charles D. Hadley and Lewis Bowman, eds. *Southern State Party Organizations and Activists* (Westport, CT: Greenwood, 1995).

[34] Charles D. Hadley and Harold W. Stanley, "Race and the Democratic Biracial Coalition," in *Party Activists in Southern Politics: Mirrors and Makers of Change*, ed. Charles D. Hadley and Lewis Bowman (Knoxville: University of Tennessee Press, 1998), 10.

ocrats to adopt positions on social issues that are more liberal than those of the Republicans. Cultural conservatives felt threatened by the challenge posed by social liberals and quickly organized. As the Republicans tend to hold positions more agreeable to social conservatives, social conservatives living in urban areas shifted toward the Republicans. In rural areas, social conservatism is almost universally accepted and propounded by both local Republicans and Democrats alike. The absence of any partisan cleavage on social issues or threat to social conservatives reduced pressure for rural social conservatives to move toward the Republicans based on their beliefs on social issues.

DELAYED PARTISAN CHANGE ON SOCIAL ISSUES IN RURAL AREAS

The nearly identical positions of local Democrats and Republicans on social issues in rural areas delayed partisan change on social issues. Utilizing survey data, Nadeau and Stanley found that rural voters were more likely to remain Democratic.[35] Analysis of aggregate data from county and state legislative elections confirms this finding. Figures 5.6, 5.8, 6.4, and 6.6 show that Republicans consistently found it more difficult in rural counties than in urban counties to both recruit candidates and win local elections even after controlling for the effects of race or income. In state legislative elections, Republicans similarly made greater inroads in suburban districts than in either urban or rural districts, as shown in figures 5.7, 5.9, 6.5, and 6.7.

At first glance, the lower success rates of Republican candidates in urban state legislative districts compared to suburban districts appears to contradict the idea that differences in positions held by candidates and party elites on social issues in urban and rural areas explain why Republicans have achieved less success in rural areas. After all, both suburban and urban districts are essentially non-rural and Democratic elites tend to hold liberal views in both areas. The difference between urban and suburban districts is that urban districts located in central cities contain more residents who support these liberal policies than suburban districts. As a result, the liberal positions held by elites cost the Democrats less in urban, central-city state House races than in suburban state House races. Democrats running in central-city urban state House districts fare just as well as their more conservative rural counterparts. Additionally, one needs to consider that county lines do not respect the boundaries between urban and suburban areas. Unlike state House districts, few southern counties contain only central-city urban areas, though many counties are entirely suburban. For example, Fulton County, Georgia, is home to both Atlanta and sizable suburbs. It is surrounded by many wholly subur-

---

[35] Nadeau and Stanley 1993.

ban counties, including Cobb, Cherokee, Clayton, De Kalb, and Gwinett Counties. In the statistical analysis of county elections, urban and suburban counties are both treated as urban and the impact of socially conservative suburban whites dominates.

The greater success of Democrats in maintaining the loyalty of rural voters did not last forever. Figure 6.8 shows that just like their urban counterparts, rural Republicans are now more conservative than rural Democrats on the abortion question. Studies of state legislative elections suggest that heightened Democratic success in rural areas declined in the late 1990s.[36] The growing link in the mind of rural voters between Democrats and social liberalism and the consequent rise in Republican partisanship would explain this shift. Democrats lost ground in rural areas in congressional elections during the 1990s and in the 2000 presidential election.

The eventual shift in rural partisanship away from the Democrats is not inexplicable. Local politicians were not the only source of information about party positions so rural areas could not remain permanently insulated from the impact of political divisions over social issues. Much as Barry Goldwater's capture of the Republican nomination permanently differentiated the two parties over racial issues, Ronald Reagan's ascension to the presidency highlighted the sharp differences between the two parties on abortion. These differences have only grown sharper over time. As pro-life advocates have become increasingly concentrated within the GOP, pro-choice proponents find it more and more difficult to win Republican nominations for public office. The same process has occurred within the Democrats as pro-life supporters find less and less room for their views. One finds it difficult to imagine that a pro-choice Republican could win the Republican presidential nomination or that a pro-life Democrat could top the Democratic ticket.

Partisan differences over abortion are also increasingly reflected in the views of members of Congress. Figure 6.10 shows that the voting records of southern Democrats and southern Republicans on abortion have grown increasingly distinct over time as measured by scores given by the National Abortion Rights Action League (NARAL) to representatives. As with other interest-group ratings, NARAL scores range from 0 to 100 and reflect the percentage of times that a representative voted in accordance with NARAL on a number of key votes on the House floor. The gap between congressional Democrats and Republicans in their support for abortion rights ranged between 14 and 43 points between the 97th and 101st Congresses. The gap escalated to 64 points in the 102nd Con-

[36] Lublin and Voss 2000, 797–801.

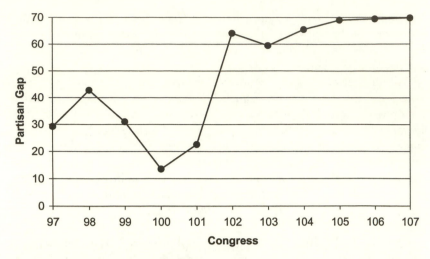

Figure 6.10. Partisan gap in NARAL scores.
Note: The partisan gap is the difference between the rating given by the National Abortion Rights Action League (NARAL) to the average Democrat and the average Republican. Every Congress is numbered sequentially with a new Congress elected every two years. The 97th Congress was elected in 1980; the 102nd Congress was elected in 1990; the 107th Congress was elected in 2000.
Source: National Abortion Rights Action League.

gress, elected in 1990, and rose further to 70 points in the 107th Congress, elected in 2000.

The Supreme Court has helped maintain the enduring national feud over abortion. Small majorities in favor of upholding *Roe v. Wade* have led pro-life activists to hope, and their pro-choice counterparts to fear, that a few more Supreme Court nominations by a conservative pro-life president might result in overturning federal judicial protections for abortion rights. Moreover, the conservative Supreme Court's constricted reading of *Roe*, even as they have upheld the broad principle of abortion rights, has expanded the fight to the states. Activists in the states now wrangle over issues such as parental consent and waiting periods.

Other issues have stoked the national debate over social issues. Gay rights may now rival abortion as a source of disputes between social conservatives and liberals. President Clinton's support for gays in the military led to sharply increased polarization over this issue at the very beginning of his presidency. As on abortion, southern Democratic members of the U.S. House are more liberal on gay rights than their Republican colleagues, though they remain more conservative than their northern Democratic colleagues.

Moreover, the insulation that rural areas experienced from the impact of Supreme Court decisions on prayer in schools has gradually declined as prayer has gradually been removed from most schools even in rural areas. National debates over social issues are thus belatedly having a direct impact on rural southern life. Local Democratic elites could delay the shift in party identification toward the Republicans over these issues by taking conservative positions. However, they could not totally insulate rural residents from the highly partisan debate over these issues. Partisan change related to beliefs about abortion and other social questions may have arrived ten years later in rural areas, but it did arrive.

COMPARING THE IMPACT OF RACIAL, ECONOMIC,
   AND SOCIAL ISSUES

One can examine the effect of social issues on partisanship and voting behavior in presidential elections using surveys like the National Election Studies. In order to assess the relative importance of racial, economic, and religious issues in shaping southern white partisanship, I estimated the impact on party identification of shifting from the conservative to liberal extreme on each issue, as measured by the seven-point scale derived from the responses to survey questions, after controlling for the other issues. Figure 6.11 shows the estimated difference in the probability of someone identifying as a Republican between someone who responded at the conservative end of the scale compared to someone who responded at the liberal end, assuming that they took the middle position on the other two issues.[37] For example, in 1980–82, the probability of someone who took a strongly conservative position on economic issues being a Republican was 38 percent higher than someone who took a strongly liberal position. Similarly, in 1996–98, an individual who strongly opposed abortion was estimated to be 14 percent less likely to identify as a Democrat than someone who strongly favored allowing women to choose for themselves whether to have an abortion.

Economic Issues Remain Paramount

Economic issues have consistently remained the best predictor of partisanship among white southerners. Between 1980 and 2000, beliefs about whether it was up to the government or the individual to promote em-

[37] These estimates were derived from probit models of party identification using data gathered by the National Election Study (the 1948–98 Cumulative Data File and the 2000 Pre/Post Election Study). The dependent variable was derived from the standard collapsed measure of partisanship (Republicans = 1, Democrats = 0, Other or Independent excluded).

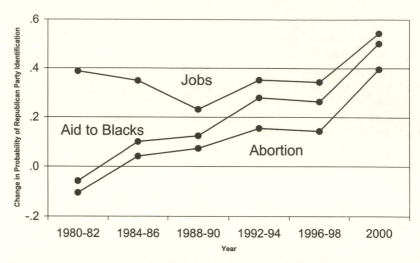

Figure 6.11. Impact of issues on Southern white partisanship.
Note: The predicted impacts of the various issues on white partisanship are based on the models presented in table 3A of the appendix. Each model included responses to survey questions on each of the three issues (economic, racial, and social) with a 7-point scale ranging from liberal to conservative extremes on the issue. See footnote 15 for the exact wording of the survey questions. The vertical axis measures the estimated difference in the probability of someone identifying as a Republican between someone who responded at the conservative end of the 7-point scale compared to someone who responded at the liberal end.

ployment and a high quality of life had a powerful relationship to partisanship. In an average year, people who believed that the responsibility lies with the individual, rather than government, were 38 percent more likely to identify with the GOP. Class issues have not been eclipsed by either racial or social issues. Even as these other issues grew in importance, beliefs on economic issues retained a greater influence over partisanship. In 2000, strong supporters of economic conservatism were 54 percent more likely to view themselves as Republicans compared to believers in a major role for government.

These results contradict the notion that economic issues are fading and being replaced by other new issue cleavages. Instead, the influence of economic issues on white southern partisanship has remained surprisingly steady despite regional and global changes that might have been expected to have a contrary impact. Socialism, always regarded with great disdain in the South, has been on the wane globally with the collapse of the Soviet system throughout eastern Europe. Even in western Europe, traditional social democratic approaches are increasingly viewed as unlikely to promote economic prosperity and left-wing parties such as the British Labour Party and the Italian Communist Party have moved to the right. The South's growing prosperity has arguably dimmed the appeal of economic populism, particularly for whites who have especially benefited from the South's excellent record of economic growth.

Others might contend that rising prosperity makes social welfare programs more affordable to formerly impoverished southern states. State governments can afford to provide a number of benefits that simply were not feasible in the past. Expansion in the number of affluent and middle-class southerners may also emphasize the economic divide to a greater degree to those who have not benefited as greatly from the South's impressive economic development. Improved communications may also make poor southerners more acutely aware of their relative deprivation compared to the wealthy.

There is little evidence that economic issues are waning from either national or state campaigns. The core dispute between the Democrats and the Republicans still rests on whether government should expand social welfare benefits or curtail them in order to provide greater tax relief. The centerpiece of Al Gore's 2000 presidential campaign was a promise to provide prescription drug coverage to retired Americans, a very costly new addition to the social safety net. George W. Bush campaigned on a promise to cut taxes. Providing new prescription drug coverage would undoubtedly disproportionately benefit poor Americans who cannot afford private coverage. On the other hand, tax cuts, especially the permanent elimination of the inheritance tax, would especially gratify rich Americans. The spending versus tax cuts and poor versus rich debate retains a central place in national politics.

Economic issues retain potency at the state level as well. Democratic governors often campaign on improving education and expanding opportunities for college education. Georgia's Hope Scholarship program, promoted by former Democratic Governor Zell Miller, makes it far more affordable for Georgians to attend public colleges if they maintain a sufficiently high grade point average in high school and college. Funded by a state lottery, the program has proved enormously popular as it improved access to higher education without requiring a tax increase. Other successful Democratic candidates have been quick to imitate it. South Carolina Governor Jim Hodges and Alabama Governor Don Siegelman were both elected in 1998 on platforms to implement a similar program. In contrast, Republican Jim Gilmore won election as governor of Virginia in 1997 on a promise to eliminate his state's car tax.

Continuing partisan differences over economic issues combined with growing southern prosperity could explain at least part of the Republican growth among white voters. As more white southerners became middle class or affluent, more became likely to benefit from Republican efforts to trim taxes. At the same time, fewer white southerners would benefit from social welfare programs designed to aid the poor or have need of them. Economic growth has been rapid in the South since the Civil Rights Movement, allowing the region to narrow considerably the gap in prosperity between the South and the rest of the nation. Growing Republicanism might unsurprisingly accompany this rise in prosperity.

Racial and Social Issues Have Grown in Importance

Even as economic issues have retained a critical place in shaping southern partisanship, the importance of racial and social issues has grown substantially. As figure 6.11 shows, race and abortion had a comparatively low impact on party identification as late as the mid-1980s. However, the impact of each issue on partisanship has steadily increased. By 2000, this gradual increase resulted in a strong relationship between both racial and social issues and southern white partisanship. In 2000, staunch opponents of abortion were 40 percent more likely to identify as Republicans than strong supporters of abortion rights. At the same time, strong opponents of government aid to blacks were 50 percent more likely to think of themselves as Republicans than passionate believers in greater aid to blacks.

The growth in the importance of racial and social issues meant that their impact on white southern partisanship lagged only a little behind that of economic issues by 2000. Indeed, the impact of the rising racial and social issues on partisanship in 2000 actually exceeded the impact of economic issues prior to 2000. Only the continued growth in the strength of the relationship between economic issues and party identification prevented these new issues from surpassing economic issues in their effect.

Examining the role of these same issues and white behavior in presidential and congressional elections presents a similar though more complex and erratic picture. Figures 6.12 and 6.13 suggest that racial and social issues had a more sizable impact on voting in federal elections than on partisanship in the late 1980s. In 1988, a shift from one extreme to the other in attitudes on abortion caused a shift of 29 points in voting behavior in both presidential and congressional elections, but a change of only 7 points in partisanship. At the same time, moving from the liberal to the conservative end of the spectrum on racial issues made voters 23 percent more likely to vote Republican in presidential elections and 41 percent more likely in congressional elections. However, a comparable shift in attitude positions was related to only a 12-point change in party identification.

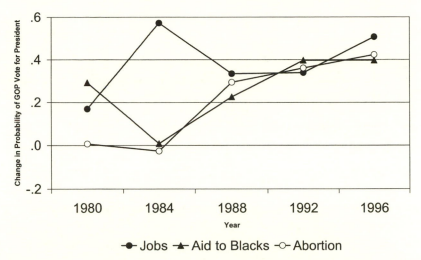

Figure 6.12. Impact of issues on Southern white presidential voting behavior.
Note: The predicted impacts of the various issues on white partisanship are based
on the models presented in table 3B of the appendix. Each model included responses to survey questions on each of the three issues (economic, racial, and
social) with a 7-point scale ranging from liberal to conservative extremes on the
issue. See footnote 15 for the exact wording of the survey questions. The vertical
axis measures the estimated difference in the probability of someone voting Republican for president between someone who responded at the conservative end
of the 7-point scale compared to someone who responded at the liberal end.

The earlier effect of issues on voting reflects at least partly that many
older voters who supported Republican candidates nevertheless continued to identify as Democrats. Over time, they have gradually been replaced by younger voters whose party identification is more consistent
with their presidential votes. At the same time, Republicans may have
attracted Democrats to vote for their presidential candidates who only
later converted their party identification to match their voting habits.
Conservative Democratic voters may have originally perceived their defection to support Republican presidential candidates as a temporary ab-
erration from the habits of a lifetime. However, as the Democrats continued to offer liberal candidates, these votes may have become a pattern
and formed the basis for a more permanent shift in party identification.

The relative impact of economic, racial, and social issues on votes for
U.S. President and the U.S. House appears more erratic than their impact on party identification. These differences likely reflect the stability
of partisanship compared to voting behavior over time. They may also

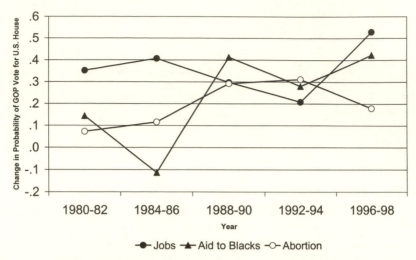

Figure 6.13. Issues and Southern white congressional voting behavior.
Note: The predicted impacts of the various issues on white partisanship are based on the models presented in table 3C of the appendix. Each model included responses to survey questions on each of the three issues (economic, racial, and social) with a 7-point scale ranging from liberal to conservative extremes on the issue. See footnote 15 for the exact wording of the survey questions. The vertical axis measures the estimated difference in the probability of someone voting Republican for the U.S. House between someone who responded at the conservative end of the 7-point scale compared to someone who responded at the liberal end.

reflect that the greater number of cases available to study party identification make it easier to establish consistent relationships between issues and partisanship.[38]

[38] Presidential elections occur only once every four years; in any four-year cycle, there are more than twice as many cases available to study party identification than presidential voting behavior. Congressional elections occur every two years; however, voters living in districts without a Democratic or a Republican candidate are excluded. On average, the number of cases available over a four-year cycle is less than one-half of the cases utilized in the study of party identification.

The relative stability of partisanship could conceivably reflect that the importance of issues shifts from campaign to campaign in response to short-term trends and choices by candidates even if the relationship between issues and partisanship is more stable. However, there appears to be little evidence to support this theory. For example, in 1992 the impact of economic issues on both presidential and congressional voting behavior declined compared to 1988 even though the country was experiencing a recession and the Democrats relentlessly emphasized economic issues.

Conclusion

In the one-party South, all strands of public opinion were contained within the Democratic Party. The exclusion of large sections of the population from the electorate by undemocratic rules and procedures facilitated this containment of public opinion in one party. Nonvoters, especially blacks, remained unrepresented in the southern Democratic Party, so there were fewer factions to appease than if the electorate had been representative of the general population. The dominance of the Democratic Party provided further incentive for members of otherwise divergent groups to remain Democratic as the party remained the path to power. The critical role of the Democratic Party in maintaining this racially based system of exclusion kept a wide array of interests within the Democratic Party. Division might threaten the status quo. In any case, defection to the Republicans invited social and even stronger forms of disapproval from one's neighbors.

The clash around racial issues centered on the 1960s ended the artificial dominance of the Democrats. The movement of the national Democratic Party from a bulwark of the southern racial status quo to the party of civil rights and voting rights alienated many southern white Democrats from their party's presidential nominee, even though they continued to identify as Democrats and supported the mostly racially moderate or conservative Democratic officials who continued to dominate southern politics in the new small-d democratic era. The conversion of the Republicans to racial conservatism under Goldwater rendered the GOP more acceptable than in the past to southern whites, even as it permanently alienated formerly loyal blacks. Southern Democrats could no longer claim to be the bulwark of the old system as federal intervention forced by the Civil Rights Movement had shattered it irretrievably. At the same time, Republicans, now the party of racial conservatism, finally began to lose the taint of identification with the North and the Union that rendered the GOP unacceptable to many white southerners a century after the conclusion of the Civil War.

Conceivably, the South might have immediately seen enormous partisan change around racial issues, seemingly the polarizing issues of the era. Puzzlingly, partisan change centered around the old New Deal cleavage on economic issues instead. The continuing conservatism or moderation of most southern Democratic officials on racial issues muted the impact of the racial liberalism of the national Democratic Party. Political parties in the United States remain an amalgamation of highly decentralized state parties. The national Democratic Party could not force southern Democratic officials to act against their political interests by quickly adopting a racially liberal platform. Outside of presidential elections, racial issues provided little reason for most racially conservative white southerners to vote Republican. When candidates from the two major parties do not disagree about an issue, their positions cannot spur partisan change.

Despite their concentration within the Democratic Party, southerners remained aware of the longstanding national cleavage within the two parties over economic issues. Moreover, many southern Democratic officials had long adopted more moderate stands on economic issues even as they supported racially conservative parties. Recall that President Franklin Roosevelt had purposefully sidelined racial issues in order to assure southern Democratic support for his New Deal initiatives. In 1964, the clash between Democratic President Lyndon Johnson and Republican Senator Barry Goldwater revitalized partisan differences over economic issues. Commitment to shrinking the size of the federal government had always been Goldwater's most ardent and vocally articulated passion. Johnson was determined to enter the pantheon of great Democratic presidents through his relentless push for adoption of Great Society programs designed to end poverty in America.

The 1984 battle between Republican President Ronald Reagan and Senator Walter Mondale further stimulated national debate over economic issues. Ronald Reagan, the first Republican president in the Goldwater mold to win election, had spent his first term hacking away at the cherished programs of Johnson's Great Society so he could shrink the size of domestic programs and reduce taxes. Walter Mondale not only promised to defend these programs, but to raise taxes in order to do it. Economic issues did not disappear from American politics; they remained at the center of it. While southern Democrats remained more conservative than their northern counterparts on economic issues, they were more likely to support liberal economic programs, especially since they tended to bring large sums of money into a relatively poor though rapidly growing region.

The rise of race as a national question destroyed the old southern political system, but it did not assure that racial issues would assume center stage in the new one. Excepting some presidential elections, economic issues divided the parties more clearly and more immediately in the eyes of southern whites. Affluent southerners and believers in economic conservatism were the first to rally to the Republicans as a result. Economic issues promoted most Republican growth in the wake of the Civil Rights Movement. Aggregate data from local and state legislative elections as well as survey data on voting in federal elections and partisanship presented in this chapter support this conclusion. Republicans found it difficult to gain adherents in areas without affluent voters or ideological supporters of their economic agenda. Strategic politicians perceived this link and Republicans could not attract candidates in these areas. As chapter 3 drives home, parties find it hard to win elections when they cannot attract strong candidates.

Race nevertheless continued to retain importance, though in a different manner than generally realized. As outlined in chapter 5, the near unanimous support for the Democrats among black voters severely constrained Republican opportunities. As the share of blacks rises, Republicans find it harder to win elections. Moreover, racial issues finally started to impinge more strongly on southern politics in the 1980s as the elected officials of the two parties began to disagree more noticeably on racial issues. The retirement of the old segregationist Democratic elite and the rise of new Democrats elected with biracial coalitions caused this shift. White southern voters now had a new reason to discriminate between the two parties, and many more white southerners chose to vote Republican as the differences on racial issues between the two parties gradually rose.

The focus of much past scholarship on racial issues may be seen not so much as incorrect as overstated and ahead of its time. Racial issues were a rising source of partisan cleavage, though their major impact on white southern partisanship was substantially delayed. Debates over racial issues like affirmative action continue to shape southern politics. Equally important, race often serves as a prism through which other issues, like the death penalty, are viewed. Indeed, as the Edsalls perceived, racial conservatism may work in synergy with economic conservatism to the advantage of the Republicans.[39]

More recently, social issues have arisen as a new source of cleavage between Democrats and Republicans. Republican President Ronald Reagan attracted increasingly organized religious conservatives through his advocacy of their positions. Pressed by more socially liberal Democrats, urban southern Democrats often adopted more socially liberal positions. Running in a more homogeneously socially conservative environment, rural Democrats were more likely to retain conservative positions and not provoke a backlash from the Christian Right. In effect, rural Democrats in the 1980s mimicked the strategy of their southern predecessors on racial issues. Initially, as with racial issues, this strategy prevented Republicans from making gains in rural areas. Perhaps because the GOP already had a foothold in the region and because of the divide among southern Democrats on social issues, rural Democrats managed to delay the rise of social issues as a partisan cleavage for a relatively short period.

[39] Edsall and Edsall 1992.

The arrival of mass enfranchisement destroyed the old party system. African Americans quickly rallied to the Democrats because of their support for civil rights. More whites gradually became Republican due to their support for economic conservatism. As racial and then social issues arose as new sources of cleavage between the parties, these issues began to attract more southern whites to the GOP even as economic issues remained highly important.

The Future of Southern Politics

PARTISAN CHANGE in the South is a complex, multifaceted process that has occurred over a long period. Indeed, partisan change continues in the South today. It would be convenient for scholars if one issue clearly had sparked massive shifts in party preferences by the electorate over one election. Certainly, this book would have been a lot shorter. However, the growth of the Republicans as a serious force in southern politics did not happen that way. One suspects that partisan change does not really occur that way at all. Even Sundquist, one of the major proponents of the classical school of realignment in which massive upheavals remake the political landscape in one critical election, ultimately cannot defend this theory. His work constantly describes the buildup of fissures in the parties prior to the critical election and "minor" realignments that occur before and after the so-called critical election.[1]

Partisan change may not even necessarily require new issues or one central issue. The breakdown of old institutions that maintained the southern system of white supremacy allowed the national cleavage surrounding economic issues to enter into southern politics. More recently, racial and social issues have come to play a greater role in explaining partisanship and voting behavior among white southerners. Partisan change has tended to be gradual in the South, especially because southern Democratic elites tenaciously fought Republican advances. Their monopoly on power and their slowness to cede advantageous ground on issues greatly impeded Republican advances. Republican efforts to sell themselves to voters as the only acceptable conservative party often fell on deaf ears while most Democrats continued to advocate conservative or moderate stands on the key issues of the day. Moreover, Republicans often left many offices uncontested.

Racial context and racial issues play an important role, though perhaps a different one than outlined by previous scholars of southern politics. Federal involvement combined with the Civil Rights Movement to shatter the South's old racial order. Progress on racial issues allowed long suppressed nonracial ones to emerge. However, racial issues continue to explain why African Americans almost unanimously support one party rather than the other. Strong black support for the Democrats constrains

---

[1] Sundquist 1993.

where Republicans may advance. Racial conservatism also explains why some whites abandoned the Democrats and continue to support the Republicans. However, there is little evidence to support the white backlash or racial threat hypothesis. Whites who live in majority-black counties actually support Republicans at a lower rate than other whites.

Nevertheless, racial issues are not receding from southern politics; the evidence suggests quite the opposite. Racial context and racial issues condition elite behavior and the operation of southern institutions. It was hard for mass partisan change to occur while elites successfully straddled a potential source of voter cleavage. Only when one party moves toward a new position can partisan change around the issue occur.[2] The entry of blacks into the Democratic primary process promoted the departure of conservative elites and voters for greener Republican pastures. The resulting divergence in the positions of southern Democratic and Republican elites on these issues extended the national-level cleavage on racial issues to the South and made it possible for the GOP to attract voters based on these issues. Racial redistricting further aided the Republicans by concentrating the most loyal Democrats in the South into a few districts. Partisan polarization over racial issues increased as a result of the election of greater numbers of liberal black Democrats and conservative white Republicans.

The above discussion indicates that even leaving aside the role of race, one needs to incorporate elites and institutions to gain a deeper understanding of the process of partisan change. Focusing too much on issues at the expense of elites or institutions, or vice-versa, causes even the keenest observer of the political scene to miss key portions of the political picture. Candidates are not just the source of quirky stories that enliven descriptions of southern politics. Nor are institutions merely amusing regional or national antiques. Both elites and institutions are central to explaining partisan change and evolution.

A New "Solid South"?

Observers of southern politics often discuss the rise of the Republican Party as if the result of the process must be the rise of a new "Solid South." Just as the mighty Democratic Party once held sway with only insignificant opposition, the Republicans are now the coming dominant force. This goal-oriented view of southern politics is most closely held by Republicans themselves, who view their ascension as rightful and inevitable as the vanquishing of evil at the end of a fairy tale. Some Republicans

[2] Sundquist 1993, 19–34.

no doubt hold that the decline of the Democrats is the deserved fate of a party that abandoned its strong regional heritage, with all of the ugly racial connotations of that viewpoint. Others view continued GOP growth as the reward for long decades spent toiling in the political vine- yards to build the party while the overconfident Democrats simply stag- nated. Finally, many Republican leaders believe that modern conserva- tism with its belief in revitalized federalism and free enterprise, but shorn of the racism historically associated with "states rights," is the wave of the future.

While the Republican Party has made impressive gains and is probably the dominant party already in several of the region's states, the Republi- cans will never become as regionally dominant as the Democrats once were. It is imperative to remember that the overwhelming dominance of the then-white supremacist Democrats was not built so much on popu- larity as the institutional exclusion of opposition. Southern Democrats faced vibrant opposition from Republicans, Populists, and other anti- Democratic movements after the conclusion of the Civil War. This op- position did not cease until Democratic elites successfully excluded most of their opponents from the franchise. Systematic disfranchisement not only kept most blacks away from the polls; it also resulted in the dra- matic shrinkage of the white electorate in most southern states.[3] More- over, as V. O. Key perceptively identifies, the confining of true political contests to the primary elections of one party made it easier for conser- vative elites to maintain control over the region's politics even when faced with an insurgency against their control.[4]

The Voting Rights Act of 1965 is one piece of legislation that truly changed America. Responding to the demands for justice by courageous civil rights protestors, the federal government finally forced the region to admit African Americans as full citizens. White registration dramatically increased as well. This infusion of new blood into the political system ultimately toppled the calcified structure of white supremacist Demo- cratic dominance despite impressive efforts by Democrats to adapt to their greatly altered environment. Even though Democrats continued to maintain control in most areas, the party was rapidly forced to abandon its conservative racial stance due to internal pressure from newly enfran- chised blacks and external pressure from a racially liberal national Demo- cratic Party.

The Republicans will not achieve the same level of control over the region's politics as the Democrats of old because they will not be allowed to gain control over the composition of the electorate in the way that the

[3] Keyssar 2000, 114–15; Kousser 1974; Perman 2001.
[4] Key 1949, 146; Kousser 1974.

Democrats did. Section 5 of the Voting Rights Act plays an important role in protecting minority voting rights by placing the burden on "covered jurisdictions" to prove that new voting requirements do not adversely effect minority voting strength relative to the status quo. However, the Act expires in 2007 unless it is renewed by Congress.

The historic hyperdominance of the Democrats was perpetuated by discriminatory institutions, rather than the will of the voters. Such dominance by one political party is more characteristic of illiberal, undemocratic regimes. Even if they had the unlikely goal of re-creating the institutions that permitted unfettered dominance by Democrats, the Republicans would hopefully not be allowed to do it by the federal government, the courts, or the people. The GOP will continue to face real opposition, even if it succeeds in consolidating its impressive gains.

Recent presidential election results make this clear. During the 1980s, observers saw hints of a new Solid South in the region's overwhelming support for GOP presidential candidates. In 1980, Ronald Reagan carried every southern state except for Georgia, the home of incumbent President Jimmy Carter. The popularity of the conservatism espoused by the Republicans combined with the nomination of northern liberals by Democrats helped the Republicans win impressive victories in 1984 and 1988. Running as an incumbent, President Reagan not only carried every southern state but defeated former Vice President Walter Mondale by impressive margins throughout the region. Running against Massachusetts Governor Michael Dukakis, George Bush repeated the feat in 1988.

Earlier predictions by observers like Kevin Phillips that the GOP would achieve national political dominance by gaining southern support on racial issues appeared to have come true.[5] The GOP "lock" on the South's electoral votes appeared to some to give them a similar "lock" on the electoral college.[6] Republicans laughed that Democrats could depend on the electoral votes of Massachusetts, Minnesota, and the District of Columbia. Meanwhile, the Republicans had the votes of a large and growing South sewn up.

The Reagan-Bush era proved the enduring power of racial issues to many observers. Reagan deeply alienated blacks with his talk of "welfare queens," his staunch racial conservatism, and his appointment of very few blacks to prominent positions. Tom and Mary Edsall convincingly argue that Reagan's marriage of racial and economic issues successfully allowed to the GOP to overcome the traditional strength of Democrats on economic issues. Instead of being perceived as advocates for the working and

---

[5] Phillips 1969.
[6] Black and Black 1992.

middle classes, the Democrats were perceived by many whites as advocates for minorities who benefited disproportionately from federal programs.[7]

Despite his appeals for a "kinder, gentler nation," Bush continued the Reagan racial legacy by making Willie Horton the poster child for his campaign. Horton, a fearsome-looking black man convicted of rape and murder, committed new heinous crimes while on a furlough from prison in Massachusetts. While crime is surely a legitimate issue, the use of the picture of a black man convicted of raping a white woman, one of the oldest racial stereotypes in America, smacked of race baiting in some camps.[8] Bush's opposition to racially liberal legislation on civil rights also eroded his reputation among African Americans. During his term, he vetoed civil rights legislation on the grounds that it promoted racial quotas. President Bush also vetoed the National Voter Registration Act, ultimately signed into law by President Clinton.

Election results during the 1990s refuted the idea of a Republican lock on either the South or the electoral college. Arkansas Governor Bill Clinton carried four southern states in both 1992 and 1996. Al Gore lost all of the region's electoral votes in 2000, though Democrats fiercely dispute that he really lost Florida. Perhaps more important, the Democratic share of the presidential vote held up in much of the region. Gore may have lost but he was no Walter Mondale. For that matter, even Walter Mondale won a much larger share of the vote in 1984 than the Republicans did historically during the heyday of Democratic hegemony. Today, the Democrats are clearly the minority party in the South at the presidential level. However, they remain competitive in many states and seem likely to win at least some of the region's electoral votes when they win a national majority and the presidency.

ISSUES AND SOUTHERN POLITICS

The comeback of the Democrats in the 1990s suggests that race in isolation does not explain southern politics. If white voters were completely in thrall to racial issues, it seems unlikely that the Democrats could have achieved such successful inroads in 1992. Some ascribe Clinton's initial success to his calculated attacks on blacks, like Sister Souljah, designed to attract white support but without going so far as to promote large-scale defections by blacks eager to elect a Democrat to the presidency. Throughout the 1992 campaign, Clinton repeatedly attacked the Republicans as

[7] Edsall and Edsall 1992.
[8] Mendelberg 2001, 134–88.

dividing Americans and played a unifying theme that *all* people who worked hard and paid their taxes ought to be able to get ahead. By the time of his 1996 reelection campaign, his support for racial liberalism was readily apparent to all observers. Clinton's identification with the black community was sufficiently strong that Toni Morrison, the first African American to win the Nobel Prize for Literature, labeled Clinton the first black president. If racial issues dominated white voting behavior, it seems unlikely that Clinton would have carried four states in the region in both 1992 and 1996.

Racial issues have nevertheless played a role in shaping southern politics and voting behavior, though they have not always worked as anticipated. The relative liberalism of the Democrats and the unacceptable conservatism of the Republicans on racial issues maintains nearly monolithic support for the Democrats by African Americans. The impact of racial issues on white southern partisanship and voting behavior was less immediate. The average white southern Democrat did not even become more liberal than the average white southern Republican on racial issues until the mid-1980s. There is only meager evidence that white backlash against the presence of blacks continues to influence southern white voting behavior.

Race nevertheless remains a powerful influence on southern politics even if its role is much debated and often misunderstood. The presence of African Americans conditions the decision by elites to seek election under the Republican or Democratic banner and the probability of a GOP victory even if the Republicans successfully recruit a candidate. The presence of African Americans has also helped liberals gain control of the Democratic Party and spurred white conservatives to abandon the party of their forebears as a consequence. Moreover, the influence of racial issues has risen substantially since the mid-1980s as southern Democratic and southern Republican disagreements on racial questions grew more acute. By 2000, racial issues rivaled both the traditional economic cleavage and the rising division over social issues in terms of influence on southern white partisanship and voting behavior.

Unfortunately for Democrats, the other major cleavages influencing white southern partisanship have likely not worked to their advantage. Democratic appeals on economic and social welfare issues may increasingly fall on deaf ears as a greater share of the white population joins in the South's remarkable economic progress. The rise of social issues, like abortion and gay rights, seriously eroded support for the Democrats during the 1990s. Social conservatives, who had continued to support the Democrats in large numbers in the past, fled the Democrats for the Republicans as Democrats became identified with the pro-choice side of the abortion debate and Republicans picked up the pro-life banner. For most of the 1990s, battles in the culture wars took place primarily in urban areas so Democrats suffered relatively little damage in rural areas. Unlike in urban areas, rural Democratic elites continued to profess socially conservative positions that did not arouse anti-Democratic (and pro-Republican) organization on the part of social conservatives associated with religious conservative groups like the Christian Coalition. The spreading from urban to rural areas of the perception of Democrats as liberal on social issues in the late 1990s means that rural Democrats have also lost ground.

It is unclear how racial, economic, and social issues will influence southern politics in the future. Republicans may try to play down racial issues and emphasize social issues as part of an effort to recruit African Americans and Latinos into their coalition. Efforts by the Democrats to emphasize broad-based social welfare programs, like prescription drug insurance for the elderly, may help Democrats attract middle-class southerners who have little need for programs designed to help the poor. This strategy paid some dividends for Al Gore in 2000. Alternatively, the white middle class may solidify its belief that the Democrats are the party of the poor and racial minorities. As in other parts of the nation, young southerners are more liberal on social issues than their elders. If they do not become substantially more conservative on issues like abortion and gay rights as they age, partisan divisions on social issues may gradually work to the advantage of the Democrats instead of the Republicans.

Do Long-Term Trends Favor the Democrats?

Several long-term demographic and institutional trends may benefit Democratic candidates seeking office in the South. Minorities who overwhelmingly support the Democrats, especially Latinos, form the most rapidly growing sector in the electorate. Several opinions issued by the Supreme Court interpret the Voting Rights Act in a manner that may result in redistricting plans more favorable to the Democratic Party.

Rising Minority Population

African Americans and Latinos will play a growing role in southern politics as their share of the southern population and electorate continues to grow. As in the rest of the nation, the Latino share of the southern population is rising faster than the African-American share. Many Latinos currently cannot or do not register or vote, so they have yet to realize even their current potential influence on southern politics.

AFRICAN AMERICANS

As racial oppression in the South substantially declined as a result of the Civil Rights Movement, national migration patterns changed with more African Americans migrating to the South than leaving the region. African Americans additionally have a higher birthrate than white southerners. As a result, the black share of the population of southern states has reversed its historical trend of decline. In all southern states, the black share of the population has begun to rise slowly, or at least stabilize. The relatively high birthrate of African Americans means that blacks form a smaller share of the voting-age population than in the total population. Nevertheless, as table 7.1 shows, blacks compose over 10 percent of the voting-age population in all eleven southern states. In the five states of the Deep South, African Americans form approximately one-quarter to one-third of the voting-age population.

Table 7.1 further shows that the Civil Rights Movement and the Voting Rights Act have largely been successful in assuring black access to the ballot. These gains are even more impressive when one considers various factors that continue to impede black turnout. Felon disfranchisement disproportionately affects the black community. Studies show that the educational level of an individual is the strongest predictor of whether that individual will register and vote. While blacks have made strong educational gains since the 1960s, the average black American still receives less education than the average white American. The black share of the electorate nevertheless closely tracks the black share of the voting-age population throughout the South. In 2000, the largest gap between the black share of the voting-age population and of the electorate was in South Carolina where black participation lagged five percent behind the black share of the eligible population. However, according to the polls, the black share of the electorate exceeded their share of the population in Florida, Tennessee, and Texas. Relatively low participation rates by another minority group, Latinos, probably explain the disproportionate share of the electorate formed by African Americans in Florida and Texas.

Despite talk of increased black interest in the GOP, Republicans still usually receive minimal support from black voters. George W. Bush's efforts to attract racial minorities did not succeed among southern blacks. As table 7.1 indicates, Bush probably received more than 10 percent of the black vote in only two southern states. Newspapers widely reported that Bush's share of the black vote was the lowest in Republican history.

Any growth in the black share of the electorate should benefit the Democrats unless these patterns change. Republicans already have to win an especially high share of the white vote to carry Deep South states.

TABLE 7.1
Black and Latino Share of the Population and Electorate

	Voting-Age Population		In the Electorate		Support for Bush in 2000		
	Blacks	Latinos	Blacks	Latinos	Blacks	Latinos	Anglos
Alabama	24	2	25	0	8		72
Arkansas	14	3	11	1	12		56
Florida	12	16	15	11	7	49	57
Georgia	26	5	25	1	7		71
Louisiana	30	2	29	1	6		72
Mississippi	33	1	30	0	3		81
North Carolina	20	4	19	0	9		68
South Carolina	27	2	22	0	7		70
Tennessee	15	2	18	1	8		60
Texas	11	29	15	10	5	43	73
Virginia	18	4	16	3	14		60

Sources: Data on voting-age population from the U.S. Census. Data on share of the electorate and support for Bush in 2000 from the VNS (Voter News Service) polls published on CNN's web site at http://www.cnn.com/ELECTION/2000.

Based on the black share of the electorate in 2000 and the black support for Bush in 2000, the minimum share of the non-black vote required for a Republican victory in the Deep South ranges from a low of 62 percent in South Carolina to a high of 70 percent in Mississippi. Peripheral South states contain a lower share of blacks, so Republicans require fewer non-black votes to win a majority. The lowest share of the non-black vote George W. Bush could have received and still carried the Peripheral South states ranged from a low of 55 percent in Arkansas to a high of 60 percent in North Carolina. Note that these are the figures for a bare majority. A convincing victory by Republican presidential candidates necessitates an even higher share of the non-black vote.

Republicans now manage to carry most southern states in most presidential elections despite their desultory share of the African-American vote. As the black share of the voting-age population and electorate continues to increase, the required share of the non-black vote for a GOP victory will rise. Moreover, local Democratic candidates who do not carry the political baggage of northern presidential candidates often experience greater success in attracting white votes in southern elections. Republicans either need to figure out how to win a greater share of the black vote or to further unify whites behind their banner in order to win. Efforts by the Republicans to win more black votes would obviously do more to ameliorate the racial divide in southern politics than efforts to achieve ever greater levels of racial polarization. Greater competition for their votes would expand black political influence and integrate them more strongly into the political system.

The rewards for the Republicans would be even higher. If Republican candidates could win even 20 percent of the black vote on a regular basis, it would be extremely difficult for Democrats to win many statewide contests. At this point, this sort of GOP effort appears unlikely. The racial and economic conservatism of the GOP alienates many blacks. Republicans believe that black votes are too difficult to attract and that the effort might alienate racially conservative whites who form a key part of the Republican base. The overwhelmingly white nature of the southern Republican Party further means that the party has few links to the African-American community on which to build support. However, the Republicans started from nothing in the South before, so gaining a greater share of the black vote should not be viewed as inherently impossible, especially with the greater resources possessed by Republicans today.

LATINOS

Democrats and Republicans alike see Latinos as an expanding portion of the electorate that they simply cannot afford to ignore in many key states around the nation. The South is no exception. Latinos compose 29 percent of the voting-age population in Texas and 16 percent in Florida. The 2000 Census further revealed that Latinos compose 5 percent of the voting-age population of Georgia and 4 percent in North Carolina and Virginia—a marked rise that is likely to continue as Latino migration to states with strong economies but historically without many Latino residents continues.

Unlike blacks, the Latino share of the electorate falls far short of the Latino share of the voting-age population (see table 7.1). Citizenship and language barriers explain much of this disparity. Many Latino residents of the United States are relatively recent immigrants and have yet to qualify for citizenship. Moreover, many Latinos come from countries where political activity is hazardous and may be chary of any involvement in politics. Language barriers further make it difficult for many first-generation immigrants to navigate the registration process. The cumulative result is that Latino influence falls short of their share of either the voting-age population or even the citizen voting-age population. Latino Texans compose only one in ten voters even though they form nearly three in ten of the voting-age population. Florida Latinos composed only 16 percent of the voting-age population but only 11 percent of the electorate according to surveys from the 2000 election.

The smaller gap in Florida can be attributed to greater levels of organization and mobilization among Cuban Americans compared to Latinos of other national origins. Most Cubans arrived in the United States as refugees from the Castro regime and American law made it easier for Cubans to acquire American citizenship than immigrants from other nations. Cuban Americans remain ardently opposed to the repressive Castro regime in Cuba. They have achieved a high degree of political organization as part of their effort to encourage the American government to place pressure on Cuba's Communist government to democratize and respect human rights.

Despite the gap between current levels of Latino influence and their potential influence, both political parties recognize the rapidly growing importance of the Latino vote. Mike Dukakis, the 1988 Democratic nominee for president, would have carried California if Latinos composed the same share of the electorate then that they do now. Latino influence can only expand through the first decade of the new century as the Latino share of the population continues to grow. Even if Latino participation rates remain static, Latinos will form a fast-growing sector of the electorate. As Latinos spend more time in this country, greater numbers of Latinos can be expected to naturalize. The original welfare reform law passed by congressional Republicans essentially created an incentive program for Latinos to naturalize because it denied benefits to noncitizens. Despite changes in the law, the experience likely connected the lack of citizenship with second-class status in the minds of many legal immigrants and continues to encourage them to complete the naturalization process.

The big question is which party Latinos will support over the long term. Currently, Latinos divide by national origin. Like African Americans, Puerto Ricans vote overwhelmingly Democratic. In contrast, Cuban Americans tend to support the Republicans due to the stronger anti-Communist and anti-Castro credentials of Republicans. Some Democratic candidates, like Bill Clinton in 1996, have been able to attract a significant share of the Cuban vote. Moreover, Cuban Americans and their representatives tend to support economic liberalism and tolerance toward immigrants at a higher rate than other Republicans.[9] The Elian Gonzalez controversy caused the Democratic share of the Cuban vote to dip sharply in 2000 despite Al Gore's public sympathy with the Cuban position. Gore probably would have won the election if Elian had never landed on American shores.

Mexican Americans, by far the largest group of Latinos, tend to vote Democratic. However, a minority vote Republican and the GOP aspires to win a greater share of votes of this critical group. In particular, George W. Bush has aggressively pursued Latino votes both as governor and

---

[9] de la Garza et al. 1992; Lublin 1997, 70.

president. President Bush speaks Spanish, though some political observers doubt his claim of fluency.[10] More important, Bush has consistently promoted close relations with Mexico and articulated his view that America benefits from Latino immigrants. His Latino nephew, George P. Bush, campaigned in Latino communities during the 2000 campaign. Bush's efforts have won him a greater share of the Latino vote than other Republican candidates. According to the Voter News Service poll, Bush won 43 percent of the Latino vote in his home state of Texas. In Florida, Bush won just under one-half of the Latino vote. His failure to win an outright majority reflects great increases in the non-Cuban Latino population of Florida. For example, many Puerto Ricans have settled around Orlando.

If Bush successfully attracts Latinos to the Republican banner, it will be a great victory for his party. However, his first battle may be against Anglos in his own party. Powerful Texas Republicans in Congress immediately nixed Bush's proposal for amnesty for illegal Mexican immigrants. Former California Republican Governor Pete Wilson won reelection in 1994 by running a campaign perceived as hostile to Latinos. Several initiatives sponsored by Republicans and perceived as hostile to Latino immigrants to varying degrees passed at the same time. The anti-immigrant provisions of the welfare reform legislation passed shortly thereafter. The share of new Latino voters who chose to register as Republicans in California collapsed to near zero in the wake of this spate of anti-Latino activity.[11] The ability of the Texas Republican Party to continue to attract the same share of new registrants as in the past under the leadership of then-Governor George W. Bush appears more impressive in light of the negative national image created by the Republicans.[12]

Despite Bush's efforts, the rise of Latinos appears likely to help the Democrats considerably over the long term. Most Latinos remain far poorer than the average American and are likely to benefit from Democratic social welfare initiatives. Latino workers have already helped revitalize the union movement, a key Democratic constituency. Bush's public support for Latinos and ability to win Latino votes remains an exception rather than the rule within his party. Even the one incumbent non-

[10] Ivins and Dubose 2000.

[11] Matt A. Barreto and Nathan D. Woods, "Latino Voting Behavior in an Anti-Latino Context" (paper presented at the Conference on Minority Representation: Institutions, Behavior, and Identity, Claremont Graduate University, Claremont, CA, February 2–3, 2001).

[12] Arturo Vega and John Bretting, "Political Participation and Representations of Mexican Americans: Recent Trends in San Antonio, Texas" (paper presented at the Conference on Minority Representation: Institutions, Behavior, and Identity, Claremont Graduate University, Claremont, CA, February 2–3, 2001).

TABLE 7.2
Minimum Required Share of the Anglo Vote for Republican Victory

	Percentage of Latinos Voting Republican				
	10	*20*	*30*	*40*	*50*
Alabama	64	64	64	64	63
Arkansas	**58**	**57**	**57**	**57**	56
Florida	**66**	**64**	**62**	**60**	57
Georgia	*69*	*69*	68	67	67
Louisiana	*70*	*70*	*70*	69	69
Mississippi	74	74	74	74	74
North Carolina	63	62	62	61	61
South Carolina	*68*	*67*	*67*	*67*	66
Tennessee	*58*	*58*	*58*	*58*	57
Texas	**77**	72	68	63	58
Virginia	**61**	*60*	*60*	*59*	*59*

Note: The table shows the percentage of the Anglo vote that the Republicans must win to carry the state depending on the percentage of Latinos voting Republican. The table assumes that the African-American and Latino share of the electorate is the same as their share of the 2000 voting-age population. **Boldface** indicates that the GOP would lose the state if their share of the Anglo vote does not increase. *Italic* indicates that the GOP would lose the state if their share of the Anglo vote declined by 3%.

Cuban Latino Republican, Texan Henry Bonilla, cannot attract a majority of the Latino vote in his district; Bonilla's victories rest on strong Anglo support.[13]

Table 7.2 shows the scope of the danger to Republicans in the future if they cannot win a sizable minority of the Latino vote. The table shows the percentage of Anglo votes that the Republicans must win depending on the percentage of Latino votes won by Republicans. Unlike 2000, the table assumes that the Black and Latino share of the electorate equals their current share of the voting-age population. However, even if Republicans attract 40 percent of Latino votes, a somewhat optimistic assumption, Republican percentages will drop in many states. Percentages in boldface indicate that the Republicans would lose the state unless their share of the Anglo vote rises to compensate for increased Latino participation. Similarly, percentages in italics indicate that the Democrats will win the state if Latino participation rises and the Democrats can attract a mere 3 percent more of the Anglo vote.

[13] Jonathan N. Katz, "Report on Texas Congressional Redistricting: Minority Opportunities and Partisan Fairness," unpublished manuscript from *Del Rio* case on Texas state legislative districts, August 27, 2001, 23.

Increased Latino participation should gradually erode Republican dominance of the South's electoral votes. Republicans need to win an optimistic 40 percent of the Latino vote to continue to win Arkansas and Florida. As the fourth most populous state in the country, Florida is a major prize in terms of electoral votes. If the GOP share of the Anglo vote declines by even a small amount, Republicans might also lose Louisiana and Virginia. Texas forms a critical part of the Republican base. However, control of the electoral votes of the nation's second largest state could fall to the Democrats if Latino participation rises and Anglo support for the GOP does not match that of 2000. Since the Republicans nominated the incumbent governor of Texas in 2000, Anglo support for the top of the GOP ticket was unusually high in the 2000 election. One suspects that Texas might become hotly contested between the two parties if Democrats can raise Latino mobilization and the Republicans do not nominate another highly popular Texan.

One should note that the Republican share of the total vote should decline as the Latino share of the electorate rises even if they manage to win one-half of all Latino votes. Anglos provide majority support to the Republicans throughout the region, so the rise of a group that splits its votes evenly between the two parties would actually harm the Republicans. On a more positive note for the GOP, Republicans will likely retain control of most of the region's electoral votes if they can win more than 40 percent of Latino votes. As noted above, this will take a great deal of effort and luck on the part of Republicans. Regardless of the difficulty, attracting a sizable minority of Latino votes is vital to the future of the GOP. Republicans may now get a taste of the traditionally Democratic problem of cobbling together a diverse coalition without irrevocably alienating key members.

Supreme Court Attacks on Racial Redistricting

In the wake of the 1990 Census, new majority-black districts were created at all levels of government under the aegis of the Voting Rights Act as interpreted by the Justice Department and the Supreme Court in *Thornburg v. Gingles*. Beginning with their decision in *Shaw v. Reno*, the now conservative Supreme Court attacked efforts to maximize the number of majority-minority districts through the creation of bizarrely shaped districts that contain a majority-minority electorate. As a result, black-majority congressional districts in Florida, Louisiana, North Carolina, Georgia, Texas, and Virginia were either redrawn or eliminated. South Carolina also agreed to redraw its majority-minority district in a more compact fashion and with fewer minorities by 2002 as part of a settlement. Despite the focus on congressional redistricting, one should remember that these decisions affect redistricting at every level of government, including local and state legislative redistricting. The Supreme Court's 2003 decision in *Georgia v. Ashcroft* approving a state legislative plan that reduced minority strength in several districts should further aid efforts to unpack some majority-minority districts.

Eliminating majority-minority districts or at least reducing the share of minorities in the districts aids Democratic prospects over the long term. Dismantling majority-minority districts requires placing additional minorities to neighboring districts and raises Democratic chances of victory. In the short term, Democrats gained few new seats as district boundaries were redrawn. Republican incumbents survived strong challenges from Democrats due to the resources that accompany incumbency and efforts to protect them by state legislatures.[14] However, as these seats become open, Democratic chances of retaking them will be greater than they would otherwise be due to the addition of minority voters.

The creation of additional districts favorable to white Democrats should encourage local elites to pursue election as Democrats rather than Republicans because of expanded opportunities for Democratic candidates. Of course, if fewer minorities win as a result, dissatisfaction with the Democratic Party among minorities, especially minority elites aspiring to hold elected office, will rise. So far, the number of minorities has not decreased much as a result of districts redrawn in the wake of *Shaw v. Reno*. However, Democrats will likely have to promote minority candidates in majority-white districts with a strong minority presence if they hope to continue to increase the number of minority officials in order to at least partially satisfy the desire by minorities for greater representation.

The discussion in this chapter indicates that southern politics is likely to remain interesting. Key questions for the future of southern politics include: Will the Republicans continue to extend their dominance down to the bottom of the ticket? Will Republicans manage to consolidate their majority by gaining an even higher percentage of the white vote? Or will their conservative social issue stances spur young southerners to vote Democratic? Alternatively, can the GOP manage to attract new African-American or Latino supporters without alienating their current core constituency? Or can the Democrats begin to reverse the Republican tide by mobilizing Latinos and earning the lion's share of their votes?

These questions suggest that the Republicans will find it far from easy to become the region's permanent majority party. Republicans will find it

---

[14] Lublin and Voss 1998.

difficult to win ever-increasing shares of the white vote now that most southern whites already vote Republican. The racial and economic conservatism of the GOP offers little to many blacks and Latinos, who will make up a greater share of the region's voters in the future. As the institutional exclusion of opposition voters that worked so well for the Democrats for decades is not an option available to the Republicans, southern politics should become even more hotly contested over the next decade.

Appendix

TABLE 1
Bivariate Probit Model for Open County Offices

	Full Model		Stripped Model	
	Coefficient	SE	Coefficient	SE
Republican Candidate				
Proportion for Republican Presidential				
Candidate	.54	.13		
Proportion Black	−1.87	.18	−1.98	.16
Proportion Hispanic	−2.26	.77		
Median Household Income ($1000)	.03	.01	.03	.00
Proportion Native to the South	−1.01	.31		
Proportion Rural	−.54	.10	−.62	.09
Year (1978 = 0, 1979 = 1 . . .				
1999 = 21)	.06	.01		
Republican Governor	.33	.06		
Sheriff	.48	.06		
Coroner	.13	.08		
Virginia	−.33	.08		
Constant	−.61	.37	−.15	.16
Republican Winner				
Proportion Black	−2.10	.23	−2.08	.21
Proportion Hispanic	−2.37	.90		
Median Household Income ($1000)	.04	.01	.04	.01
Proportion Native to the South	−.94	.31		
Proportion Rural	−.43	.13	−.56	.11
Year (1978 = 0, 1979 = 1 . . . 1999 = 21)	.03	.01		
Republican Governor	.35	.07		
Sheriff	.13	.08		
Coroner	.33	.09		
Virginia	−.26	.09		
Constant	−1.19	.35	−1.21	.19
/athrho	1.51	.09	1.53	.08
rho	.91	.02	.91	.01
Likelihood ratio test of rho = 0: chi2(1)	670.65		760.18	
Number of Cases	3127		3127	

Sources: Political data were collected by author. Demographic data are from the U.S. Census.

TABLE 2
Bivariate Probit Model for Open State Legislative Seats

	Coefficient	SE
Republican Candidate		
Proportion Black	−1.51	.22
Proportion Hispanic	−1.76	.38
Median Household Income ($1000)	.03	.01
Suburban District	.24	.13
Constant	−.03	.25
Republican Winner		
Proportion Black	−3.26	.38
Proportion Hispanic	−1.05	.45
Median Household Income ($1000)	.05	.01
Suburban District	.33	.11
Constant	−1.48	.23
/athrho	1.03	.12
rho	.77	.05
Likelihood ratio test of rho = 0: chi2(1)	105.296	
Number of Cases	911	

Sources: Political data were collected by the author. Demographic data can be found in William Lilley III, Lawrence J. DeFranco, and Mark F. Bernstein, *The Almanac of State Legislatures: Changing Patterns 1990–1997* (Congressional Quarterly, 1998).

TABLE 3
Probit Coefficients for Models of White Party Identification, Vote for President, and Vote for U.S. House

A. Party Identification

Year	Constant	Jobs	Aid to Blacks	Abortion	Number of Cases
1980–82	−.73***	.18***	−.03	−.05	455
1984–86	−.77***	.15***	.04	.02	482
1988–90	−.78***	.10***	.05^	.03	615
1992–94	−1.09***	.15***	.12***	.07**	723
1996–98	−1.08***	.15***	.11**	.06*	590
2000	−1.98***	.25**	.23**	.17**	147

B. Vote for President

Year	Constant	Jobs	Aid to Blacks	Abortion	Number of Cases
1980	−.49	.07	.13^	.00	179
1984	−.41	.29***	.00	−.01	220
1988	−.94***	.15*	.10^	.13**	208
1992	−1.82***	.15**	.18***	.16***	273
1996	−2.11***	.24***	.18*	.19***	258
2000	−.74	.03	.07	.00	106

C. Vote for U.S. House

Year	Constant	Jobs	Aid to Blacks	Abortion	Number of Cases
1980–82	−.64^	.15*	.06	.03	215
1984–86	−.12	.20**	−.05	.05	202
1988–90	−1.34*	.13	.18*	.13*	159
1992–94	−1.12***	.10*	.10*	.13***	365
1996–98	−2.47***	.29***	.23**	.09*	271

Note: *** p < .001, ** p < .01, * p < .05, ^ p < .10. The collapsed version of the standard party identification question is used in table A as the dependent variable with party identification is coded 1 for Republican and 0 for Democrat; independents are excluded. In tables B and C the dependent variable is coded 1 for vote for the Republican candidate and 0 for vote for other candidates. In the model of vote for U.S. House, respondents were included only if both major parties fielded candidates. Additionally, this model controlled for the presence of a Democratic or Republican incumbent, though these coefficients are not presented here. All of the independent variables were (re)scaled from 0 to 6 with the jobs and aid to blacks questions taking on all integer values from 0 through 6, and the abortion question taking on only the values of 0, 2, 4, and 6.

Data Source: NES Cumulative Data File 1948–98, NES 2000 Data File.

TABLE 4
Large Models of White Party Identification, Presidential Vote, and
Congressional Vote

	Models Including Proportion Non-Hispanic Black					
	Party Identification		Presidential Vote		Congressional Vote	
	Coef.	SE	Coef.	SE	Coef.	SE
Jobs Scale (0–6)	.141	.019	.163	.034	.140	.033
Aid to Blacks Scale (0–6)	.012	.037	.012	.062	.017	.062
Year × Aid to Blacks Scale	.007	.004	.011	.008	.010	.006
Abortion Scale (0–6)	−.009	.028	−.002	.044	.038	.043
Year × Abortion Scale	.009	.003	.019	.005	.010	.004
Year (1980 = 0, 1982 = 2, . . .)	−.039	.016	−.122	.033	−.057	.027
Income Percentiles (0–4)	.075	.028	.156	.055	.100	.049
Educational Level (0–3)	.180	.036	.071	.063	.078	.056
Age Cohort (0–6 with 6 oldest)	−.132	.026	−.068	.049	−.105	.045
Suburb (1 = Yes, 0 = City, Rural)	.167	.064	.179	.115	−.094	.102
Gender (1 = Male, 0 = Female)	−.145	.059	−.166	.106	−.018	.096
Proportion Non-Hispanic Black	−.515	.236	−.164	.415	−1.111	.386
Democratic Incumbent					−.735	.138
Republican Incumbent					.511	.149
Constant	−.664	.213	−.259	.370	−.296	.378
Number of Cases	2027		689		859	
LR chi2(13)	279.63		127.86		251.06	
Pseudo R2	.100		.142		.212	

	Models Excluding Proportion Non-Hispanic Black					
	Party Identification		Presidential Vote		Congressional Vote	
	Coef.	SE	Coef.	SE	Coef.	SE
Jobs Scale (0–6)	.143	.018	.161	.031	.140	.031
Aid to Blacks Scale (0–6)	.013	.035	−.002	.056	.019	.058
Year × Aid to Blacks Scale	.008	.003	.013	.005	.011	.005
Abortion Scale (0–6)	−.017	.026	.019	.040	.048	.040
Year × Abortion Scale	.010	.002	.015	.004	.008	.004
Year (1980 = 0, 1982 = 2, . . .)	−.044	.014	−.111	.023	−.057	.022

TABLE 4 Continued

| | Models Excluding Proportion Non-Hispanic Black | | | | | |
| | Party Identification | | Presidential Vote | | Congressional Vote | |
	Coef.	SE	Coef.	SE	Coef.	SE
Income Percentiles (0–4)	.097	.027	.219	.048	.141	.044
Educational Level (0–3)	.184	.033	.059	.055	.082	.051
Age Cohort (0–6 with 6 oldest)	−.121	.024	−.026	.043	−.076	.041
Suburb (1 = Yes, 0 = City, Rural)	.177	.059	.162	.098	−.043	.091
Gender (1 = Male, 0 = Female)	−.155	.055	−.168	.091	−.004	.087
Democratic Incumbent					−.743	.127
Republican Incumbent					.537	.133
Constant	−.822	.193	−.541	.315	−.723	.341
Number of Cases	2358		931		1065	
LR chi2(13)	361.14		210.60		329.42	
Pseudo R2	.111		.172		.304	

Note: Only southern white respondents from 1980–2000 included. All dependent variables were coded 1 for Republican and 0 for Democrat; cases with other values were excluded. The congressional vote data set excluded races without two major-party candidates. The models including proportion non-Hispanic black exclude cases from 2000 because data on the home county of the respondent were unavailable. The party identification model including proportion non-Hispanic black was used in the construction of figure 5.14. For estimation purposes in that figure, all variables other than proportion black were held constant (all three issue scales coded as 3; year = 18; income = 2; education = 2; age = 3; suburb = 1; woman = 1). In the party identification model, the coefficient on proportion non-Hispanic black changes little if the two terms including the aid to blacks scale are excluded from the model (coefficient = −.675, SE = .213).

Data Source: NES Cumulative Data File, 1948–2000.

Index

abortion, xvii, 175–76, 193, 196–98, 201, 205–8, 210–12, 222–23; clinics for, 20, 51, 197

Abromowitz, Alan, 174–75

accountability. *See* one-party system

Adams, Greg D., 175, 182

affirmative action, 27, 102, 145–46, 165–66

AFL-CIO's Committee on Political Education (COPE), 188–89

African Americans: competition for votes from, 139–40; counties with a majority of, 148–49; and Democrats, 100, 119–20; and economic issues, 141–42; felon disfranchisement of, 148; increased voting power of, 223–25; inhibiting GOP growth by, 161–62; participation of, xviii, 219; partisanship of, 135–46; population share of, 97, 147–48, 155, 164, 224; presidential voting by, 136; and racial issues, 27, 134–35, 217; and racial redistricting, 23; religious leaders of, 201; and Republicans, xviii, 10–11, 24, 34, 96–97; share of primary voters made up by, 119–23; shift to Democrats by, 9, 25, 42, 138–41; and states rights, 141–42; voting rates of, 148; white majority places electing, 103–4

Aistrup, Joseph, 60–63

Alabama, 42, 45–46, 48, 52, 69n.11, 79–80, 97, 99–100, 108, 162, 164, 166, 209; felon disfranchisement in, 148

Aldrich, John H., 62–63

Allain, Bill, 44

Allen, George, 108n.24

Allen v. State Board of Elections, 22–23, 97

Anderson, Marian, 139

Appalachia, 43, 47–48, 166

apportionment, xv. *See also* malapportionment; reapportionment

Arkansas, 26, 40, 43–44, 48, 52, 55–58, 60, 69n.11, 76n.24, 77, 79–80, 162–64, 225; term limits in, 126–27

Atlanta, 79, 104, 152, 197; suburban, 148–49, 204–5

Baker, Thurbert, 103

Baker v. Carr, 47n.22, 50, 148

Baptists, 198

Barnes, Roy, 46, 144–45

Barnett, Ross, 44

Barr, Bob, 143

Bartels, Larry, 7

Battle, William, 43

Beasley, David, 45, 144

Bethune, Mary McLeod, 139

Bible Belt, 142

biracial coalitions, 38, 118

Bishop, Sanford, 105

Black, Earl, and Merle Black, 19, 38, 175

Black Belt, 12, 147, 152, 166

Black Cabinet, 139

blacks. *See* African Americans

Blatt, Sol, 198

Bonilla, Henry, 229

Bourbons. *See* Democrats

Bredesen, Phil, 46

Britain, 102, 102n.13, 209

Bryan, William Jennings, 138

Bullock, Charles S., 60–61

Bumpers, Dale, 43–44, 76n.24

Bush, George, 38, 43, 159, 188, 195, 220–21; total support by county for, 152–54; white support by county for, 163

Bush, George P., 228

Bush, George W.: black support for, 224; economic positions of, 188; Governor, 45, 47, 145; and Latinos, 227–28; President, 34, 46, 125, 137, 146, 159, 209; total support by county for, 152–54; white support by county for, 165–66

Bush, Jeb, 45; and racial issues, 145

Calhoun, John, 140n.12

California, 227–28

Cameron, Charles, 113

Campbell, Carroll, 45

Campbell, Ralph, Jr., 103

Canada, 102, 102n.13

candidate pool, 77–78, 95

candidate quality, 70, 72, 77–78, 93